# How to access the supplemental web resource

We are pleased to provide access to a web resource that supplements your textbook, *StarGuard: Best Practices for Lifeguards, Fourth Edition.* This resource offers over 45 interactive and multimedia learning activities covering surveillance techniques and prevention strategies to first aid and emergency care, as well as quizzes for each book chapter.

## Accessing the web resource is easy!
## Follow these steps if you purchased a new book:

1. Using your web browser, go to the Human Kinetics Online Education Center at **http://education.humankinetics.com**.

2. Click the **Sign in** link at the top of the page, and then enter your e-mail address and password.

3. If you do not have an account with Human Kinetics, click the **Create an Account** link at the top of the page and you will be prompted to create one.

4. Once you are signed in, click the **Keycodes** button near the top of the page.

5. Enter the key code that is printed at the right, including all hyphens. Click the **Submit** button to unlock your web resource.

6. After you successfully enter your key code, you can access your web resource at any time by clicking on the **My Courses** button near the top of the page at **http://education.humankinetics.com**. You no longer need to use your key code after initial entry.

7. Your access to the web resource and its test will expire 1 year after you first access the web resource.

→ This key code can only be used once, as per the instructions in step 5.

For technical support, send an e-mail to:
support@hkusa.com . . . . . . . . . . . . . . . . U.S. and international customers
info@hkcanada.com . . . . . . . . . . . . . . . . . . . . Canadian customers
academic@hkeurope.com . . . . . . . . . . . . . . . . . . European customers
keycodesupport@hkaustralia.com . . . . . Australian and New Zealand customers

**Product:** StarGuard, Fourth Edition, web resource

**Key code:** STARGUARD-4TGGSA-OSG

**This unique code allows you access to the web resource.**

**HUMAN KINETICS WEB RESOURCE**

**HUMAN KINETICS**
*The Information Leader in Physical Activity & Health*

12-2011

# StarGuard

## BEST PRACTICES FOR LIFEGUARDS

**FOURTH EDITION**

# StarGuard

## BEST PRACTICES FOR LIFEGUARDS

## Jill E. White

STARFISH AQUATICS INSTITUTE

**Human Kinetics**

**Library of Congress Cataloging-in-Publication Data**

White, Jill E., 1955-
  Starguard : best practices for lifeguards / Jill E. White. -- 4th ed.
    p. cm.
  Includes bibliographical references.
  ISBN-13: 978-0-7360-9835-9 (soft cover)
  ISBN-10: 0-7360-9835-6 (soft cover)
  1.  Lifeguards--Training of--Handbooks, manuals, etc.  I. Title.
  GV838.74.W45 2012
  797.2'00289--dc23

                    2011042383

ISBN-10: 0-7360-9835-6 (print)
ISBN-13: 978-0-7360-9835-9 (print)

Copyright © 2012, 2006 by Jill E. White and Starfish Aquatics Institute
Copyright © 2002, 1999 by Starfish Aquatics Institute and American Safety & Health Institute

The web addresses cited in this text were current as of October 11, 2011, unless otherwise noted.

**Acquisitions Editor:** Scott Wikgren; **Managing Editor:** Amy Stahl; **Assistant Editor:** Rachel Brito; **Copyeditor:** Patricia L. MacDonald; **Permissions Manager:** Dalene Reeder; **Graphic Designer:** Robert Reuther; **Graphic Artist:** Denise Lowry; **Cover Designer:** Keith Blomberg; **Photographer (cover):** Jill E. White; **Photographer (interior):** © Jill E. White, unless otherwise noted. Photo on page 197 provided by Aquatic Exercise Association. Photos on pages 26, 113, 115, 119, 124, 125, 141, 142, 144, 147, 148, 149, 150, 154, 155, 156, 157, 158, 161, 162, and 163 provided by American Safety & Health Institute. Photo on page 137 courtesy of Cardiac Science. Photo on page 221 provided by Rich Irish. Photo on page 228 © i Stock International Inc. Photos on pages 5, 14, 16, 24, 25, 40, 41, 55, 72, 78, 79 (top 3), 82 (top 3), 83, 84, 85, 86, 96, 97, 99 (bottom 3), 101, 105, 106, 107, 170, 184, 191, and 201 © Human Kinetics. Photo on page 205 © Justin S. Padgett. Photos on pages 179 and 183 provided by Park District Risk Management Agency. Photo (a) on page 12 © Tom Griffiths; **Photo Asset Manager:** Jason Allen; **Art Manager:** Kelly Hendren; **Associate Art Manager:** Alan L. Wilborn; **Illustrations:** © Human Kinetics; **Printer:** McNaughton & Gunn, Inc.

Printed in the United States of America     10   9   8   7   6   5   4   3   2

The paper in this book is certified under a sustainable forestry program.

**Human Kinetics**
Website: www.HumanKinetics.com

*United States:* Human Kinetics, P.O. Box 5076, Champaign, IL 61825-5076
800-747-4457
e-mail: humank@hkusa.com

*Canada:* Human Kinetics, 475 Devonshire Road Unit 100, Windsor, ON N8Y 2L5
800-465-7301 (in Canada only)
e-mail: info@hkcanada.com

*Europe:* Human Kinetics, 107 Bradford Road, Stanningley, Leeds LS28 6AT, United Kingdom
+44 (0) 113 255 5665
e-mail: hk@hkeurope.com

*Australia:* Human Kinetics, 57A Price Avenue, Lower Mitcham, South Australia 5062
08 8372 0999
e-mail: info@hkaustralia.com

*New Zealand:* Human Kinetics, P.O. Box 80, Torrens Park, South Australia 5062
0800 222 062
e-mail: info@hknewzealand.com

E5241

# CONTENTS

# PREFACE

**W**ater hides and water suffocates. This inherent danger of water is the essence of the StarGuard training program. This text is designed to prepare you to earn a StarGuard course completion certificate and will help you recognize the important role you play in keeping patrons safe.

The information is concise, clear, and designed to develop your confidence and competence. The text and supplemental online resources, when combined with the training sessions taught by authorized StarGuard instructors, will teach you the essentials of lifeguarding by focusing on what is important.

In this edition, we continue to focus on the StarGuard Risk Management Model, updated to help you understand the factors that contribute to saving lives. The model includes five components:

1. prevention strategy,
2. surveillance,
3. response and rescue,
4. emergency care, and
5. workplace environment

with one part of this text devoted to each. Once you understand the model, learning best practices for applying that knowledge are the next step. The training program continues to be unique in its experiential methodology and integrated approach, combined with a team and leadership development foundation.

## What's New in the Fourth Edition?

The fourth edition of *StarGuard: Best Practices for Lifeguards* and its online resource bring an increased emphasis on evidence-based practices and how those apply in the real world. The text has an expanded international focus to reflect the growth of the StarGuard program beyond the United States.

The content in the fourth edition has been updated to include new research. The reference list is now organized by chapter to increase its usefulness. The CPR, AED, and first aid content has been provided by the Health and Safety Institute (HSI) through its American Safety and Health Institute (ASHI) brand and is based on *2010 International Consensus on Cardiopulmonary Resuscitation and Emergency Cardiovascular Care Science With Treatment Recommendations, 2010 American Heart Association Guidelines for Cardiopulmonary Resuscitation and Emergency Cardiovascular Care*, and *2010 American Heart Association and American Red Cross International Consensus on First Aid Science With Treatment Recommendations*. The consensus on science process occurs every five years, with the purpose of identifying and reviewing international science and knowledge relevant to emergency care. At the suggestion of instructors who used previous editions, first aid and CPR have been consolidated and included in the StarGuard text.

Complementing the HSI/AHSI content is an expanded chapter specific to adapting CPR and rescue skills for an unresponsive drowning victim. A new chapter explores the important step of deciding to act and a systematic method of emergency response. Other new or expanded content can be found for victim recognition, workplace safety, workplace culture, and site- and situation-specific considerations. The goal is to emphasize reducing risk at an aquatic facility by using a team approach that includes parents or caregivers, users, facility managers or supervisors, and your employer. This approach will help us return to reasonable expectations for the role of a lifeguard without diluting high performance mandates.

In contrast, some detail has been removed from the fourth edition and is available within other resources. The content specific to lifeguarding in a wilderness setting more than one hour from medical care is available through Landmark Learning, our education partner for that specialty training. Visit www.landmarklearning.org for more information.

The most significant addition to the fourth edition is the web resource, which you can access using the key code instructions at the front of the book. More than 95 highly interactive and multimedia learning activities will help you apply the material in the text and prepare you to successfully complete the course. If you are enrolled in a StarGuard lifeguard certification course delivered through blended learning (part online, part face-to-face), the online activities, chapter quizzes, and the online test are required and designed to help you prepare for the certification exams.

## Features of the Book

The fourth edition of *StarGuard: Best Practices for Lifeguards* includes several new or revised features designed to streamline your learning experience:

- **Chapter objectives.** Each chapter's learning objectives appear at the beginning of the chapter rather than at the beginning of each part, as in the previous edition.
- **Skill guides.** Chapters that describe physical skills that you will practice during the in-person part of your training include concise charts with descriptions and photos of how to perform the skill.
- **Best practices.** Key points appear as best practices periodically throughout the book and can be found in the margins of the text.
- **Knowledge into practice.** At the end of each chapter is a section that helps you integrate the concepts you've learned throughout the chapter.
- **Visit the web resource.** This element encourages you to visit the website and lists the learning exercises you'll find there.
- **On the job.** This final section helps you understand how you will be expected to perform on the job by listing key competency requirements found in most international qualification standards.

## Assistance in Meeting National and International Standards

The fourth edition continues to assist lifeguard candidates in meeting standards. The content is consistent with the guidelines for supporting the development of minimum competencies as outlined in numerous guidance documents, including but not limited to the Model Aquatic Health Code sponsored by the U.S. Centers for Disease Control and Prevention (CDC), the UK National Pool Lifeguard Qualification, the minimum competencies recommended by the International Life Saving Federation, and Australian NTIS training package qualifications. As mentioned previously, the CPR, AED, and first aid curricula integrated into the StarGuard program are at the forefront of international standards.

# Organization

Organization changes you will notice in this fourth edition of *StarGuard: Best Practices for Lifeguards* include a revised sequence of chapter order to better flow with the way the course is taught. As in the third edition, the five parts of the text follow the five components of the StarGuard Risk Management Model.

Part I contains three chapters of fundamental concepts about **prevention strategies** to reduce the risk inherent at a recreational aquatic venue. Chapter 1 identifies misconceptions about lifeguarding and the need for best practices. Chapter 2 offers strategies to reduce the risk of aquatic emergencies. Chapter 3 explains how to prevent exposure, for yourself and others, to potentially disease-causing bloodborne and waterborne pathogens.

Part II examines **surveillance** and the concepts and techniques that underlie what you will do for almost every minute you are on active lifeguard duty. Chapter 4 will help you recognize distress and drowning. Chapter 5 gives you strategies for learning to look for distress and drowning.

Part III describes the skills necessary for **response and rescue**. Chapter 6 stresses the importance of deciding to act and gives steps for taking action when an emergency situation is identified. Chapter 7 focuses on skills for land-based assists and water rescue. These chapters provide much detail related to how to perform the specific rescues as well as the objective that is meant to be achieved. This objective-based approach will help you develop decision-making skills.

Part IV looks at the **emergency care** skills necessary if a drowning, injury, or illness occurs. The goal is to prepare you to provide care until emergency medical services (EMS) arrives. Chapter 8 provides skills for managing suspected spinal injuries on land or in the water. Chapter 9 presents skills for providing basic first aid for injury and care during sudden illness. Chapter 10 presents skills for how to provide basic life support for an adult, child, or infant, including rescue breathing, CPR, AED use, and response for choking. Chapter 11 considers the unique circumstances created by a submersion incident and suggests a protocol for responding to an unresponsive drowning victim.

Part V focuses on the **workplace environment** and explores key concepts that affect how effective and safe you will be on the job. Chapter 12 provides strategies for minimizing the risk of workplace injury. Chapter 13 identifies common professional behavior and performance expectations for both you and your employer and explores the importance of workplace culture on risk management. Chapter 14 identifies site-specific and situation-specific considerations (e.g., when lifeguarding at single-guard facilities or for special events). Chapter 15 explains how to adapt your knowledge and skills for the water-park setting and chapter 16 for the waterfront setting.

The appendix provides information about using supplemental emergency oxygen. It is presented as an optional training module for use in facilities that have emergency oxygen equipment.

# Web Resource

As mentioned earlier, the web resource can be used for enriching the content in each chapter. Use the instructions and key code in the letter bound into the front of the book to access the web resource.

# Terminology

The terms used in this text for *drowning*, *drowning victim*, *drowning survivor*, and *drowning fatality* are based on definition guidelines developed at the World Congress on Drowning (WCD), approved at a meeting of the International Liaison Committee on Resuscitation (ILCOR), and adopted by the World Health Organization (WHO). (See definitions on page 37.)

The term *lifeguard* generally refers to a person primarily responsible for monitoring patrons in an aquatic environment by providing constant, dedicated surveillance; enforcing the facility's risk reduction strategies; and responding during an emergency.

The terms *swimmer*, *patron*, *bather,* and *guest* are used interchangeably to refer to people who are in or near the water at an aquatic facility.

The terms *victim* and *casualty* are used interchangeably to refer to people who may be in distress, drowning, or in need of emergency care.

The terms *rescuer* and *responder* generally refer to a person responding to an emergency either in or out of the water and providing care. The terms may refer to a lifeguard as well as to other personnel, bystanders who are assisting, or emergency medical services.

# Compliance and Constraints

This text is solely intended to facilitate certification in a StarGuard lifeguard training class. The information is furnished for that purpose and subject to change without notice. Recommendations in this text do not replace those of local regulatory agencies or authorities, which you should consider to be primary. When an emergency occurs, the circumstances of each incident will vary, and guidelines for aquatic safety and emergency care that apply exactly in all cases do not exist. The publisher and authors make no representations or warranties with respect to any implied future performance by persons using this text or completing StarGuard training.

StarGuard certification may only be issued when an SAI-authorized instructor verifies that you have successfully completed the required core knowledge and skill objectives of the program. Lifeguard training and certification is simply the first step in becoming a competent lifeguard. The documentation you receive upon successfully completing the course verifies that you had certain skills and understanding at that time. The responsibility for future performance lies with you, your supervisor or manager, and your employer.

The Starfish Aquatics Institute is committed to helping aquatic managers and employers of lifeguards maintain high standards by offering a comprehensive aquatic risk management service that can provide lifeguard performance audits (StarReview) and operational support. The facility where you work may have this service in place, in which case you can be assured that your employer is committed to the highest level of aquatic safety.

For StarReview information, contact the Starfish Aquatics Institute at 877-465-4545, or refer to www.starfishaquatics.org.

# ACKNOWLEDGMENTS

The StarGuard program began in 1999. Each edition of the StarGuard textbook reflects the contributions and shared knowledge of countless instructors, staff, colleagues, and dedicated aquatic professionals committed to saving lives.

I would like to especially acknowledge and thank the lifeguards and managers who have put the StarGuard program into practice the way it is intended. Good managers make good lifeguards, and the facilities listed here have voluntarily chosen to participate in the StarReview lifeguard and operational audit program and have achieved the highest level of safety excellence—the 5-Star award—since the third edition was published. Achieving the 5-Star award is difficult, and only a small percentage of facilities in the StarReview program can claim this recognition. Congratulations and thank you for setting the bar: Arizona Grand Resort, Arizona; Bend Parks & Recreation, Oregon; Bloomingdale Park District, Illinois; Bolingbrook Park District, Illinois; Carol Stream Park District, Illinois; Caribbean Cove Indoor Water Park, Indiana; Charleston County Parks & Recreation, South Carolina; City of Cape Coral Sunsplash Family Waterpark, Florida; City of Cape Coral Yacht Club, Florida; Geneva Park District, Illinois; Glenview Park District, Illinois; Homewood-Flossmoor Park District, Illinois; Indy Parks & Recreation, Indiana; Knights Action Park, Illinois; Land of Make Believe Water Park, New Jersey; Leawood Parks & Recreation, Kansas; Lee County Parks & Recreation, Florida; Lombard Park District, Illinois; Midwest Pool Management, Missouri; Midwest Pool Management, Kansas; Mundelein Park District, Illinois; Niles Park District, Illinois; Northbrook Park District, Illinois; Oregon Park District, Illinois; City of Overland Park, Kansas; River Road Park District, Oregon; Roselle Park District, Illinois; Skokie Park District, Illinois; The Champion Corporation, Chatham County Aquatic Center, Georgia; Tinley Park Park District, Illinois; Urbana Park District, Illinois; Village of Orland Park, Illinois; West Chicago Park District, Illinois; Wilmette Park District, Illinois; Woodridge Park District, Illinois. Of special note is the City of Cape Coral Sunsplash Family Waterpark in Florida. The exceptional staff have achieved a 5-Star award in over 20 consecutive operational audits over the past six years.

Many thanks are also due to our education partners, the American Safety and Health Institute (a brand of the Health and Safety Institute) and Landmark Learning. We have enjoyed a long relationship and respect your expertise and willingness to break new ground with us.

Special thanks to the following individuals, who have contributed greatly to the field of aquatic safety and whose ideas have been adapted and included in the StarGuard program: Tom Griffiths (5-minute scanning strategy and "disappearing dummies"); Robert Ogoreuc and Kim Tyson (STAAR rescue model); Frank Pia (RID factor); Terri Smith (vigilance voice) along with Jeff Ellis and Dr. John Hunsucker, who paved the way for innovation in vigilance and victim recognition training.

To Human Kinetics, thank you for your commitment to SAI and the StarGuard program, and special thanks to the dozens of people who make this book an outstanding product that stands above others in the aquatics industry.

Special thanks to Lake White, director of training, and the hundreds of instructors and faculty who excel at instilling the vision of the StarGuard program.

## PART I

# Prevention Strategy

# Foundation of Best Practices

## CHAPTER OBJECTIVES

This chapter

▶ identifies what is important in saving lives,
▶ explores some misconceptions about lifeguarding,
▶ introduces the concept of best practices, and
▶ explains the need for a team approach to best practices.

# Identifying What Is Important in Saving Lives

There are two kinds of lifeguards: Those who get it and those who don't. Those who get it are lifeguards for life.

What is *it*? The understanding that drowning can happen quickly, silently, with deadly consequences in a matter of minutes, and that it can happen to anyone, even in a facility where nothing has happened in decades. And that being a lifeguard (who gets it) is one of the most valuable and demanding jobs you'll ever have.

Let's contrast this attitude and understanding with lifeguards who don't get it. They may have never been told the facts about how drowning occurs in a way that instills understanding, and they may work within a culture of complacency that has built up over the years and never been challenged because no person has drowned at that facility. These people don't want to be bad lifeguards—they just don't know what they don't know. It is the goal of the StarGuard program to counteract complacency and help you understand the importance of what you will do as a lifeguard.

Aquatic facilities can and should be fun, and working there should be, too. However, it is important that you know what your job may entail.

# Misconceptions About Lifeguarding

When you think about your lifeguarding job, what comes to mind? Do you have any of these misinformed ideas about lifeguarding?

- I'll be getting paid for hanging out at the pool and getting a tan.
- I'll be paid for hanging out at the pool with my friends.
- Nothing bad has ever happened at the pool where I'll work, so nothing ever will.
- Drowning will be easy to see, and I know rescue skills, so I am prepared.

Lifeguarding can be one of the best and most rewarding jobs you can have. It can also be the worst experience of your life if you don't understand the risks. The goal of the StarGuard training program is to help you understand these risks and know the actions you can take—best practices—to develop a high level of competency.

# The Need for Best Practices in Lifeguarding

What is a "best practice"? This term can have many meanings, but for the purpose of this text refers to actions you can take to develop a high level of competence. "Best" does not mean exclusively the only "right" practice. The intent in identifying best practices is to give you a framework so you can focus on the behaviors and skills that can make the most difference in saving lives. Best practices are highlighted in the margins of the text throughout this book with this icon: ✚.

Age and experience range widely among lifeguards. Often, lifeguarding is the first job a person has in the teen years. The excitement of entering the workforce usually creates a highly motivated person ready to accept responsibility. However, in some circumstances, the workplace culture, and even the attitudes of society, changes the lifeguard who came out of training as someone who gets it into someone who becomes complacent and doesn't get it, which can be a recipe for disaster.

StarGuard training will help you identify and focus on the few critical things that can save a life when someone is within minutes of dying, and the program prepares you to do these things extremely well:

- Recognize
- Respond and rescue
- Resuscitate

Lifeguarding can be one of the most rewarding jobs you will have.

Each of these actions is important, but 100 percent of your time as a lifeguard may be spent in recognition mode. You will be scanning to recognize drowning, enforcing rules, and making interventions to change patron behavior. The interventions you will do every day are valuable and important components of saving lives. You must realize the importance of that fact and not equate lifeguarding only with the "hero" stuff of rescue and resuscitation.

# The Need for Best Practices From Management and Patrons

You will play an important part in saving lives, but you can't do everything. Your employer will have crucial responsibilities that will allow you to do your job to the best of your ability. The guests who come to your facility should also share in the responsibility for their own actions. This team approach will create a recipe for safety rather than a recipe for disaster.

## ⭐ Knowledge Into Practice

Your attitude and understanding of your responsibilities will determine your success as a lifeguard. The best practices identified in this text will help you keep the most important aspects of lifeguard performance in mind. The learning activities at the end of each chapter are designed to help you reinforce the content in each chapter.

## @ Visit the Web Resource

The activities in the web resource will help you reinforce your learning. Follow the instructions on the key code form bound into the front of the book to access the web resource, where you will be able to navigate to the unit designed specifically for each chapter, including the following interactive online learning activities for chapter 1:

- ▶ Activity 1.1: Examine your attitudes and expectations about becoming a lifeguard.
- ▶ Activity 1.2: View videos of a lifeguard describing the realities of lifeguarding and a drowning incident that occurred while he was on duty.
- ▶ Activity 1.3: Chapter quiz. Test your knowledge, receive feedback, and print the quiz page.

## ✚ On the Job

The on-the-job element at the end of each chapter summarizes the tasks related to the chapter content that you will be expected to competently perform while working as a lifeguard.

# Reducing the Risk at an Aquatic Facility

## CHAPTER OBJECTIVES

This chapter

▶ introduces the StarGuard Risk Management Model,

▶ describes the importance of a prevention strategy and layers of protection,

▶ identifies high-risk behaviors and policies to control them,

▶ provides methods for inspections and hazard identification,

▶ suggests methods for effectively enforcing rules and minimizing risk of injury, and

▶ identifies the need to watch for threatening behaviors and how to do so.

Aquatic risk management includes all the components in place at an aquatic facility to reduce the chance that an emergency will happen. As a lifeguard, you are part of the risk management system, so it is important that you know preventive strategies and those factors that contribute to drowning, illnesses, and injuries.

## StarGuard Risk Management Model

The StarGuard Risk Management Model has five components:

1. **Prevention strategy.** This includes all the behind-the-scenes components in place to reduce the risk of patrons drowning or becoming ill or injured.

2. **Surveillance.** Watching patrons, monitoring their behavior, and recognizing emergencies play a large role in reducing risk.

3. **Response and rescue.** You must understand what needs to be accomplished and use best practices to respond to and manage the emergency.

4. **Emergency care.** If an illness, injury, or drowning occurs, you must have a plan and be prepared to provide emergency care, whether the person is responsive or unresponsive.

5. **Workplace expectations.** The site-specific training, supervision, and culture at your workplace play a significant role in your future performance and ability to follow best practices.

Each component of the StarGuard Risk Management Model is separate from but dependent on the others—just like the appendages of a starfish, as illustrated in figure 2.1. If any part is weak or missing, your ability to minimize overall risk will be reduced.

Let's look more closely at a realistic concept of prevention and how it relates to your job as a lifeguard.

## Prevention Strategy

Lifeguard training, education, and standards have changed significantly over the years. Gone are the days when a coach, teacher, or attendant could be expected to serve as a lifeguard

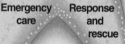

Ongoing performance assessment

Prevention strategy

Site-specific supplemental training

Workplace expectations

Surveillance

Emergency care

Response and rescue

**FIGURE 2.1** The StarGuard Risk Management Model.

while performing other duties. Today, the role of a lifeguard is extremely proactive, which involves constantly and exclusively watching the water and the patrons in it. In the past, the role of a lifeguard was more reactive, which meant being available to make a rescue when notified that someone was in trouble.

Although prevention is at the heart of your job, despite your best reasonable efforts, accidents happen. If you see dangerous or risky behavior, you can intervene and reduce the chance of an accident, but you can't watch everyone all the time. You also can't prevent accidents if patrons choose to disregard your warnings or don't use common sense, such as when caregivers leave children unattended, nonswimmers enter the water without a life jacket, or people dive into shallow water where "No Diving" signs are posted. In these instances, patron actions can cause an emergency situation.

Rather than thinking that prevention is solely the job of the lifeguard, you and the facility managers where you work should focus on your mutual responsibility for implementing prevention strategies. Having a strategy implies that several layers of protection are in place, all designed to help reduce the chance of injury, illness, or drowning. Patrons should share in this responsibility as well.

## Layers of Protection

The layers of protection that make up a prevention strategy, as illustrated in figure 2.2, include the following:

- **Design (safety) features and barriers.** The way a facility is designed (e.g., layout and barriers) and the type of materials used (e.g., nonslip flooring) can help reduce the risk of injury and control access.

- **Warnings.** Signs can help reduce injury by warning patrons of dangerous conditions or communicating important information.

- **Rules.** Rules should spell out the behavior expected at all times of everyone at a facility and should be posted in a visible location. Examples of two common rules include no running and no diving in shallow water.

- **Policies and procedures.** Policies help guide decisions and outline rules for specific circumstances that may not apply to all users. Well-designed policies that are strictly enforced can be one of the most effective layers of protection. Examples of policies include defining the age at which children may enter a facility unattended, identifying the types of flotation devices allowed, restricting nonswimmers to certain areas, requiring the use of life jackets, and restricting the use of play features to patrons of certain heights. Procedures describe actions to be taken in specific circumstances, including responding to emergencies. Procedures provide the framework for managing incidents and handling problems.

- **Surveillance.** The location and number of lifeguards and the scanning strategies expected of the lifeguards are a significant layer of protection. Regular and frequent inspections can either verify that the swim area, mechanical room, locker rooms, common areas, and facility exterior are in good condition or identify problems that need to be fixed. Performance audits can verify whether lifeguards

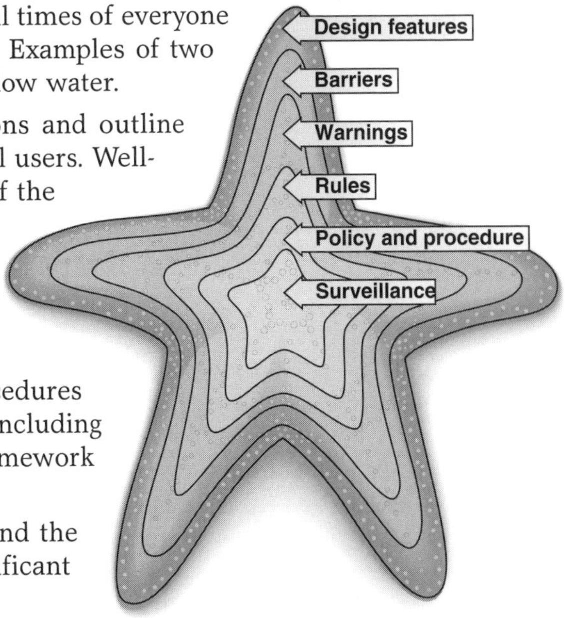

Design features
Barriers
Warnings
Rules
Policy and procedure
Surveillance

FIGURE 2.2 Layers of protection that make up a prevention strategy.

provide adequate surveillance, perform in a professional manner, and can manage an emergency or identify that remediation is necessary. A performance audit usually consists of observing and evaluating a lifeguard on duty and then conducting and evaluating a rescue scenario.

Because policies can be such an effective layer of protection, let's look at the reasons behind some of the policies that may be present at the facility where you work. Most policies have been developed to try to control dangerous patron behavior. You need to understand what kinds of behaviors can contribute to accidents so that you understand how enforcing a policy can help reduce risk.

## Controlling High-Risk Behaviors

Many known factors contribute to injuries, drownings, and illnesses in an aquatic environment. The following are the most common patron behaviors that contribute to injury at an aquatic facility:

- Running
- Horseplay
- Collision with another patron
- Diving into shallow water
- Striking the wall, diving board, or other equipment

The following are the most common patron behaviors that contribute to drowning:

- Lack of close and dedicated adult supervision for children
- Breath-holding activities or contests
- Bobbing or wading into deeper water and then choking on water or being unable to lift the mouth or nose out of the water
- Being a nonswimmer in the water without a life jacket
- Slipping off a flotation device such as a noodle or raft
- Having a seizure, heart attack, or other medical condition while in the water
- Not resting and becoming exhausted
- Being under the influence of alcohol or drugs

Finally, the following are the most common patron behaviors that can contribute to recreational water illness:

- Swallowing recreational water (treated water in pools, spas, water parks, or spray parks)
- Swallowing freshwater that contains contaminants such as wildlife feces, fertilizer runoff, or pesticides
- Fecal accidents in the water
- Diaper changing near recreational water

More information about prevention of recreational water illness can be found in chapter 3.

The following policies are suggestions that can help prevent injury, illness, and drowning by reducing the likelihood of high-risk patron behaviors. The facility where you work may have different policies that are modified based on site-specific needs, so be sure you are aware of what regulations you are expected to follow. Suggested strategies for reducing risk at water-park and waterfront facilities are provided in chapters 15 and 16.

- Restrict the use of starting blocks to those diving under the direct supervision of an instructor or coach. When not in use, mark starting blocks with warning signs, or put covers on them to prevent patrons from having access.

- Restrict all headfirst entries (dives) to deep water, and require entry with a hands above the head body position. Restrict divers from performing any technique that takes them back toward the board or side, or diving off starting blocks, unless under the supervision of a coach or instructor trained in safe diving technique and teaching progressions.

- Require that all children under a certain age be accompanied by a responsible person of a certain age (required ages will vary from facility to facility). Lifeguards are not babysitters, and they can't watch all children at all times. Parents and guardians should not leave children unattended. An even stronger policy requires that all preschool children or nonswimmers be directly supervised, within touching distance, by a responsible adult. Posting signs that clearly state the responsibility of the parent or caregiver and how this may relate to the responsibility of the lifeguard can help you enforce a supervision policy.

Active adult supervision within arm's reach helps prevent accidents or drownings.

- Prohibit breath-holding contests, underwater swimming contests, and hypoxic training drills (breath holding while swimming). These policies reduce the risk of swimmers passing out while underwater because of lack of oxygen.

- Require that nonswimmers stay in water that is less than waist deep. "Deep water" is relative to the height of a swimmer and can be considered anything above chest level for that person. A policy that requires nonswimmers to stay

### ⭐ High Risk of Parties and Group Outings

A high number of rescues and drowning incidents occur during events such as day-camp trips, group outings, and birthday parties.

Group leaders and party hosts should understand that they are responsible for the direct supervision of the participants and should be required to maintain a reasonable leader-to-participant ratio. Often group leaders or party hosts inappropriately view a trip to the pool as a chance to relax and turn over responsibility to the lifeguards. They also may be unaware of the swimming ability of the children in attendance and not understand the need to make sure nonswimmers wear life jackets. The energy level of the participants is often high, and peer pressure can encourage children to try activities that would not be allowed under parental supervision. A badge or vest that identifies the adults with the group as "child watchers" can help you know who the group leaders are as well as communicate a sense of responsibility to those assigned the identification.

Conducting a group orientation and safety briefing before the participants enter the water helps reduce the risk during these events. The orientation should include the following:

- Identifying group leaders
- Defining the responsibilities of the leaders
- Identifying the deep and shallow areas of the facility
- Explaining the rules and policies
- Locating and sizing life jackets
- Explaining restrictions and supervision requirements for nonswimmers
- Identifying nonswimmers

in waist-deep water can reduce the risk of drowning. Placing buoyed ropes across areas to define a depth change or using buoyed ropes to enclose areas of specific depths can help keep nonswimmers and children in shallow water.

- Require that nonswimmers or weak swimmers wear a U.S. Coast Guard-(USCG) or International Organization for Standardization (ISO) PDF Standard–approved life jacket or swimming flotation suit in the appropriate size. Looseness in the shoulder area or body means the device is too big. A life jacket policy can reduce the risk of drowning because the life jacket will keep the person wearing it on the surface. However, a life jacket may not keep a struggling person face up. In the United States, Type III (figure 2.3a) and Type V (figure 2.3b) are the most functional for swimming (vs. boating) activity and provide the best comfort and mobility.

- Restrict the use of flotation devices (such as noodles, rafts, and float toys) to certain

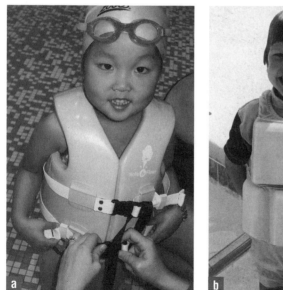 

**FIGURE 2.3** *(a)* USCG-approved Type III life jacket; *(b)* USCG-approved Type V swim flotation suit.

activities or areas to help reduce the risk of drowning if a nonswimmer or weak swimmer falls off a device. Restricting the use of large float toys also helps keep your underwater view clear.

■ Request physician approval in writing before allowing patrons to participate in certain activities, such as exercise classes. This policy may reduce the risk of a medical emergency happening at your facility.

■ Require a rest break by clearing the water on a prescribed schedule. Rest breaks can help reduce the risk of swimmers, particularly children, becoming overtired.

■ Prohibit alcohol and drug use in the facility, and have a procedure for evicting patrons suspected of being intoxicated or using drugs. This policy reduces the risk of impaired swimmers being in the water.

**When feasible, screen for nonswimmers.**

## Conducting Swim Skill Tests

If a policy at your aquatic facility allows only swimmers with demonstrated swimming skills to use certain areas of depth or requires nonswimmers to wear life jackets, you must have a way of determining skill level. Swim skill tests will determine whether someone can meet the requirements. It is not practical to conduct swim skill tests on every patron who enters an aquatic facility, but a testing method should be in place to screen users as needed. Screening for nonswimmers may be prioritized to include:

▶ First: any child under age 12 that is part of a group such as camps, field trips, or parties

▶ Second: all children under age 7 and anyone under 48 inches (1.2 meters) tall

▶ Third: children ages 8-12

A swim skill test places a person with unknown and untested skill in a high-risk situation. Therefore, you must minimize the risk and provide constant and dedicated attention to the swim test participant. You can accomplish this by doing the following:

▶ Be aware that a person's self-assessment of her swimming ability may not be accurate.

▶ Test in water no more than waist deep for the participant.

▶ Test along a wall or dock if possible, and walk along the edge to watch the swimmer. Allow only feetfirst entry during the test—no diving.

▶ Test no more than two swimmers at a time, except when testing swimmers of known skill for endurance (completing a distance swim of a predetermined length).

▶ Make sure rescue equipment is ready.

▶ Keep a written record of all swim skill evaluations that you conduct. Include the date, time, and swimmer's name and age. Detail which skills were evaluated, including the distance and time (e.g., swim 30 feet or 9 meters, tread water for 1 minute). Indicate the skill assessment outcome, such as passed/failed or satisfactory/unsatisfactory, according to the criteria set up at your facility.

After the results of the screening have been noted, you should have an action plan for those individuals who are nonswimmers or who do not pass your criteria. One effective method is to "float" nonswimmers by requiring that a life jacket be worn. An additional step to identify individuals who should be wearing a life jacket is to issue a wrist band of a certain color or style that can be seen by lifeguards or those responsible for supervising groups. See the Bibliography and Resources section for more information on life jackets.

Policies that can help prevent waterborne illnesses are described in detail in chapter 3 and include the following:

- Ask parents to instruct children not to swallow or drink water in which they swim or play. Your facility's procedures to regularly test the level of sanitizing chemicals in the pool or contaminants in freshwater should help reduce the amount and risk of disease-causing germs in the water.
- Require the use of swim diapers by anyone who does not have bowel control, and prohibit changing diapers on the pool deck.

# Minimizing the Risk of Injury

Three effective ways to minimize the risk of injuries are to eliminate or reduce known hazards, be prepared for environmental hazards such as weather, and enforce rules and policies.

## Inspections and Hazard Identification

Part of your job as a lifeguard is to watch for hazards or conditions at your facility that might threaten patrons' safety. This is true whether you are working at an indoor or outdoor facility. Examples of hazards include equipment defects; fall-causing hazards; security risks; air, water, or chemical hazards; and missing items.

### Equipment Defects

Inspect your facility for hazards daily.

- Broken or nonfunctioning equipment
- Loose bolts
- Rust on support beams
- Loose railings or handrails
- Loose stairs or footholds
- Broken grates
- Cracked or broken lane-line floats
- Broken fixtures
- Sharp edges or protrusions
- Leaks
- Cracks
- Exposed wires or overloaded plugs

### Fall-Causing Hazards

- Loose carpet
- Debris
- Standing water
- Obstructions
- Inadequate lighting

## Security Risks

- Damaged locks
- Doors that do not latch or open properly
- Suspicious people

## Air, Water, or Chemical Hazards

- Poor air or water quality
- Unsanitary conditions
- Improperly stored chemicals or cleaning products

## Missing Items

- Missing signs or markings
- Missing equipment or supplies

# Outdoor and Waterfront Area Hazards

Additional hazards at outdoor and waterfront areas may include the following:

- Wildlife
- Extreme temperatures
- Weather conditions
- Glare
- Currents, riptides, or undertows
- Submerged rocks or stumps
- Turbid (cloudy or dark) water
- Sharp objects or debris
- Holes or drop-offs
- Falling limbs or trees
- Obstructions
- Watercraft
- Unstable docks or piers
- Rotting or broken pier slats
- Changing water levels under platforms
- Missing or inadequate buoy line to mark swim area

Your employer should have a system for frequently inspecting the areas used by patrons. This is especially important for waterfront areas where natural hazards may form over time or debris may wash up on the shore. If you find a hazard that can't be immediately removed or fixed, you must limit access to the area and point out the dangerous condition to patrons. When possible, post warning signs or use barricades to keep people out of the hazardous area. Report hazards to your supervisor, or follow the procedure at your facility.

# Electrical Safety

In addition to the physical hazards in an aquatic facility, electricity can pose a risk. Electricity is present in the wiring used to power the pool pumps, lights, and other systems as well as in the outlets used for equipment. Electricity can also be present in the form of lightning, so you should understand the strategies for electrical safety and how to monitor thunderstorms.

Water and electricity can create a deadly mix. Take these precautions to prevent electrical shock:

- Keep electrical devices away from the water's edge.
- Elevate cords or cover cords on the ground with a mat or tape to prevent tripping.
- Know where the main power switch is for your facility; shut off power in the event of an injury from electrical shock. If the power cannot be turned off, use something that does not conduct electricity, such as wood, to remove the source of voltage from contact with the victim.

## Severe Weather Conditions

To reduce the risk of injury from severe weather, closely monitor weather conditions and be prepared to quickly direct swimmers out of the water and the surrounding area. Here are ways to monitor the weather:

- Emergency weather radios are inexpensive and provide warning signals when severe weather statements are issued.
- Live satellite and radar images and local forecasts are available on The Weather Channel and on weather information websites.
- Lightning detectors provide an early warning of approaching lightning. These devices measure the lightning strike distance, track the storm direction, and sound an alert when lightning is within a dangerous range. Lightning detectors, which are shown in figure 2.4, come in two forms: (1) a device permanently mounted to a pole attached to a building or (2) portable devices that can be clipped to a belt or carried.

**FIGURE 2.4** Portable lightning detectors.

Be familiar with weather conditions unique to your location. Knowledge of local weather patterns, such as where storms usually form and the direction they take, can be useful in making safety decisions. To determine if a storm is approaching your location, do the following:

- Watch the movement of the clouds; a storm may move in a different direction than the wind at ground level.
- Note abrupt changes in wind direction and speed as well as a sudden drop in temperature; both can be signs that you are in the path of a storm.

Emergency action plans (EAPs) are needed for severe weather as well as for aquatic emergencies. Learn the steps in your facility's EAP for severe weather. The EAP should detail evacuation procedures for a tornado warning and lightning-generating storms.

Instruct swimmers who are outdoors to exit the water and patrons to leave the surrounding area whenever storms are approaching. Lightning can develop a great distance ahead of a storm cloud and may appear to come out of clear blue sky. Consider yourself in striking distance whenever you can hear thunder from an approaching storm.

Keep swimmers out of the water until a passing storm is at least 10 miles (16 km) away. In most instances, the storm has moved on and threat is minimal when 30 minutes have passed since the last lightning or thunder.

If an electrical storm approaches and you are outdoors, direct patrons out of the water and to the closest safe location. A primary safe location is any building that people normally or frequently occupy. A secondary safe location could be any vehicle with a hard metal roof and rolled-up windows. If an electrical storm approaches and you are at an indoor aquatic facility, instruct patrons to exit the water. Follow the EAP for severe weather at your facility. When patrons are out of the water and located in a primary shelter, prohibit using landline telephones, taking a shower, and touching surfaces exposed to the outside, such as metal doors, windows, electrical wiring, cable, and plumbing. Electricity can travel indoors through these paths and could cause injury to people in these situations.

The most dangerous hazard in an aquatic facility is the behavior of the people who use the facility. Rules are made to help control dangerous behavior and actions. Because enforcing the rules will be an important part of your job, let's explore some ways to effectively communicate the rules to patrons.

> **Monitor severe weather conditions, and know the evacuation procedures at your facility.**

## Enforcing Rules and Policies

First, you need to know the rules at your facility and the reason for each rule. Make sure you understand each rule and that your fellow lifeguards understand it in the same way. Then, you need to effectively enforce the rules. You will have the most success getting patrons to follow the rules at your facility if you take a positive, professional approach. To be effective when enforcing a rule, follow these steps:

1. Signal to get a patron's attention, using the method designated at your facility. If your facility is crowded and noisy, you may need to blow a whistle or speak into a megaphone to attract attention; if it is less crowded, you may be able to speak directly to the patron more discreetly.

2. Use verbal or nonverbal communication to indicate to a patron that what he is doing is not acceptable. If the person does not understand or does not respond, then ask the person to come talk to you.

3. Once the patron comes to you, keep watching the water and explain to the patron that you are required to keep your attention on the swimmers in the water while you are talking. That

Enforce rules in a positive manner.

**Be consistent when enforcing your facility's rules and policies.**

way the patron won't mistake your lack of eye contact for a lack of respect or poor customer service.

4. Be courteous and positive when you talk to the patron. Use phrases such as "Please walk" instead of "Don't run," or "We allow only plastic bottles" instead of "You can't have glass in here." Briefly explain that the reason for a rule is to keep patrons safe, not to restrict their fun or enjoyment.

5. Use a "sandwich approach" when discussing a rule or policy infraction. Say something positive to the patron, state what you want the patron to do, and then say something positive again. Here's an example: "Ma'am, we're glad you are enjoying our pool today with your children. I want you to be aware that we have a policy that all small children need to be within arm's reach of an adult when they are in the water, so please stay in the water with your children. Thank you, we want everyone to be safe while having fun."

Whenever you are guarding, be consistent; enforce the same rule or policy the same way for everyone, each time. If a patron refuses to comply with a rule or policy, notify your supervisor, using the communication system in place at your facility.

## Identifying Threatening Behaviors

Besides knowing how to reduce hazards and enforce rules, you also must watch for behaviors that might be harmful to others. Aquatic facilities are usually open to the general public, and although the aquatic playground setting attracts people who want to enjoy themselves, it can also attract people with other intentions. For example, child predators go where children go. The threat of gang violence, terrorism, sexual predation, and other antisocial acts is present in any public location that attracts large crowds. If you notice suspicious behavior or activity, report it immediately to your supervisor. This behavior may include the following:

- Leaving unidentified packages unattended and where they should not be left
- Videotaping children without their knowledge
- Making frequent physical contact, especially in the water, with children in a crowd, or "by accident"
- Using the locker rooms and changing rooms frequently or for prolonged amounts of time
- Loitering or interacting with children without any apparent relation
- Entering the locker room or changing room of the opposite sex
- Loitering in a facility and not dressed in swimwear
- Congregating outside the fence
- Talking about violence or showing off a weapon
- Indecent exposure
- Sexual activity, gestures, intimate contact, or harassment

**Watch for threatening or suspicious behaviors and, if observed, notify your supervisor.**

Most of these behaviors by themselves are not threatening. You will need to consider the circumstances as you notice behaviors. If the behavior of another person makes you uneasy, further evaluation by others is a reasonable next step.

If you encounter serious disturbances such as violence among patrons, follow your facility's emergency action plan for these incidents. Any time a behavior is suspicious enough for concern, notify your supervisor and call for police assistance and have them address the situation.

## Performing Lifeguard Interventions

Every time you enforce a rule or correct a behavior, control admission of non-swimmers or weak swimmers into deeper water, or talk to a patron to educate her about safer behavior, you have performed a lifeguard intervention. Watching your zone and performing interventions will be the critical skills you will use the vast majority of the time you are a lifeguard. Rescue skills will (hopefully) be rarely used. It is important to understand that every time you perform an intervention, you are saving lives.

### ⭐ Knowledge Into Practice

You can't prevent all incidents from happening, but having knowledge of prevention strategies that can reduce risk will go a long way toward minimizing the chance that someone will need emergency care at your facility.

### @ Visit the Web Resource

You can reinforce your learning by visiting the web resource, where you can do the following in the interactive online learning activities for chapter 2:

▶ Activity 2.1: Build the StarGuard Risk Management Model.

▶ Activity 2.2: Test your skills for conducting a swim test and logging results.

▶ Activity 2.3: Evaluate real-life scenarios that could occur at an aquatic facility and build your decision-making skills.

▶ Activity 2.4: Listen to weather reports, and decide whether or not to clear the pool.

▶ Activity 2.5: Chapter quiz. Test your knowledge, receive feedback, and print the quiz page.

### ⊕ On the Job

These are the tasks related to reducing risk that you will be expected to competently perform while working as a lifeguard:

▶ Develop mutual responsibility between you, your facility, and patrons for following prevention strategies.

▶ Minimize the risk of injury by reducing known hazards, being prepared for environmental hazards, and enforcing rules and policies that protect patrons.

▶ Undergo ongoing training and skills assessment (provided by your employer) related to the site-specific needs at the facility where you will work.

## CHAPTER 3

# Managing Bloodborne and Recreational Water Illness

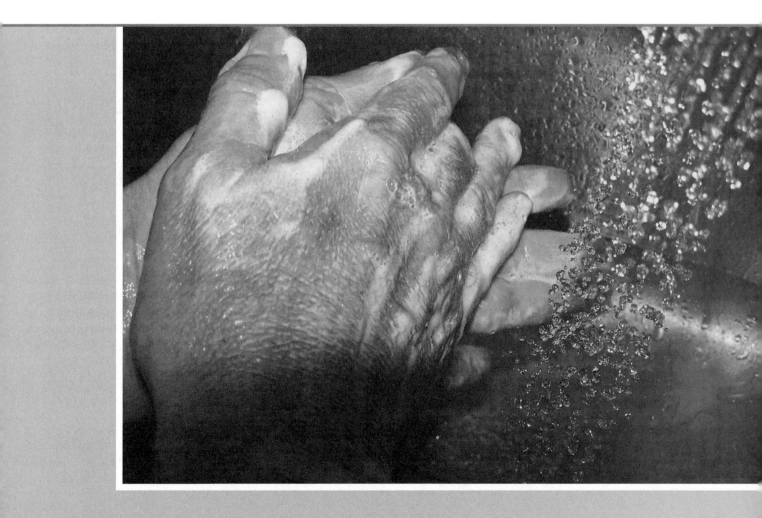

## CHAPTER OBJECTIVES

This chapter

▸ defines bloodborne pathogens,

▸ explains what to do in case you are exposed to bloodborne pathogens,

▸ defines recreational water illness (RWI),

▸ introduces a model for cleaning up bodily fluid spills on pool surfaces, and

▸ introduces a model for in-water vomit and fecal incident response.

This chapter explains how to prevent workplace exposure to potentially disease-causing pathogens and how to reduce the risk of exposure to waterborne pathogens. When lifeguarding, you may come in contact with blood, vomit, or fecal matter that can contain pathogens. When lifeguarding, you need to be aware of patron behaviors and incidents in or around the pool that can contaminate the water.

## Disease Transmission and Swimming Pools

A decade ago, few people would have linked getting sick with swimming in treated swimming pools. Today, however, media reports from around the world frequently contain stories of outbreaks: 3,000 illnesses that spread to 36 New York counties in 2005; 185,000 falling ill after a 2007 outbreak in Japan; and that same year, 1,902 cases in Utah. Many more outbreaks have gone unreported or are of smaller scale and did not get worldwide media attention. All aquatic recreation facilities seem to be vulnerable—even those that are well managed. Outbreaks are often hard to identify quickly because it takes many people reporting an illness before a pattern can be established and it can be determined whether all the people had visited the pool. The consequences of an outbreak can be high: Several people have died, thousands have been hospitalized, facilities have been shut down for extended periods of time for expensive cleanup, and multimillion-dollar lawsuits have been filed. What is behind the surge of outbreaks? Is there a new "superbug"? Are we more aware because of better monitoring? Is it media hype? Are our immune systems weakening? Have our chemicals become less potent? Are people less careful of toilet habits? There are no simple answers to these questions, but this chapter explores how you can play a role in preventing exposure to potentially disease-causing pathogens.

Most bodily substances, especially blood, vomit, and fecal matter, can contain disease. The germs that can be transmitted through direct contact with blood and some bodily fluids are called bloodborne pathogens. The germs that can be transmitted by swallowing contaminated water are called waterborne pathogens. Let's look at bloodborne pathogens first.

## Bloodborne Pathogens

You may have contact with blood or bloody bodily fluids when you are involved in a rescue, performing first aid or CPR, or performing cleaning duties at the aquatic facility where you work. In these circumstances, you need to use infection control guidelines to minimize the risk of yourself and others becoming ill. The two primary diseases caused by bloodborne transmission are HIV and hepatitis.

HIV and AIDS are acronyms for human immunodeficiency virus and acquired immune deficiency syndrome. AIDS applies to the most advanced stages of HIV infection. By killing or damaging cells of the body's immune system, HIV progressively destroys the body's ability to fight off certain bacteria, viruses, fungi, parasites, and other microbes.

Hepatitis is the name of a family of viral infections that affect the liver. The most common types are hepatitis A (HAV), hepatitis B (HBV), and hepatitis C (HCV).

■ HAV infection is primarily transmitted by the fecal–oral route, by either person-to-person contact or through consumption of contaminated food or water. Hepatitis A vaccination is the most effective measure to prevent HAV infection.

■ HBV infection is transmitted through contact with infectious blood or bodily fluids and can cause acute illness and lead to chronic or lifelong infection, cirrhosis (scarring) of the liver, liver cancer, liver failure, and death. Hepatitis B vaccination is the most effective measure to prevent HBV infection.

■ HCV is spread by contact with the blood of an infected person. Exposure sometimes results in an acute illness but most often becomes a silent, chronic infection that can lead to cirrhosis, liver failure, liver cancer, and death. Most HCV-infected people do not know they are infected since they have no symptoms. There is no vaccine for hepatitis C.

## Hepatitis B (HBV) Vaccine

The HBV vaccine is delivered by injection and is used to prevent infection by the hepatitis B virus. The vaccine works by causing your body to produce its own protection (antibodies) against the disease. The vaccine is made without any human blood or blood products or any other substances of human origin. It cannot give you the hepatitis B virus (HBV) or the human immunodeficiency virus (HIV).

In the United States and many other countries, occupational safety regulations require that an employer make the hepatitis B vaccination available if you are assigned to a job with occupational exposure to blood or bodily fluid and have not previously been vaccinated. In the United States you may decline the hepatitis B vaccination but decide to accept it at a later date. If you decline the vaccine, you must sign a declination document.

# Reducing Exposure to Bloodborne Pathogens

You can prevent transmission of bloodborne pathogens by isolating yourself and others from contact. The first step in isolating a bodily substance is to use universal precautions, which means that whether or not you think the victim's blood or other bodily fluid is infected, you act as if it is. The next step is to protect yourself from becoming exposed through the use of protective equipment.

## Personal Protective Equipment

Because you cannot look at a bodily substance and know if it is infected, assume that all bodily fluids and feces could contain pathogens. Always use personal protective equipment (PPE) when you are at risk of exposure to any type of bodily substance. The minimum personal protective equipment available for your use while lifeguarding should include disposable gloves, protective eyewear, protective footwear, and a barrier mask for use during resuscitation.

### Disposable Gloves

Use disposable, single-use gloves to protect your hands. If a glove is damaged, don't use it! Wearing two pairs of gloves can provide an additional barrier and further reduce the risk of transfer of bloodborne pathogens.

When taking contaminated gloves off, do it carefully. Don't snap them. This may cause blood to splatter. See the skill guide on this page for the recommended technique.

Never wash or reuse disposable gloves. Make sure there is always a fresh supply of gloves in your first aid kit. If you find yourself in a first aid situation and you don't have any gloves handy, improvise. Use a towel, plastic bag, or some other barrier to help you avoid direct contact.

Some people are allergic to natural rubber latex, which can be a serious medical problem. You may be at risk for developing latex allergy if you use latex gloves

## SKILL GUIDE

## Removing Contaminated Gloves

| **Grasp First Glove** | **Remove Inside out** | **Slide Finger Under** | **Throw Gloves Away** |

**Grasp First Glove**

Always remove contaminated gloves carefully. Never snap them, as this may cause blood to splatter. Without touching the bare skin, pinch the glove at the base of either palm, pulling it slightly away from the hand.

**Remove Inside out**

Gently pull the glove away from the palm and toward the fingers, turning the glove inside out as you remove it. Gather the removed glove inside the palm of your gloved hand.

**Slide Finger Under**

Without touching the outside of the contaminated glove, slide the ungloved index finger inside the wristband of the gloved hand. Gently pull outward and downward so that the glove comes off inside out, trapping the first glove inside.

**Throw Gloves Away**

Throw away both gloves in an appropriate container to prevent any further contact. Wash your hands immediately with warm running water and soap, or use an alcohol-based hand rub.

frequently. Allergic reactions may include skin rashes; hives; nasal, eye, or sinus symptoms; asthma; and (rarely) shock.

If you are allergic, take steps to protect yourself from latex exposure and allergy in the workplace. Taking simple measures such as using nonpowdered latex gloves and nonlatex gloves can stop the development of latex allergy symptoms and help you prevent new cases of sensitization.

It is difficult to put dry gloves onto wet hands, especially when you are in a hurry. If your hands are wet, and you are near the water, it may help to fill your glove with water and then slip your wet hand into the wet glove.

**SKILL GUIDE**

## Putting on Gloves With Wet Hands

**Get Gloves**

When possible, carry gloves with you.

**Fill Glove With Water**

Open the wristband and scoop in water.

**Insert Hand**

Line up your fingers with the water-filled glove.

**Lift Hand**

Repeat with the other glove and hand.

### Protective Eyewear and Footwear

In the presence of large amounts of blood or vomit, wear some type of covering for your eyes to reduce the risk of bodily fluids splashing into your eyes and entering your body. Bloodborne viruses can be transmitted through the mucous membranes of the eyes from blood splashes or from touching the eyes with contaminated fingers or other objects. Eye protection provides a barrier to this transmission.

Goggles or glasses with solid side shields or a chin-length face shield should be worn whenever splashes, sprays, or spatters of blood or bodily fluids are present or reasonably anticipated. Appropriately fitted, indirectly vented goggles with a manufacturer's antifog coating provide the most reliable practical eye protection from blood splashes and sprays. Regular prescription eyeglasses and contact lenses are not considered eye protection. Contact lenses, by themselves, offer no protection against infection.

Whenever you are cleaning up bodily fluids, you also need to wear some type of footwear to prevent contact with your bare feet. At a minimum, wear sandals. When large amounts of bodily fluids are present, consider footwear with more coverage and protection.

### Barrier Masks

Resuscitation devices (pocket masks, face shields, or bag-valve mask devices) must be made readily available to employees who are designated or can reasonably be expected to perform resuscitation procedures.

Your employer must provide you with proper training in the specific type, use, and location of the devices present where you work, according to the manufacturer's instructions or acceptable medical practice.

There are several styles of barrier masks:

- A shield-style device provides a minimal barrier and is compact enough to be carried on a keychain or in a pocket. This type of barrier is designed for use by laypeople and is not the best choice for use in the aquatic workplace.

- Masks designed for professional rescuers have a larger mouthpiece and a one-way valve, and they create a seal over the mouth and nose for maximum ventilation. These barrier masks may also contain a port for an oxygen tube and may come in different sizes for use on an infant, child, or adult.

- Bag-valve mask devices (also known as a BVM) come in various sizes (see figure 3.1). It is very important to select the proper size of bag-valve mask device, especially for an infant or small child.

**FIGURE 3.1**  Bag-valve mask (BVM).

Always place a barrier between you and another person's blood or body fluid.

Once you are protected by PPE, your risk of transmission is greatly reduced. However, incidents may occur when you are unexpectedly not protected by PPE. If a *significant amount* of blood or bodily fluids comes in contact with your unprotected skin or eyes, or you have been stuck with a needle, you may be considered exposed and should follow specific steps after the incident.

## Exposure Incidents and Follow-Up

You may be exposed to blood or bodily fluids when you provide first aid and do not use PPE, or when you are cleaning up around your facility if syringes are discarded in the trash or on the grounds. If you or others have a sharps injury such as an accidental needle stick or are exposed to blood or bodily fluids at work, immediately follow these steps:

1. Wash cuts and needle sticks with soap and water.
2. Flush splashes to the nose, mouth, or skin with water.
3. Irrigate eyes with clean water, saline, or sterile irrigants.
4. Report the incident to your supervisor.
5. Immediately seek medical treatment.

After a report of an exposure incident (and after initial first aid), an employer in the United States must make a confidential medical evaluation and follow-up immediately available to you. If you work outside the United States, follow your employer's guidance.

## Recreational Water Illness and Waterborne Pathogens

If vomit or fecal matter gets into the water, there is a slight possibility that germs may remain long enough, before being killed by the sanitizing agent such as chlorine, for a patron to become ill by swallowing contaminated water. Although incidents of transmitting serious disease in this manner are rare, you must understand how the risk for transmitting these diseases can be reduced.

A recreational water site is anywhere people enter the water such as a pool, water park, hot tub, lake, river, or ocean. Recreational water illnesses (RWIs) are caused by germs spread by swallowing, having contact with, or breathing in mists or aerosols of contaminated water in swimming pools, hot tubs, water parks, water-play areas, interactive fountains, lakes, rivers, or oceans. RWIs encompass a wide variety of infections, including gastrointestinal, skin, ear, respiratory, eye, neurologic, and wound infections. Patrons who are most at risk for getting very sick from an RWI include children, pregnant women, and those who have an immune system deficiency caused by HIV, chemotherapy, or other conditions.

Germs that cause RWIs generally enter the water when a swimmer has a fecal incident while in the water. When swimmers are ill with diarrhea, their stool can contain millions of germs and contaminate the water. In addition, on average people have about .14 gram of feces on their bottoms that, when rinsed off, can contaminate recreational water. Germs are less likely to be present in a small amount of vomit, which is a common occurrence when a child swallows too much water, especially right after eating. Viruses are more likely to be present in vomit when it contains more than just regurgitated pool water, which may indicate that a person is sick. Germs that may be present in blood don't survive in chlorinated water and do not pose a threat.

The most common RWI is diarrhea, which can be caused by germs such as the following:

■ *Crypto* (KRIP-toe, which is short for *Cryptosporidium*)
■ *Giardia* (gee-ARE-dee-uh)
■ Norovirus
■ *E. coli* (ee-CO-lye, which is short for *Escherichia coli*)

There are other germs and chemical compounds that naturally occur in the environment. If disinfection, oxidation, or pH levels of the water are not maintained appropriately, these germs can multiply and cause other types of RWIs that affect the skin, eyes, ears, or respiratory tract.

# Reducing Exposure to Waterborne Pathogens

When people swim, they always ingest a small amount of water. This is why it is so important to keep the germs out of the water in the first place and to have adequate chemicals in the pool water to kill germs that are present. Chlorine (in swimming pools and hot tubs) kills the germs that cause RWIs, but the time it takes to kill each germ varies. For example, *Crypto* can survive for days, even in a properly disinfected and sanitized pool. The aquatic facility where you work should have several strategies for reducing exposure to waterborne pathogens, including patron education, water testing, and fecal and vomit response procedures for both land-based and in-water incidents.

## Patron Education

Educating patrons about how to avoid contaminating the water is the first step in reducing the risk of RWIs. Your employer should post signs and distribute information for patrons about how to reduce the spread of recreational water illnesses. The Centers for Disease Control and Prevention (CDC) has established a list of healthy swimming behaviors for protection against RWIs that should be included as the foundation to educate patrons.

### Three Steps for All Swimmers

1. Don't swim when you have diarrhea. You can spread germs in the water and make other people sick.
2. Don't swallow the pool water. Avoid getting water in your mouth.
3. Practice good hygiene. Shower with soap before swimming, and wash your hands after using the toilet or changing diapers. Germs on your body end up in the water.

### Three Steps for Parents of Young Kids

1. Take your kids on bathroom breaks or check diapers often. Waiting to hear "I have to go" may mean it's too late.
2. Change diapers in a bathroom or diaper-changing area and not at poolside. Germs can spread in and around the pool.
3. Wash your child thoroughly (especially the rear end) with soap and water before swimming. Invisible amounts of fecal matter can end up in the pool.

> Make sure you can explain, in a way that is inoffensive and acceptable to parents, why behaviors such as using public chairs and tables for diaper changing is a health risk.

## Water Quality

Treated water should be tested several times per day using a test kit designed for measuring the chlorine level as well as other qualities of the water such as pH and temperature. The health authority regulations in place at your location will determine how often during a day these tests must be conducted. If you are responsible for adjusting chemical levels, adding chemicals to the water, or backwashing to clean the pool filters, you must obtain additional training and, depending on your location, possibly certification in pool operation and safety procedures for handling chemicals.

## Incident Management

Fecal incidents are a concern and an inconvenience for both pool staff and patrons. A written bodily fluids (blood, vomit) and fecal accident response policy will help you respond more efficiently to any problems. You may not have control over the event's occurrence, but you do have control over how you respond and document it.

### Bodily Fluid or Fecal Matter Incident Response on Pool Surfaces

Your workplace should have a specific plan for how to clean up and dispose of bodily fluids or fecal matter that is found on the pool deck or other surfaces. A cleanup procedure should consist of at least these key components:

1. Use universal precautions, and wear your personal protective equipment.
2. Contain the area of exposure. If blood, vomit, or fecal matter is on the floor or pool deck, mark and restrict access to the area to prevent others from walking through it and becoming exposed or spreading the bodily substance.
3. Remove the substance. There are many effective methods for removing a liquid substance, such as soaking it up with an absorbing material and scooping up the material into a container. Then use paper towels to absorb or pick up any remaining substance. Commercially packaged biohazard cleanup kits usually include single-use packets of absorbing material, or it is available in large containers. As an alternative, you can use other high-absorbing materials (such as cat litter) effective for the type of contaminant, the type of surface to be cleaned, or the area within the facility. Remove a solid bodily substance by scooping it up or picking it up inside a plastic bag.
4. Disinfect the area of exposure with a bleach solution of 5,000 milligrams per liter or an equivalent product that has been approved by your regulatory agency for bodily fluids disinfection. Gently pour or spray the disinfectant on the area. Leave the disinfectant on the area for least 20 minutes or as otherwise directed on the label or by your regulatory agency. Wipe up any remaining bleach solution with paper towels, and allow the area to air dry.
5. Dispose of the contaminated materials in a sanitary manner or as required by law. Place the materials in a double plastic bag, being careful not to touch the outside of the bag. Tie or close the inner bag. To prevent cross-contamination, soak any nondisposable utensils you used in bleach, and allow to air-dry. When the cleanup process is complete, remove your gloves. Place your gloves and any other soiled items in the outer plastic bag and close the bag. If the bag is not marked as a biohazard, place a biohazard label on the bag.
6. Allow others to access the cleanup area after the deck, ground, or floor is completely dry.
7. Wash your hands using hand hygiene techniques.

### Fecal and Vomit Incident Response in Chlorinated Recreational Water

Chlorine in recreational pool water kills germs that can contaminate water, but the chlorine does not work immediately on some types of pathogens. For example, in swimming pool water treated with chlorine at levels that meet most health regulations, *E. coli* can live for less than a minute, and some viruses will live for about 16 minutes. Parasites can be harder to kill. *Giardia* survives about 45 minutes, and

**If you are responsible for water testing, make sure you understand how your employer wants you to respond if the disinfectant levels are not adequate.**

**Disinfection solution can be made by slowly adding one part household bleach to nine parts of water. Gently mix the solution.**

*Cryptosporidium* can survive for almost 11 days. Guidelines have been established that help determine the amount of chlorine and the amount of time necessary to kill different pathogens. Because norovirus is more likely to be present in vomit, *Giardia* in formed stools, and *Crypto* in loose stools (diarrhea), you will handle each type of incident in a slightly different manner.

A diarrheal fecal incident is a higher-risk event than a formed-stool incident. With most diarrheal illnesses, the number of infectious germs found in each bowel movement decreases as the diarrhea stops and the person's bowel movements return to normal. Therefore, a formed stool is probably less of a risk than a diarrheal incident.

A formed stool may contain no germs, a few, or many that can cause illness. You won't know. The germs that may be present are less likely to be released into the pool because they are mostly contained within the stool. However, formed stool also protects germs inside from being exposed to the chlorine in the pool, so prompt removal is necessary.

Your facility should have a detailed response plan that follows the regulatory guidelines for your location. If your job function includes water testing, handling of pool chemicals, and water dosing, follow the guidelines and safety procedures in place at your facility. Otherwise, follow the vomit and fecal incident communication plan established by your employer to notify those who can make water adjustments.

For the most recent disinfection guidelines suggested by the CDC, go to www.cdc.gov/healthywater/swimming/pools/disinfection-remediation-pools-hot-tubs.html.

The information about fecal contamination and disinfection guidance is based on the recommendations of the Centers for Disease Control and Prevention (CDC), but it does not replace the health authority regulations in place in your location. The recommendations are revised when new research or information becomes available. Check www.cdc.gov/healthyswimming for the most recent updates.

## Freshwater Contamination

Freshwater swimming areas in lakes, streams, ponds, and rivers can also contain pathogens and germs that cause RWIs. Contamination from human bodily fluids or feces is possible, but the bacteria and other pathogens found in freshwater usually come from wildlife feces or wastewater runoff. Freshwater is not chemically treated with chlorine, so there is no way to kill the pathogens once they are present. A common testing schedule for freshwater is weekly or more frequently if required by the local health authority or if bacteria levels are above a certain point. The usual procedure is to obtain a water sample in a sterilized container and take it to a laboratory for testing. If the test results are not within the acceptable range, the swimming areas are closed until nature takes its course and the bacteria levels drop.

## Knowledge Into Practice

There are many unanswered questions about RWIs, and research is ongoing. The solution will likely involve a multifaceted approach requiring that everyone involved—patrons, pool operators, equipment designers, health agencies, media, management staff, coaches, instructors, and lifeguards—be aware of the danger and educated about prevention practices. Because it is such a complex problem, you can play an important role in reducing the spread of RWIs. For this reason, it is important that you stay informed of developments and apply that knowledge while on the job.

## @ Visit the Web Resource

You can reinforce your learning by visiting the web resource, where you can do the following in the interactive online learning activities for chapter 3:

- ▶ Activity 3.1: Obtain the CDC's latest fecal incident response recommendations for pool staff, listen to a podcast of the CDC's Dr. Michael Beach discussing the superbug *Cryptosporidium*, and explore other resources from the CDC.
- ▶ Activity 3.2: View an RWI symptoms and fecal and vomit simulation, and decide what action to take.
- ▶ Activity 3.3: Play the pathogens transmission game.
- ▶ Activity 3.4: Equip the lifeguard to protect him from bodily substances.
- ▶ Activity 3.5: Order the steps of protective glove removal.
- ▶ Activity 3.6: Review scenarios to help you practice minimizing risk of exposure.
- ▶ Activity 3.7: Chapter quiz. Test your knowledge, receive feedback, and print the quiz page.

## ⊕ On the Job

These are the tasks related to minimizing disease transmission that you will be expected to competently perform while working as a lifeguard:

- ▶ Follow exposure control procedures when cleaning up vomit, fecal matter, blood, or other bodily fluids.
- ▶ Appropriately apply procedures for fecal and vomit water contamination cleanup in accordance with facility standards, health and safety requirements, and relevant legislation and industry code.

# PART II

# Surveillance

# Recognizing Distress and Drowning

## CHAPTER OBJECTIVES

This chapter

▶ differentiates between distress and drowning,

▶ explains the drowning process,

▶ describes what a person in distress or drowning may look like,

▶ explains why time is critical when a person is drowning, and

▶ identifies why drowning victims are hard to recognize when under the water.

One of the most important skills you must develop as a lifeguard is the ability to recognize when a swimmer needs help so you can intervene quickly. A drowning person does not look like the stereotype portrayed in movies or drawings: someone frantically waving arms or shouting for help. A distressed or drowning person exhibits behaviors that are much more subtle and difficult to detect. It is also important to understand that all people in the water are at risk of distress or drowning—from nonswimmers to world-class athletes and everyone in between.

## Distress

A person in distress is still on the surface of the water but is struggling to stay afloat. The person's mouth or nose or both are above the surface, and he is still able to breathe (see figure 4.1). Some behaviors that indicate a person is in distress include the following:

■ Head back and body low in the water

■ Arms extended from the sides and moving up and down

■ Minimal use of the legs, with little support from a kick

Often, a person in distress will try to remain upright and turn to face the nearest source of assistance, for example toward a lifeguard stand, the pool wall, or shore. If this is the case, and the person is relatively close, you may be able to recognize a fearful, wide-eyed look on his face (see figure 4.2). However, you cannot rely only on facial expression to indicate distress because a person may be facing away from you or blocked from your view by other people.

If distress continues, the person's mouth and nose will sink below the surface of the water, and she will begin to drown. How quickly a person progresses from distress to drowning varies depending on many circumstances. A

**FIGURE 4.1**   Person in distress: eyes closed.

person who cannot keep his mouth and nose out of the water and breathe will die unless someone intervenes. The earlier the person receives help, the better the chance of keeping a distress situation from becoming a fatal drowning.

It is important to understand that not everyone experiences distress first, before drowning. Many drowning victims are not upright or on the surface of the water to start with and therefore never exhibit any of the observable instinctive responses to try to stay on the surface. Examples include people who submerge underwater and never surface. Chapter 5 provides more detail about the circumstances that often surround drowning without observable distress.

**FIGURE 4.2**   Person in distress: eyes opened.

## ⭐ Definitions of Drowning

Lack of agreement on a definition of *drowning* has made analysis of drowning studies difficult. In response to this problem, a group of international experts met in 2002 at the World Congress on Drowning to develop definitions and guidelines for reporting drowning data. The following is the universal definition of *drowning* that was adopted by consensus:

*Drowning* is the process of experiencing respiratory impairment from submersion or immersion in liquid. Additionally, the victim may live or die after the process, but regardless of the outcome, she or he has been a part of a drowning incident. Other definitions related to drowning include the following:

▶ *Drowning victim.* A person involved in an incident in which the airway has been covered with water, preventing her from breathing air, and being unable to surface, is considered a drowning victim. A drowning victim who is rescued becomes a drowning survivor if she remains alive after a drowning event.

▶ *Drowning survivor.* The physical condition of a drowning survivor can vary from complete recovery to having permanent brain damage or heart damage. Many drowning survivors at facilities where lifeguards are present are rescued before becoming unresponsive and recover completely. A drowning survivor who is unresponsive may be resuscitated at the scene by lifeguards providing basic life support, or during prehospital care by EMS, or at the hospital by advanced life support measures. The length of time a drowning person was unresponsive determines the amount of permanent damage sustained, in addition to other factors. Many drowning survivors must be placed on a ventilator and fed through a tube. These drowning survivors live in what is called a vegetative state and cannot function without the aid of the machines keeping them alive.

▶ *Drowning fatality.* A person who dies as a result of a drowning incident is considered a drowning fatality. The death may occur at the scene or may occur later at the hospital as a result of lack of oxygen to the organs or infections such as pneumonia.

For research and statistical purposes, the term *near drowning*, although once popular, should not be used. Now that you know the terminology associated with drowning, let's discuss the physiological changes that the body goes through during the drowning process.

# Drowning Process

A person's first response to the drowning process is to hold her breath, followed shortly by a laryngospasm. A laryngospasm is a physical reaction to water droplets at the back of the throat that causes the top of the larynx (the windpipe that carries air from the mouth to the lungs) to close. At this time the victim tries to breathe but cannot and instead may swallow large amounts of water.

As the victim's blood oxygen level falls, the laryngospasm relaxes and the victim may breathe water into the lungs. The amount inhaled is different for each person. Studies have shown the average amount of water inhaled during drowning to be relatively small and involve only 4 ml/kg of liquid.

If the victim does not return to the surface and start breathing, either on his own or after being resuscitated, the heart will stop, brain damage caused by lack of oxygen will occur, organs will stop functioning, and the victim will die. The heart and brain are the organs at greatest risk for permanent damage during drowning, even if someone interrupts the drowning process and resuscitates the victim.

Two factors to remember about drowning are that a person doesn't have to be submerged completely under the water for drowning to occur; a person can drown if her face is immersed in water. And the amount of time that passes before interruption of the drowning process is crucial to the victim's survival.

## Water Depth and Drowning

A person is drowning if the face and airway are covered with water, and the head cannot be lifted or brought to the surface to breathe. Drowning can occur through either just the face being covered with water or the entire body being underwater. It is important to understand that drowning can occur in a small amount of water, such as if a child is trapped in a bucket or toilet or is unable to get up after falling facedown in a puddle, or in the shallow water of a beachfront or stairs entry area. Remember that shallow water is relevant to a person's height. What may be considered shallow to an adult would be deep to a toddler.

## Time Factors

> ✚ Realize the importance of early recognition of distress or drowning.

You can interrupt drowning at any time by making a rescue. The earlier you interrupt the process, the better the victim's chances for survival without brain or organ damage.

The length of time a victim was submerged is the most important predictor of survival. Unless the water is very cold (less than 50 degrees Fahrenheit, or 10 degrees Celsius), brain damage and death generally occur 3 to 5 minutes after the person starts drowning, although this varies from person to person. Figure 4.3 shows how the length of submersion relates to survival outcomes.

To intervene quickly in an emergency situation, you must rely on your observation skills and understand what a person in distress or who is drowning might look like.

> ✚ Realize that drowning will not look like the drowning portrayed in movies.

# Victim Recognition

A person in distress or drowning may have certain movements or behaviors that you can observe (see figures 4.4 and 4.5). Table 4.1 provides a summary of the most common observable indications of distress or drowning.

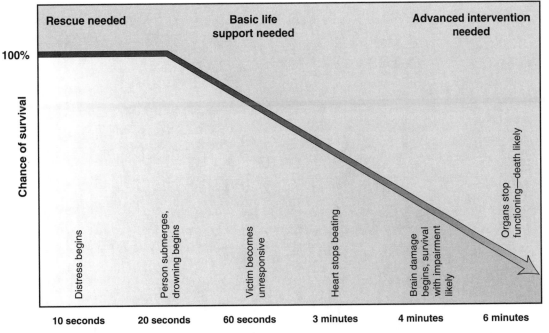

Note: This time line is a representation of general physiological responses during drowning. The individual circumstances of each drowning can cause wide variation from the times represented. Unresponsiveness and death can occur with much shorter submersion times, and survival can occur with much longer submersion times. Not all drowning victims start on the surface with distress, especially nonswimmers and young children.

**FIGURE 4.3** Time is critical in chances for survival.

**TABLE 4.1**

## Observable Indications of Distress and Drowning

| | Distress (mouth and nose are above water) | Drowning (mouth and nose are covered by water) |
|---|---|---|
| Can the person breathe? | Yes | No |
| Expression | The person's head and face may tilt back with a wide-eyed panic-stricken look, or the eyes may be squeezed shut. Hair may be over the face and eyes. | Expressions are usually not visible because the victim's nose and mouth are covered by water. |
| Movement | Limited leg movement. Arms are often out to the side, making fast back-and-forth or up-and-down movements just under the water. | If the person is still responsive, distress symptoms can occur under the water. If the person is unresponsive, the person will be limp, but the water movement may still move the body. |
| Position | Body is low in the water, with mouth at water level. Position is usually vertical or on an angle. | Any position: vertical, horizontal, or at an angle in the water. An unresponsive person may float facedown or faceup, on the surface, or submerged. |
| Depth | Usually on the surface or alternating just underneath the surface, with bobbing up to the surface for a breath. | On or just beneath the surface, submerged to mid-depth, or on the bottom. |
| What this person may look like | ▪ Someone struggling to stay on the surface<br>▪ Someone trying to swim but not moving forward<br>▪ Someone bobbing<br>▪ Someone gasping for air<br>▪ Someone struggling to get to the side of the pool<br>▪ Someone struggling to grab something to stay afloat | ▪ Someone playing underwater or bobbing<br>▪ Someone floating<br>▪ Someone trying to stand up but unable to<br>▪ A shadow<br>▪ A smudge or blur<br>▪ A towel on the bottom<br>▪ A drain on the bottom |

**FIGURE 4.4** A drowning victim at the beginning of the drowning process may still show movement in the water.

**FIGURE 4.5** A drowning victim may float on the surface with his head facedown in the water or may be faceup.

Not all drowning symptoms can be seen. The properties of the water can interfere with the ability to see a victim who has submerged under the surface (see figure 4.6).

FIGURE 4.6  Close-up view of a submerged drowning victim who is difficult to see through the water's surface.

## How the Water Hides Drowning Victims

You might think that in a pool with clear water you would be able to clearly see something on the bottom. While this might be the case when there is no one in the pool and the water is still, the circumstances change when the water begins to move.

As soon as people enter the water, it begins to move and the surface is filled with ripples and undulation. Even a breeze can cause the water surface to become impossible to see through. Add glare caused by the sun angle or reflection off of windows, and your vision underwater can be completely obscured. Figure 4.7 on page 42 shows a sequence of how a simulated drowning victim can completely disappear from view as the surface water moves.

Because distress and drowning symptoms may be subtle and silent, and the water can hide a victim, it is important for you to know how to look to give you the best chance of seeing a victim as early as possible in the drowning process. This is discussed in chapter 5.

**Realize that water hides and suffocates its victim.**

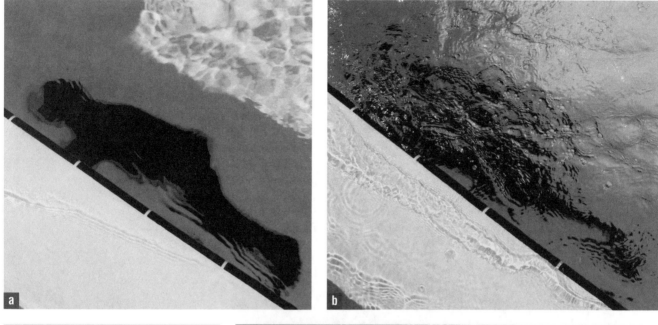

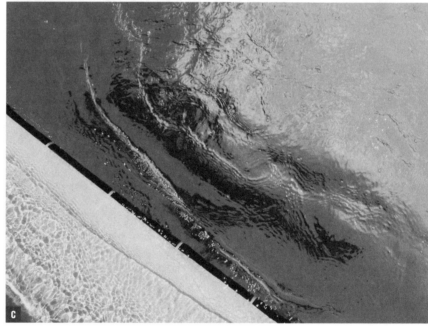

FIGURE 4.7 (a) Visible simulated drowning victim; (b) water movement begins to hide the victim; (c) victim is almost invisible.

## ⭐ Knowledge Into Practice

Knowing how to recognize a distressed or drowning person is the most important lifeguarding skill you can possess.

## @ Visit the Web Resource

You can reinforce your learning by visiting the web resource, where you can do the following in the interactive online learning activities for chapter 4:

▶ Activity 4.1: View a video of how the water hides anything under the surface.

▶ Activity 4.2: Watch video clips showing real people in distress from the view of a lifeguard chair.

▶ Activity 4.3: Complete an activity to heighten your awareness of the urgency of time.

▶ Activity 4.4: Chapter quiz. Test your knowledge, receive feedback, and print the quiz page.

##  On the Job

These are the tasks related to recognizing distress and drowning that you will be expected to competently perform while working as a lifeguard:

▶ Understand the observable symptoms that a distressed or drowning person may exhibit.

▶ Understand that a submerged victim may not be clearly visible.

▶ Understand the critical element of time and the need to act quickly when a person is drowning.

## CHAPTER 5

# Looking for Distress and Drowning

## CHAPTER OBJECTIVES

This chapter

▸ identifies critical lifeguard observation skills,

▸ explains the RID factor,

▸ describes lifeguard zones,

▸ identifies the StarGuard scanning model,

▸ provides strategies for remaining vigilant,

▸ illustrates methods for maintaining surveillance during rotations, and

▸ explores the potential of drowning detection technology.

To intervene quickly in an emergency situation, you must rely on your observation skills. These include the ability to watch the water (scan), identify anything unusual (target), and determine if there is an emergency (assess the situation).

Scanning is a combination of eye movement, head movement, body position, and alertness strategies that allow you to watch every area of the water you are responsible for. This chapter describes zones, emphasizes the importance of your scanning location and ability to see underwater, and explains the use of rotations to keep you alert as you continuously guard the water. This information allows you to develop a scanning method that is effective in your particular work environment.

## Observation Skills

To recognize distress or drowning, you must continuously perform three crucial observation skills: scan, target, and assess. To *scan* means to watch the water, using specific patterns and timing. If you notice a situation that might indicate a problem, you will *target* the person or people and look more closely. The next step is to *assess* the situation and determine your course of action. The following scenario illustrates how you would use your observation skills:

■ **Scan.** While you are watching a crowded pool, you notice a man holding a young child. He is standing in shoulder-deep water, and they are located near a gradual slope into deeper water. Neither exhibits distress symptoms. However, you notice several things about the situation that could indicate a potential problem, so you briefly target your attention on the father and child.

■ **Target.** You target the father and child for closer examination for the following reasons: The father's bobbing movements are gradually pushing him toward deeper water. The child does not appear comfortable in the water. The crowded conditions may prevent the father from quickly changing position and moving toward shallow water.

■ **Assess.** You assess the situation and realize with one more step the father could quickly become submerged just enough to be unable to breathe or to recover to a standing position. You decide to take action and intervene to get the attention of the father, directing him to move back toward shallower water.

Let's consider another example. A seven-year-old child is playing in the shallow end, which for him is water that is chest deep. He and a friend decide to move out a bit from the edge, pushing off the bottom and bobbing or maybe "wall walking" (holding on to the side) a couple of feet into slightly deeper water. The water is just deep enough that when the child pushes up off the bottom to get to the surface for a breath, his mouth does not clear the water. The child gulps a mouthful of water instead of air. In this situation, the child is not able to cry out for help because he is already underwater. The child's movements may make him appear to be swimming underwater, and if you don't have a clear underwater view, you may not notice anything extraordinary during your scan. You may not recognize the situation because there are no signs of distress until the child stops moving and is unresponsive. In this case, the lack of movement you notice when you scan, if the movement of the water is not obstructing your

Scanning is your primary job function.

view, is what causes you to target the situation for further examination, assess it as an emergency, and begin a rescue. In many instances it will be a nearby patron, with a clear view, who may notice the victim first. Whenever someone in the water requests your attention and has concerns about another person in the water, respond immediately and check it out.

Anytime you see something and are not sure what you are looking at, check to make sure it is not a drowning victim. Lifeguards who have seen a submerged drowning victim often describe what they saw as a "shadow" or a "smudge." Statements such as "I thought it was a towel on the bottom" or "It looked like the drain but it was in the wrong place" or "I thought the person was swimming underwater" are common. Lifeguards who have seen a drowning victim floating on the surface often claim, "I thought she was relaxing" or "I thought she was playing." Do not make assumptions about what a person may or may not be doing if he is submerged for much longer than 10 seconds or not actively and obviously swimming and exhibiting signs of life.

In some instances, a change in movement may cause you to target in on a situation. For example, if a patron has been swimming laps and her stroke pattern, tempo, or body position changes, this could signal distress. If a person enters deep water and begins to ineffectively move his arms to try to keep on the surface, this person could be in distress and need your immediate intervention. A drowning person may still be moving, submerged but near the surface, with a wide-eyed and panic-stricken look and not able to call out or wave for help.

# The RID Factor

Each year, people drown in swimming pools with lifeguards on duty. The first question people usually ask is "How could this happen?" In many cases, the drowning was a result of medical conditions or environmental factors. However, in some instances, the lifeguards didn't recognize that a person was drowning because they did not know what to look for.

Frank Pia was the first to analyze distressed or drowning swimmers' behaviors. After analyzing film of hundreds of distressed and drowning swimmers in real situations, Pia recognized three factors that contribute to a lifeguard's inability to respond to a drowning victim. Although Pia's film study was limited to swimmers in an ocean setting, the fundamental concepts he defined as the RID factor can help identify the need for constant and dedicated surveillance.

The following are the three factors:

- **R**ecognition. The lifeguard did not recognize that a person was in distress or drowning because the victim did not splash or cry for help; the victim's struggle was silent and lasted a short time.
- **I**ntrusion. The lifeguard did not watch patrons closely because other nonsurveillance tasks, such as maintenance or cleaning, intruded on his ability to scan.
- **D**istraction. The lifeguard was distracted because she was bored or engaged in conversation with peers or patrons.

Adapted from Pia 1984.

The RID factor explains why it is important to know what distress or drowning may look like, to constantly scan as your only dedicated responsibility when you are on station, and to use vigilance strategies to remain alert and keep from being distracted. It may not be physically possible for you to see every instance of distress or drowning, but understanding the RID factor will help you perform to the best of your ability and meet your lifeguard responsibilities.

# Zones

A *zone* refers to the area of the water you are responsible for when scanning. A zone is three dimensional and includes the water surface, the bottom, and everything in between. No matter where patrons are located or the number of patrons in your zone, the physical area that you scan does not change.

You should be able to describe the exact boundaries of your zone. Your primary zone is the physical area you are responsible for, and your secondary zone is everything within range of your sense of sight, sound, and smell. If you work at a facility with several lifeguards, the water area is divided into multiple zones with overlapping coverage. If you are the only lifeguard at your facility, your zone is the entire pool. The size of the zone you are responsible for may change with the conditions at your facility. You also must be aware of transition zones and how to handle zone coverage during a rotation and during an aquatic emergency.

## Zone Size

A zone should be of a size that you can do the following:

- Scan the three-dimensional (3-D) area within 10 seconds
- Get to the farthest part of the zone within 20 seconds

Zone size at your facility may change based on the number of patrons, the nature of pool activities, the time of day, or other conditions. For example, as more patrons enter your zone, it may take longer to scan or longer to swim across because of the crowded conditions. If the zone can't be scanned in 10 seconds, or if you don't think you could get to the farthest area of the zone within 20 seconds, the zone should be made smaller by adding another lifeguard and reassigning the zones.

Zone charts that clearly mark the location of each site-specific protection zone should be posted in the lifeguard office or on the stands. A common method to indicate specific zones is to assign each zone configuration a color code and post zone charts for each. For example, zone assignments when two lifeguards are on duty may be code yellow. Later in the day, when the facility is more crowded and additional lifeguards are on duty, the zone assignments switch to code red.

## Transition Zones

When more than one activity takes place in a facility, many facilities use a transition zone, or safety zone, such as an area between swimming and diving activities or swimming and boating areas. Participants are not allowed in this zone. Even though this area is not used, it is still part of your zone, and you should scan it just as thoroughly as if swimmers were present.

## Emergency Zone Coverage

Be prepared to cover another lifeguard's zone if she enters the water to make a rescue. When lifeguards scan adjacent zones, it is usually the lifeguard to the rescuer's left who takes over the zone. Follow the plan in place at your workplace.

When you scan during emergency coverage, watch for a signal for assistance from the lifeguard making the rescue. If he needs help, transfer emergency zone coverage to another lifeguard or clear the zone of swimmers according to the plan in place at your facility.

Now that you understand the concept of zones, let's look at where lifeguards should be placed and at scanning methods for effectively monitoring your zone.

## Zone Verification to Determine Location of Lifeguards

The ideal location for scanning is a place where you can see your entire zone. This may be from an elevated lifeguard stand, or an alternative location may be better if the stand has blind spots or a glare problem from the sun during certain times of the day. In some conditions, the only way you are able to cover your zone is by roaming the deck and scanning the water while you walk.

Depending on the features at your facility, some lifeguard locations may be in the water, such as at the bottom of a waterslide, or on floating docks. Chapters 15 and 16 describe strategies for determining locations and surveillance strategies at site-specific attractions.

Before establishing or changing a zone plan for a facility, zones should be tested at various times of day and in different patron level conditions to verify the ability to see the entire zone (no blind spots) from the lifeguard location. One method of zone verification is to station a lifeguard in the stand and have a person submerge to the bottom in various places of the zone. Start under the lifeguard stand and continue in a grid-like pattern being sure to verify all corners and potential blind spots. Another method is to use a submersible mannequin to conduct the zone verification.

In addition to verifying that there are no blind spots, verify that the submerged person or mannequin can be viewed within 10 seconds as the eyes scan from the furthest area of the zone back to the area of submersion. Then place the submerged person or mannequin in the furthest area of the zone and verify that the rescuer can reach the area from the lifeguard stand within about 20 seconds.

# The StarGuard Scanning Model

Constant visual contact with the water, including dedicated attention to the activity in and around it (surveillance), is your primary responsibility. The two key words in this statement are *constant* and *dedicated*. The StarGuard scanning model illustrated in figure 5.1 represents the why, when, where, what, and how of scanning.

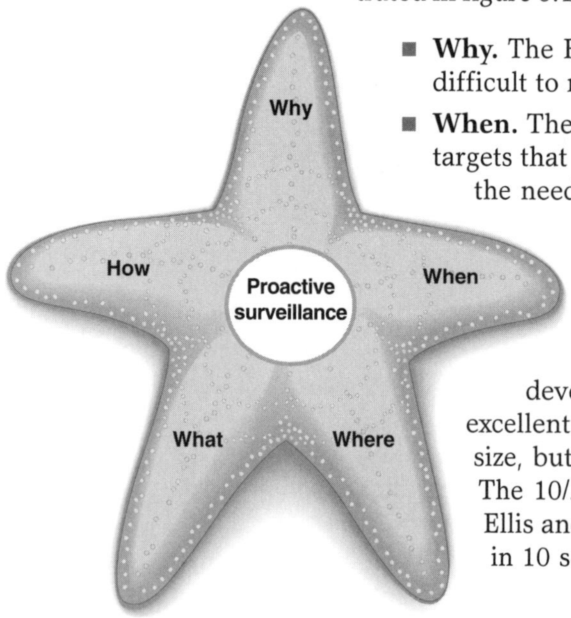

■ **Why.** The RID factor reinforces the fact that a drowning victim may be difficult to recognize.

■ **When.** The timing of your scans will vary based on the zone, number of targets that you assess as you sweep your eyes, and other factors such as the need to stop scanning for brief periods to enforce rules or other interventions. In general, effective scanning should be timed to allow you to respond to a victim as early as feasible and ideally within 30 seconds. Sweeps of your entire zone with your eyes every 10 seconds will be effective in most circumstances. Over the years various scanning "rules" have been developed by training organizations based on time. These rules are excellent training tools and methods for determining appropriate zone size, but cannot be considered mandates effective in every situation. The 10/20 rule, developed by the aquatic safety consulting firm Jeff Ellis and Associates, says you should be able to scan your entire zone in 10 seconds, and you should be able to reach the farthest point of the zone in 20 seconds.

**FIGURE 5.1**  The StarGuard scanning model.

■ **Where.** 3-D triage scanning, developed by the Starfish Aquatics Institute, states that the person who most urgently needs rescue is the one who is submerged and may be on or near the bottom.

■ **What.** Scanning should be constant and dedicated. Constant means that nothing interrupts scanning. Dedicated means that scanning is all you do.

■ **How.** Moving your head and eyes are critical for effective scanning when your zone is not entirely in front of you. You also need to know how to remain alert, and the 5-Minute Scanning Strategy is one method that provides ideas for improving vigilance.

**Move your eyes and your head when you scan.**

Let's look more closely at 3-D triage scanning, how to move your head and eyes, and what to look for.

## 3-D Triage Scanning

In the medical field, the term *triage* refers to sorting patients in order to provide treatment first to those with the most need for, and likelihood to benefit from intervention. In your zone, where would the most severely endangered victim—one with the most critical need—be located? Remember that once the drowning process has begun and a victim is submerged and cannot breathe, it takes just a few minutes before brain damage or death occurs. Thus, the most critical victims are those who have already completely submerged and drifted toward the bottom.

Triage your scanning by first looking for anything out of the ordinary on the bottom and under the surface (vitally urgent). Then scan looking for other distress or drowning indications from people on the surface (urgent). Then scan looking for behavior situations that may require rule enforcement (important).

## Head and Eye Movement

Most zones will be large enough to require some head movement (from side to side or up and down) to position your eyes and enable you to see the entire area. Small zones, such as catch pools or areas limited to directly in front of the lifeguard station, will not require head turn.

Regardless of the zone size, your eyes should make sweeping movements across the zone so you can conduct your 3-D scan. As you sweep your eyes, pause occasionally to focus on a segment of the zone, and target any symptoms of distress or drowning. Time the combination of head turn, eye sweeps, and focusing on segments so that your eyes look at each area of the zone about every 10 seconds. This timing does not have to be exact, but it helps give you a sense of the need to frequently look at every area.

> Scan every area of your zone about every 10 seconds to look for symptoms of distress or drowning.

## What to Look for When Scanning

Do the following while you are scanning:

1. Look for someone who may be submerged and drowning. Target anyone who is submerged and verify that the person comes to the surface within a few seconds. This includes anyone who is
   - bobbing up and down or
   - appears to be swimming or playing underwater.
2. Look for symptoms of distress.
3. Look for high-risk behaviors and rule infractions.

> Target anyone bobbing or under the water, and assess the situation. If you don't know, go!

Frequently review the symptoms of distress and drowning described in chapter 4, and remember that there may be others. If you don't know, go!

# Strategies for Improving Vigilance

*Vigilance* means to be watchful, attentive, alert, and aware. When you are vigilant you have a sense of urgency and understand why it is important to focus on your task. You are expected to be vigilant when you are on station, but it can be difficult, especially in conditions of heat and during times of low activity in your zone. There are some strategies you can consider to help you remain vigilant and keep your attention from drifting.

## 5-Minute Scanning Strategy

This strategy keeps your scanning efforts organized and your attentiveness high. Follow these steps to perform the 5-Minute Scanning Strategy:

1. Consistently scan your zone, sweeping your eyes and turning your head so you can see every area of the zone every 10 seconds.
2. Use the same scanning pattern for 5 minutes. A scanning pattern is the direction of head movement and eye sweeps you use to be sure you cover each area of the zone. Scanning patterns should be simple and not require thought. For example, first sweep your eyes side to side, and then switch to sweeping your

eyes up and down across the zone. The goal is to institute a change to avoid monotony and keep you alert, not burden your mind with patterns to follow.

3. As you scan, triage your efforts by first looking at the bottom and under the water. Then assess the patrons in your zone that are on the surface, looking for behaviors that may indicate distress or drowning.

4. Make frequent changes (about every 5 minutes) in posture, position, and pattern. The goal is to keep you alert through physical movement and variation. The exact timing and what changes you make are not as important as the fact that you do something.

Reprinted, by permission, from Dr. Tom Griffiths.

One way to make significant position and posture changes is by switching from sitting to standing or to strolling. For example, during the first 5 minutes of your rotation, sit. During the next 5 minutes, stand. Then stroll for the next 5 minutes. The goal is to do some type of movement rather than sit in the same place and position for a long period of time.

If your facility has elevated lifeguard stands with only a small step for your feet, it may not be practical to stand or stroll. In this instance, you will have to identify other ways to meet the objective of keeping alert through physical movement.

A strategy for keeping your mind active and engaged in scanning is to "touch" each person with your eyes as you scan. If you are moving your head and sweeping your eyes, but your mind is thinking about things other than the behaviors of the patrons, you will not be focused enough to notice situations that may need intervention.

Your facility may have a communication system in place so you can signal to other lifeguards at the end of each 5-minute scanning segment that your zone is okay. Common signals used during the 5-minute increments include a raised "thumbs-up," a raised rescue tube, or a short whistle blast. This type of communication system helps you know when it is time to change position, posture, and pattern.

> **Use vigilance strategies to remain alert.**

## Surveillance Breaks

Research from other professions that require high vigilance, such as air traffic control, has shown that the ability to remain focused starts to decrease significantly after about 30 minutes. When feasible, the rotation schedule at your facility should be established so you are not in any one location for a long time. The short break from surveillance to move from station to station will help you be vigilant. It also helps to alternate periods of nonsurveillance duties, as well as breaks when you can get out of the sun, with periods when you are on station and actively scanning.

## Vigilance Voice

The vigilance voice technique is a method to help you explore your zone by putting a voice to what you see. The method was developed by Terri Smith after experiencing "commentary drive" techniques used by emergency response teams when teaching driving skills. Your facility may use vigilance voice as part of organized training, or you may find it helpful to do on your own. By talking through every detail of what you see while you scan, you will remain focused and be able to identify problem areas you may not have noticed before. The StarGuard web resource contains a video clip of how to perform the vigilance voice.

## Site-Specific Victim Recognition Training

Another common method that facilities use to maintain lifeguard vigilance and help you learn to identify a submerged drowning victim is mannequin or shadow drops.

This type of site-specific training activity is feasible at facilities where it is possible to place a small waterproof training mannequin, or a body outline that lies flat on the pool bottom, into the water without a lifeguard noticing (see figure 5.2). These unexpected scenarios help you remember to perform a 3-D triage scan, allow you to practice actually seeing something on the bottom, and are also a good way to test and develop zones by verifying that the item can be seen in any location within the zone.

## Shadow Guarding

Sometimes it is helpful to learn from others. Shadow guarding pairs up two lifeguards, usually one more experienced than the other. The less experienced lifeguard "shadows" the other and learns by observing and discussing (such as through the

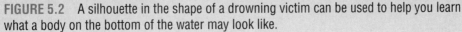

**FIGURE 5.2** A silhouette in the shape of a drowning victim can be used to help you learn what a body on the bottom of the water may look like.

vigilance voice activity) the best strategies for scanning the zone. If you are assigned to a shadow guard position, remember that your conversations and attention should remain on being vigilant, not on socializing.

## Lifeguard Reviews or Audits

Your facility may have a system in place to conduct unannounced lifeguard reviews, which are also known as audits. These reviews may be conducted by a member of the management staff (internal) or by someone not affiliated with your facility (external). Reviews keep your vigilance high because you never know if someone is watching and documenting your performance while you are on station. More information about reviews can be found in chapter 13.

You can't provide constant and dedicated surveillance for one zone for an extended period; it becomes physically and mentally too difficult. To give you breaks away from surveillance responsibilities, your facility should have a system for frequently moving lifeguards from one location to another. When another lifeguard comes to take over your zone, this change is called a rotation.

## Proactive Rotations

Rotations help you keep your attention level high. The shorter your time at a zone and the more frequent your rotations, the more attentive you are likely to be. Rotations generally involve the lifeguard on break coming back into a lifeguard zone and the other lifeguards moving in sequence to new locations. Rotation timing varies from facility to facility, but it generally occurs every 15 minutes to every hour. Rotation charts should be present at your facility to diagram the movement of the lifeguards from station to station.

The lifeguard taking over a zone is known as the incoming guard, and the lifeguard who has been scanning the zone is the outgoing guard. A well-performed rotation presents a very professional image and does not compromise the level of surveillance for the zone. A well-executed rotation

> **Scan the entire zone, including the bottom, before taking over or leaving a zone during rotation.**

- occurs quickly,
- involves limited conversation, and
- provides a systematic transfer of responsibility.

A proactive rotation begins the minute you begin to proceed to your station. Depending on the features present at your facility, your station may be a lifeguard stand of some type, a slide tower, an in-water location, or a roving position. Scan the water as you walk toward the zone so you can get a feel for the activity level and begin to prepare yourself mentally for your scanning responsibility. Scanning the zone before you take it over assures that you are becoming responsible for a "clean" zone—one that does not have a drowning victim on the bottom that the previous lifeguard missed.

If you don't have your own rescue tube as you rotate into a station, the outgoing lifeguard will have to transfer one to you. The lifeguard with the rescue tube during a rotation is responsible for scanning and would be the person to make a rescue, if needed.

The procedure description on page 55 is for a traditional lifeguard stand with several stairs along the back or front. In this procedure the rescue tube is transferred twice. If your facility has lifeguard stands that allow a side, front, or back walkout, you can modify the rotation system so the tube is transferred once.

# Proactive Rotation

### Incoming Guard Sweeps the Zone

The incoming lifeguard performs a full sweep and scan of the bottom of the pool and then says, "Bottom clear."

### Passing the Rescue Tube

The outgoing lifeguard passes the rescue tube to the incoming lifeguard.

### Incoming Guard Takes Over Zone

The incoming lifeguard positions the rescue tube, begins scanning, and says, "I have the zone."

### Outgoing Guard Climbs Down

The outgoing lifeguard climbs down from the chair and stands next to the incoming lifeguard. Both lifeguards scan. The rescue tube is passed back to the outgoing lifeguard, who positions the rescue tube and assumes responsibility by saying, "I have the zone."

### Incoming Guard Climbs Up

The incoming lifeguard climbs up into the chair. The outgoing lifeguard passes the rescue tube back up to the incoming lifeguard, who positions the rescue tube, begins scanning, and says, "I have the zone."

### Outgoing Guard Sweeps the Zone

The outgoing lifeguard does a complete sweep and scan of the bottom, then says (or signals), "Bottom clear," and leaves the zone.

- If both of you have a rescue tube, perform the rotation in the same manner except for the transfer of the rescue tube.
- Be careful not to slip while climbing up or down a chair ladder.

A proactive rotation does not end when you leave the lifeguard stand. Scan the zone as you walk away. Remember that the eyes of the patrons are on you any time you are in public view; maintain your professionalism.

We've identified the difficulty in being able to see a victim who is submerged under the water, even in a pool with clear water. In locations with turbid (dark) water, seeing under the surface is impossible. Advances in technology are resulting in the development of systems to help counter these surveillance difficulties.

# Drowning Detection Technology

Crowds, glare, ripples, blind spots, dark water, or floating rafts and tubes can make it difficult for you to see beneath the surface to scan the area you know is vitally important. Recent technology makes it possible to scan the underwater area and bottom with a clear view or to be notified if a person is submerged in dark water. This technology greatly increases your ability to be aware of a swimmer in difficulty and execute a rescue. Although it may not be feasible to have such a system at all aquatic venues, you may work at a location that does utilize technology, so you may need to be familiar with the concept. You will need to obtain site-specific training on the equipment where you work.

## Underwater Camera Systems

Underwater cameras can be linked to a small monitor on your guard chair, which gives you a real-time view under the surface to include in your scanning pattern. Do not sit and watch the screen; rather, look at the monitor about every 10 seconds as part of your regular scan. Some monitors can be programmed to sound a reminder beep at a designated interval and to track compliance when you push a button to verify that you have looked at the underwater view on the screen.

This technology greatly enhances your ability to see under the water and provide 3-D triage scanning without the limitations of surface movement or glare. In some facilities, reliable and user-friendly technology may be the only answer to full and effective water surveillance.

## Alarm Systems

Alarm systems emit a warning signal if a swimmer has been submerged under the water for a predetermined threshold of time. A system of receivers and detection devices is installed that covers the swimming area. Some systems can sense a body on the bottom. Other systems require swimmers to wear a tracking sensor device, usually inside a head band or wrist band. If the sensor submerges past a certain depth for a dangerous amount of time, the alarm sounds.

The use of technology should not de-emphasize your role as a lifeguard. Nor should these devices be allowed to create a culture of complacency because they are in place. Instead, technology should supplement your skills and reduce your limitations, because even with a diligent staff the risk of drowning is always present at an aquatic venue.

## ⭐ Knowledge Into Practice

Looking for distress and drowning is the critical skill you will use almost the entire time you are lifeguarding. While it may not be possible to always see a person who is distressed or drowning, it is your primary responsibility to stay vigilant proactively scanning when on station.

## @ Visit the Web Resource

You can reinforce your learning by visiting the web resource, where you can do the following in the interactive online learning activities for chapter 5:

- ▶ Activity 5.1: Analyze ideal locations for scanning.
- ▶ Activity 5.2: Order steps for a proactive rotation and watch video clips of lifeguard rotations.
- ▶ Activity 5.3: View video clips of how it looks to scan from a lifeguard chair, and practice virtual scanning.
- ▶ Activity 5.4: View a video clip of a lifeguard discussing the importance of scanning, and view a video clip of an actual drowning that highlights the importance of vigilance.
- ▶ Activity 5.5: Listen to a description of the vigilance voice training activity.
- ▶ Activity 5.6: Chapter quiz. Test your knowledge, receive feedback, and print the quiz page.

## On the Job

These are the tasks related to scanning and vigilance that you will be expected to competently perform while working as a lifeguard:

- ▶ Use observation skills, while systematically scanning, to look for behaviors that indicate distress (when a person can still breathe) or drowning (when a person's mouth and nose are covered with water).
- ▶ Maintain vigilance while you are on station.

# PART III

# Response and Rescue

# Deciding to Act and Emergency Response

## CHAPTER OBJECTIVES

This chapter

▶ examines legal considerations and barriers to action,

▶ defines responder chain of command and chain of survival,

▶ explains the importance of communication signals,

▶ presents the STAAR aquatic rescue model,

▶ identifies how and when to contact emergency medical services (EMS) and what to expect when you call,

▶ describes an effective emergency action plan (EAP),

▶ explains how to manage an emergency scene including providing directions to a crowd and coordinating bystander involvement, and

▶ identifies considerations when activating the EAP for a water rescue.

An emergency, such as a sudden illness, injury, or drowning, can happen at any time. A coordinated response by the people and agencies that provide care offers the best chance for a good outcome.

When an emergency happens, responders may provide different levels of care. Responders may have certain legal obligations depending on the severity of the event and their training.

## Legal Considerations

During an emergency, certain legal principles apply regarding what you are expected to do in the United States. These principles include the following:

■ **Duty to act.** If you are a lifeguard expected to give emergency medical care, including CPR, you almost certainly have a duty to act. However, emergency care performed voluntarily on a stranger in need while you are off duty is generally considered a Good Samaritan act.

Duty to act is a requirement to act toward others and the public with the watchfulness, attention, caution, and prudence that a reasonable person in the same circumstances would use.

■ **Good Samaritan principle.** Since governments encourage people to help others, they pass Good Samaritan laws (or apply the principle to common laws). These laws prevent a rescuer who has voluntarily helped a stranger in need from being sued for wrongdoing. You are generally protected from liability as long as you are reasonably careful, act in good faith (not for reward), and do not provide care beyond your skill level. If you decide to help an ill or injured person outside your job, you must not leave that person until someone with equal or more emergency training takes over (unless it becomes dangerous to stay).

■ **Consent.** A responsive adult must agree to receive care. To get consent, first identify yourself. Then tell the victim that you are a lifeguard and ask if it's

OK to help. People over the age of 18 may give oral or written consent or give consent by gesturing.

- *Implied consent* means that permission to perform care on an unresponsive victim is assumed. This is based on the idea that a reasonable person would give permission to receive lifesaving first aid if he were able.

- **When caring for children**, you should gain consent from a parent or legal guardian. However, when a life-threatening situation exists and a parent or legal guardian is not available, give first aid care based on implied consent.

- **When caring for older adults**, you must keep in mind that if they are suffering from a disturbance in normal mental functioning, such as Alzheimer's disease, they may not understand your request for consent. Consent must then be gained from a family member or legal guardian. Again, when a life-threatening situation exists and a family member or legal guardian is not available for consent, give first aid care based on implied consent.

■ **Confidentiality.** A person has the right for her name and medical history to remain confidential among care providers. Care providers may share only information pertinent to medical care. The regulation in the United States that governs confidentiality is the Health Insurance Portability and Accountability Act, which is commonly referred to as the HIPAA law.

■ **Standard of care.** This is the level of emergency care that you are expected to provide, based on the level of your training, and with a response that a reasonable person in the same circumstances would use. If a person's actions do not meet this standard, then the acts may be considered negligent, and any damages resulting may be claimed in a lawsuit for negligence.

■ **Negligence.** This occurs when an injured or ill person incurs proven damage from a trained person who has a duty to act and the person does not uphold the standard of care.

■ **Refusal of care.** A person older than 18 can refuse treatment and care if he is alert and oriented to the surroundings.

■ **Advance directives, living wills, and do not resuscitate (DNR) orders.** These are documents authorized by law and are usually witnessed or notarized. The documents allow a person to appoint someone as her representative to make decisions on resuscitation and continued life support if the person has lost her decision-making capacity (e.g., if she is in a coma). Advance directives are statements about what victims want done or not done if they can't speak for themselves. The DNR is a type of advance directive. This is a specific request not to have CPR performed. In the United States, a doctor's order is required to withhold CPR. Therefore, unless the victim has a DNR order, emergency care providers should attempt resuscitation. Victims who are not likely to benefit from CPR and may have a DNR order include those with terminal conditions from which they are unlikely to recover. Outside the hospital, rescuers should begin CPR if there is a reasonable doubt about the validity of a DNR order or advance directive, the victim has changed his mind, or the victim's best interests are in question.

■ **Documentation.** All emergency care provided must be recorded in writing. This document serves as a medical record and legal documentation.

# Legal Liability

The legal system in the United States and most countries allows a lawsuit to be filed any time there is a perceived wrong. Filing a lawsuit puts into motion a series of events to determine the details of the alleged wrongdoing. The person filing the lawsuit, called the plaintiff, must prove that the other person, called the defendant, caused the injury either through action or inaction and that the injury could have been anticipated and therefore could have been prevented.

Only a judge or jury can decide whether the people named in the lawsuit were guilty of negligence. Before going to trial, a judge may determine that there is not enough evidence of wrongdoing or refuse to hear the case, or the parties involved may settle the case. In any event, simply naming someone in a lawsuit does not mean she is guilty; she must be found to be so in a court of law.

The legal process is time consuming, emotionally draining, and expensive. If an injury or drowning event happens while you are lifeguarding and a lawsuit is filed, it would likely name your employer, you, and possibly others as defendants. In most instances, your employer would cover the legal costs to defend you. In some locations, if you work for a governmental agency, you cannot be held liable.

However, if you are working as an independent contractor or for someone other than your primary employer (such as at an after-hours party for which the host is paying you directly), you can be held liable and may not be covered under an insurance policy. It is important for you to understand the different types of employment status and the possible consequences in the event of legal action. If you are unsure of your status, be sure to ask, and consider legal advice.

In most countries, to be considered an employee, you are required to fill out government withholding tax forms. In the United States, legitimate employers follow state and federal labor laws as well as occupational safety regulations, pay employment tax, and provide worker's compensation insurance in case you are injured on the job. All these provisions are designed for your protection. If you are asked to work without filling out employment tax forms, the person hiring you may be considering you an independent contractor, and you will likely not be covered by worker's compensation or liability insurance should you get injured or should a lawsuit be filed against you. In this instance, you should consider purchasing liability insurance. Be sure you understand your employee status and the possible consequences before accepting any lifeguarding job.

# Responder Chain of Command

People trained in basic life support (BLS) and basic first aid at the first-responder level (such as lifeguards) can provide care in the critical time after an emergency occurs and before emergency medical services (EMS) responders arrive.

Emergency medical responders consist of people with various types of training who respond when an emergency number such as 9-1-1, 0-0-0, or 1-1-2 is called. EMS units are usually staffed with emergency medical technicians (EMTs) or paramedics. Emergency medical technicians have completed extensive hours of advanced training, particularly in advanced cardiac life support (ACLS), and they can perform additional emergency medical procedures under the authorization of a physician designated as a medical director for the local EMS unit. Paramedics are additionally trained to use specialized equipment, administer medications, and perform medical procedures under the direction of a physician.

The care that any of these people provide is prehospital care because it takes place either at the site of the emergency or in an ambulance on the way to the hospital. The EMS responders decide whether or not to transport an ill or injured person to a hospital for additional care. Once at the hospital, if necessary, the emergency room medical team can provide advanced life support care. This medical team may determine that additional specialized care is necessary and transfer the injured or ill person to another hospital, such as a regional trauma center.

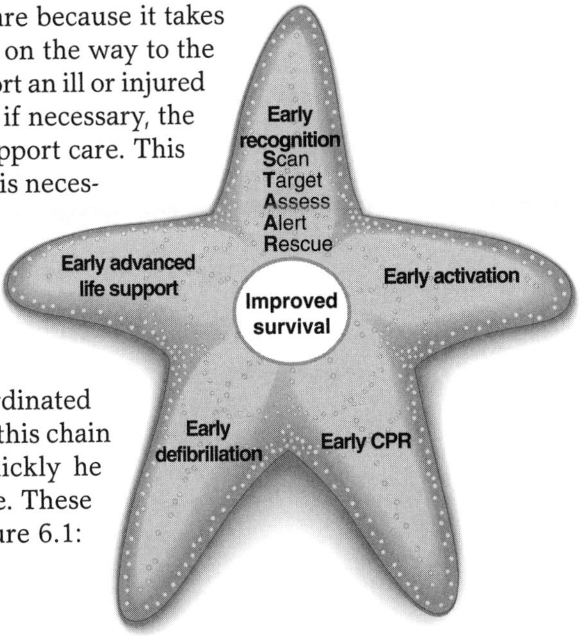

## Chain of Survival

When an emergency occurs at an aquatic facility, particularly if it involves an unresponsive drowning victim, a coordinated response is important. You, as a lifeguard, are the first link in this chain of survival, and the victim's survival depends on how quickly he progresses through the required sequence of emergency care. These actions include the following and are also highlighted in figure 6.1:

- Early recognition and response
- Early activation of EMS
- Early CPR
- Early defibrillation
- Early advanced life support

Because a coordinated response is important in prehospital emergency care, let's look at communication signals that should be established at an aquatic facility.

## Communication Signals

Clear communication signals are vital to the operation of an aquatic facility. Your facility should have a system of communication signals that allow you to indicate that a rescue is in progress, call for help, request coverage of your zone, and activate the emergency action plan (EAP).

Most communication signals are based on a combination of whistle and hand movements, such as the signal shown in figure 6.2. At a minimum, you should have a whistle with you at all times. Know and practice the communication signals designed for your workplace. Following is a list of communication signals that should be in place and some of the most common signals used:

- Standard rescue: long whistle blast or air horn blast
- Major rescue (e.g., unresponsive person): two long whistle blasts or air horn blasts
- I need help: raised fist
- I need another lifeguard's attention: two short whistle blasts
- Cover my zone: two short whistle blasts; tap top of head
- Clear the pool: series of whistle blasts
- Zone clear and covered, resume activity: thumbs-up

**FIGURE 6.1** The StarGuard aquatic survival model highlights the five actions that improve chances for survival.

*(Starfish diagram labels: Early recognition — Scan, Target, Assess, Alert, Rescue; Early advanced life support; Early activation; Improved survival; Early defibrillation; Early CPR)*

**FIGURE 6.2** A system of communication signals is important between lifeguards.

# Emergency Action Plans

Each person will play an important role in the event of an aquatic emergency. The role you will play depends on many factors, including your training, government regulations, local guidelines, and the decisions the managers of your facility have made.

An emergency action plan (EAP) is a written document detailing who does what and when in the event of an aquatic emergency. An EAP should be

- posted in key areas for quick reference;
- simple and easy to follow;
- practiced regularly;
- designed to include everyone who will respond; and
- developed for different types of emergencies: not just drowning but also other situations such as injury, severe weather, or fire.

Some of the duties to be defined for an emergency at your facility may include, depending on the emergency and site-specific considerations, responsibilities such as the following:

- Calling EMS
- Signaling for equipment and help
- Maintaining surveillance
- Removing or controlling dangerous conditions (e.g., shutting off gas and electricity or neutralizing chemicals)
- Evacuating patrons
- Bringing equipment to the scene
- Attending to the victim and providing care
- Meeting EMS personnel, leading them to the scene, and unlocking gates or doors, as necessary
- Notifying parents or relatives
- Obtaining and securing the victim's personal belongings
- Obtaining witness statements
- Writing reports
- Notifying supervisors
- Serving as a spokesperson and providing information to the media

Figure 6.3 on page 67 is an example of an emergency action plan for an unresponsive drowning victim when there are three lifeguards plus one supervisor or manager on duty. This is an example only; you must follow the EAP specifically designed for the facility where you work.

> **Practice and execute site-specific emergency action plans for various emergencies.**

# STAAR Aquatic Rescue Model

When an emergency occurs, it is helpful to have a systematic method for responding to aquatic emergencies. The StarGuard program uses the acronym STAAR (scan, target, assess, alert, rescue; see figure 6.4) to maximize the key elements you will perform in an aquatic emergency to activate your emergency action plan, call EMS, and make a rescue.

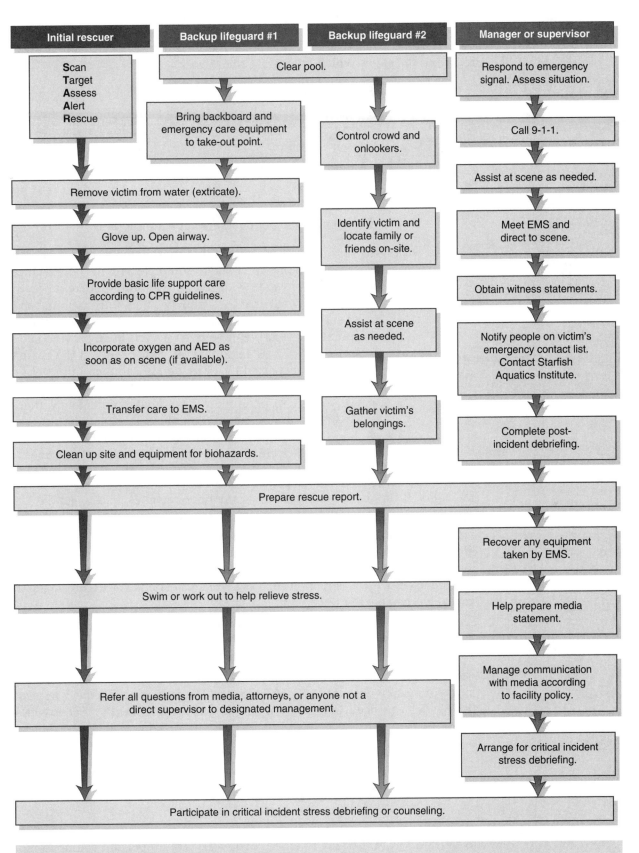

| Initial rescuer | Backup lifeguard #1 | Backup lifeguard #2 | Manager or supervisor |
|---|---|---|---|

**Initial rescuer**

- Scan
- Target
- Assess
- Alert
- Rescue

Remove victim from water (extricate).

Glove up. Open airway.

Provide basic life support care according to CPR guidelines.

Incorporate oxygen and AED as soon as on scene (if available).

Transfer care to EMS.

Clean up site and equipment for biohazards.

**Backup lifeguard #1**

Clear pool.

Bring backboard and emergency care equipment to take-out point.

**Backup lifeguard #2**

Control crowd and onlookers.

Identify victim and locate family or friends on-site.

Assist at scene as needed.

Gather victim's belongings.

**Manager or supervisor**

Respond to emergency signal. Assess situation.

Call 9-1-1.

Assist at scene as needed.

Meet EMS and direct to scene.

Obtain witness statements.

Notify people on victim's emergency contact list. Contact Starfish Aquatics Institute.

Complete post-incident debriefing.

Prepare rescue report.

Recover any equipment taken by EMS.

Swim or work out to help relieve stress.

Help prepare media statement.

Manage communication with media according to facility policy.

Refer all questions from media, attorneys, or anyone not a direct supervisor to designated management.

Arrange for critical incident stress debriefing.

Participate in critical incident stress debriefing or counseling.

**FIGURE 6.3** Unresponsive drowning victim emergency action plan.

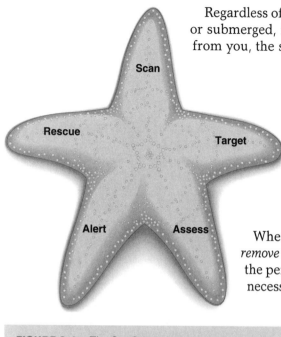

**FIGURE 6.4** The StarGuard aquatic rescue model.

Adapted, by permission, from K. Tyson and R. Ogoreuc, 2002, "S.T.A.R.R: Method for responding to aquatic emergencies," *American Lifeguard Magazine*, Winter: pages 15, 17, 18.

Regardless of whether the person to be rescued is on the surface of the water or submerged, is responsive or unresponsive, or is facing toward you or away from you, the steps, which follow, are the same:

Scan the zone.

Target the area with your eyes if you recognize distress or drowning behavior or if something unknown catches your attention.

Assess the situation and decide whether or not to take action.

Alert others with a whistle or other device.

Rescue the person; decide what action to take.

When the rescue has been accomplished, the two final steps are to *remove* the person from the water and to complete a rescue *report*. Once the person is out of the water, your role is to monitor her condition. If necessary, provide first aid or, if the victim becomes unconscious, basic life support care until EMS arrive. Fill out the rescue report after all necessary emergency care has been provided and before the injured person leaves your facility. If the person is being transported by EMS, obtain as much information as possible and complete the report later.

If you are responding to a land-based emergency, there are similar emergency action steps that you should take as you provide care. Follow these to respond to an emergency and manage life-threatening airway, breathing, and circulation problems in a victim of any age.

■ **Assess the scene.** Whenever you recognize an emergency, assess the scene for safety. If the scene is not safe or at any time becomes unsafe, get out!

In most cases you should not move an ill or injured person. Emergency services personnel are best trained and equipped to do this. However, in a life-threatening emergency or catastrophic disaster, you may not have time to wait for professional help. In these cases, you might have to perform an emergency move. In a situation such as a fire, explosion, or structure collapse, you might be able to drag a victim to safety.

■ **Assess the victim.** If the scene is safe, pause for a moment as you approach the victim. What is your first impression? If the victim is unresponsive or appears badly hurt, looks or acts very ill, or quickly gets worse, then begin the alert.

■ **Alert EMS or activate the emergency action plan.** You should call your local emergency number (e.g., 9-1-1) to alert the emergency medical services (EMS) that you need help, or you should follow your facility's emergency action plan.

## Early Activation of Emergency Medical Services

Early activation of EMS is a critical component in the chain of survival. Knowing how to call EMS from the facility where you work is an important component of your lifeguard responsibilities. Most countries have a single three-digit emergency telephone number that allows a caller to contact local EMS for assistance. Most communities in the United States use 9-1-1 as the emergency number for calling EMS, although a few still use special seven-digit emergency numbers. The 9-1-1 number is used by many other countries worldwide. In the European Union, 1-1-2 is the common emergency call number. The emergency number in Australia is 0-0-0. For successful early activation, the following should occur:

- All staff members must know how to dial out if your facility requires special access to an outside line. For example, in many situations you must first dial 9 to get a line before dialing the emergency number.

- The name, address, and phone number of your facility should be posted next to all telephones.

- If the emergency number is something other than 9-1-1 (or other than the local emergency number in your area), all staff members must memorize the number and the dialing instructions, and the emergency number should be posted next to all phones.

Many EMS agencies have enhanced computerized systems that instantly provide the dispatcher with the address and telephone number of the caller if the person is calling from a landline phone. However, this system does not work with all wireless or cell phones, so it is your responsibility when calling on a cell phone to identify your location by a street name, a street number, a landmark, or directions. If you do not know your location, the dispatcher will work with you to help determine your exact location or where to send help.

**Know what to dial to reach EMS from your facility.**

## When to Call EMS for Help

Research has shown that people have difficulty recognizing medical emergencies or they underestimate the seriousness of emergencies and fail to call for help. Remember, if you *think* you or someone you know is experiencing a medical emergency, call for help immediately. If someone experiences any of the following, you should call 9-1-1 (or your local emergency number):

- A snakebite
- A bee sting that causes a reaction
- An allergic reaction of any kind
- A seizure or convulsion
- Uncontrollable jerking movements
- Burns over an area larger than the palm of your hand
- Electrical burn or shock
- Severe injury, trauma, or an attack
- Bleeding or spurting blood that you can't stop
- Difficulty breathing or cessation of breathing
- Gasping for air or turning blue or purple or very pale
- Choking and the inability to clear the obstruction
- Altered mental status: unresponsiveness, fainting, lack of alertness, and emission of strange noises
- Chest pains, chest pressure or constriction, or crushing discomfort around the chest (even if the pain stops)

- Unusual numbness, tightness, pressure, or aching pain in the chest, neck, jaw, arm, or upper back
- A temperature of 105 degrees Fahrenheit (41 °C) or higher (heatstroke)
- Severe stiff neck, headache, and fever

## Deciding to Act

The signs and symptoms of a medical emergency can be vague or unusual. For example, the classic symptom associated with heart attack is an uncomfortable, dull feeling of pressure or tightness in the chest. However, some people experiencing a heart attack may simply feel light-headed, short of breath, or sick to the stomach, or they might break out in a cold sweat. These less well-known heart attack symptoms might be dismissed as a minor illness.

Another reason for failing to call EMS in an emergency is that ill or injured people frequently refuse to accept that something is wrong. They may believe the illness is not serious enough for a call to EMS, or they may be worried about the long-term effect the emergency might have on such things as work, child care, or finances. They want to believe they are OK, so they try to convince themselves that they don't need emergency help.

Providing help in an emergency may involve acting in the face of uncertainty. You may have to force yourself to take action even though you are not sure it is a real emergency or when the sick or injured person actively denies that she needs help. Never be afraid to call EMS just because you are unsure a real emergency exists. Let the dispatch center and emergency service professionals help you in times of confusion or doubt. That's what they are there for.

The signs and symptoms of a victim in distress or drowning may also be vague or unusual. During your assessment of the situation, there will always come a point when you will need to decide whether or not to take action and then what action to take. "When in doubt, check it out" and "If you don't know, go!" are helpful phrases to help you decide to act.

## What to Expect When You Call 9-1-1 in the United States

Typically, a professional emergency dispatcher with specialized training to deal with crises over the phone will answer your 9-1-1 call. Be prepared to briefly and accurately explain your situation. Many dispatchers today are trained to provide real-time instruction in CPR and lifesaving first aid while simultaneously dispatching emergency medical service professionals to your location. Listen to the dispatcher, and follow his instructions.

Most public safety agencies have access to a variety of highly trained personnel and specialized equipment and vehicles. To ensure that the right people with the right equipment are sent to the correct location, the 9-1-1 dispatcher must ask you specific questions. Sometimes it may seem that the dispatcher is asking these questions to determine whether or not you need help. In actuality, she is asking them to determine the level of help you need. Remember, trained dispatchers never ask unnecessary questions.

The dispatcher will always ask you to state the address of the emergency and your callback number for verification. You must state this information (or state it twice if there is no computerized 9-1-1 screen) to be sure the dispatcher hears it and copies it down correctly. The dispatcher knows how important it is to do it right and not just fast. The dispatcher asks four universal questions in order to put his knowledge and experience to work for you quickly and effectively after he has verified the address and callback telephone number at the emergency site:

1. Exactly what happened? (person's problem or type of incident)
2. What is the victim's approximate age?
3. Is the victim responsive?
4. Is the victim breathing?

Getting this critical information from you typically takes less than 30 seconds. After that, you may be asked to do nothing, to get out of an unsafe environment, or to stay on the line and assist in providing care for the ill or injured person. Working with 9-1-1 callers, emergency medical dispatchers (EMDs), professionals trained to provide telephone instruction in CPR and lifesaving first aid, have helped save thousands of lives during the 5 to 10 minutes it usually takes EMS professionals to arrive at the scene of an emergency.

**Know the address of your facility, especially if you call from a cell phone.**

In all cases, remember that the most important thing you can do when calling 9-1-1 is to *listen carefully*. Always do whatever the dispatcher asks you to do. Don't tell her to hurry; she already knows that. Every question from the dispatcher is asked for an important reason; that's why it's in the protocol.

## Crowd and Bystander Management in an Emergency Situation

During crowded conditions or emergencies, your ability to manage large groups of people will be very important. You may have to deal with a crowd to communicate safety information, make emergency announcements, provide direction, control violence, or evacuate the facility.

### Providing Direction

First, get the crowd's attention and make sure that patrons can hear you. Use a microphone or megaphone if available. Then give directions in short phrases, spoken in a loud, clear voice. Repeat the announcement several times. Provide information that is accurate but simple; skip unnecessary detail or explanation. An example of poor communication might be the following announcement: "May I have your attention. We've just been notified by the National Weather Service that a tornado warning has been issued for Clark, Wayne, and Green counties until 7:30 p.m. A tornado has been sighted near Eldorado and is heading this way. Please get out of the water, gather your belongings, and seek shelter. If you don't have transportation, go to the locker rooms. If you have questions, see the pool manager." A better way to communicate this information would be like this: "Attention. Severe weather is approaching, and a tornado warning has been issued. Please clear the pool immediately." Additional details or assistance could be provided by staff as people leave or seek shelter.

Make announcements in the language of the majority of patrons. If large groups of patrons speak other languages, make announcements in more than one language. It is also helpful if the signage at your facility is in more than one language or uses descriptive pictures to illustrate safety and emergency instructions.

## Evacuating the Pool or Facility

The emergency action plans for your facility should include predetermined evacuation routes or shelter areas for emergency hazards such as fire, chemical spills, or inclement weather. You should also have a predetermined method of evacuating patrons from the water during a rescue involving a suspected spinal injury or unresponsive drowning victim. If you need to evacuate patrons, first scan for obstacles, and then initiate your EAP. Announce clearly the need to move from the area. Calmly direct patrons along the prepared evacuation routes, or direct them to walk to a designated shelter area. When possible, it is a good idea to position staff between the crowd and the pool area to monitor and control access during the evacuation period.

## Bystander Involvement

During an emergency, it is common for bystanders to attempt to help. You will need to be familiar with the policy for bystander involvement at your facility. In some locations, bystanders are not allowed to assist for legal or other reasons. In other circumstances, you may need to solicit help from bystanders and to tell them specifically and clearly what to do.

FIGURE 6.5  A whistle signal, or other site-specific communication device, activates the emergency action plan for your facility.

# Activating the Emergency Action Plan for a Water Rescue

When you activate the emergency action plan for an aquatic rescue, you put into motion a system of backup and support. Your whistle signal, or other site-specific communication device, alerts others that a rescue is taking place (see figure 6.5). In multiguard facilities, a rescue team will respond.

The members of a rescue team vary from facility to facility, but generally, the lifeguards on break from surveillance and supervisors on site respond to the EAP signal. This plan of response allows the lifeguards on station to continue to supervise their own zones during a rescue or coordinate clearing patrons from the area. Your rescue team's ability to make a successful rescue is only as strong as your weakest rescue team member and is directly related to your team's ability to work together. Therefore, you and your rescue team must simulate real-life situations when practicing the emergency action plan. Rescue team members should be prepared to provide the following assistance:

- Cover your zone while you make the rescue or clear the zone.
- Enter the water and assist with the rescue if you signal for help.
- Bring rescue equipment to the pool edge, beach entry, or other designated point.

- Call EMS if necessary.
- Provide crowd management.
- Help remove the person from the water.
- Assist with follow-up care or basic life support on deck or on the shore.

## Knowledge Into Practice

Deciding to act, and then knowing how to start the sequence of response by you and others is critical in the chain of survival. You will play an important part in this chain.

## Visit the Web Resource

You can reinforce your learning by visiting the web resource, where you can do the following in the interactive online learning activities for chapter 6:

▶ Activity 6.1: Review scenarios and identify the legal concept that applies.

▶ Activity 6.2: Listen to whistle signals and identify what they mean; listen to sample announcements for managing crowds.

▶ Activity 6.3: Watch a video clip of a lifeguard describing the important actions that are part of an emergency action plan.

▶ Activity 6.4: Evaluate emergency action plan scenarios and decide if the correct action was taken.

▶ Activity 6.5: Listen to an EMS dispatcher and select an appropriate response.

▶ Activity 6.6: Chapter quiz. Test your knowledge, receive feedback, and print the quiz page.

## On the Job

These are the tasks related to emergency response that you will be expected to competently perform while working as a lifeguard:

▶ Appropriately assess the situation and decide to act.

▶ Call emergency medical services (EMS).

▶ Activate and follow an emergency action plan (EAP).

▶ Understand and use communication signals.

▶ Manage crowds and bystanders.

## CHAPTER 7

# Performing Assists and Rescues for Responsive Victims

## CHAPTER OBJECTIVES

This chapter

▶ suggests rescue equipment for aquatic facilities,

▶ identifies methods of land-based assists,

▶ describes entry and approach skills,

▶ describes skills for rescue on the surface and under the surface of the water,

▶ considers special-situation rescues and emergency escape skills, and

▶ explains responsibilities after the rescue.

If you are able to recognize distress or drowning symptoms soon after they begin, it is likely that the majority of the people you rescue will be moving and responsive. In this chapter we discuss how to rescue someone who is responsive. We start by examining the various types of rescue equipment. We then talk about how to perform land-based rescues or assists, followed by the details of how to enter the water and approach a distressed person or drowning victim, execute a rescue, remove the person from the water, release her from the scene, and report the incident.

**FIGURE 7.1** Rescue tubes provide flotation support for you and the distressed swimmer or drowning victim.

## Rescue Equipment

Most aquatic facilities operate under local regulations that require basic rescue equipment, such as a reaching pole, ring buoy, and telephone, readily available for emergency use by untrained bystanders when lifeguards are not present. Lifeguards generally use a rescue tube to perform rescues. A rescue tube is a length of dense foam fitted with a strap. The tube is usually 42 to 54 inches (107 to 137 cm) long, 6 inches (15 cm) tall, and 4 inches (10 cm) thick. Rescue tubes are designed for use by trained aquatic rescuers, and you should have one with you whenever you are on duty (see figure 7.1). The rescue tube will do the following:

- Provide flotation support for you
- Provide flotation support for the distressed swimmer or drowning victim
- Eliminate body-to-body contact with the distressed swimmer or drowning victim
- Improve the likelihood of a successful rescue

Rescue tubes have revolutionized the ability of lifeguards to make safe and effective rescues in a wide range of conditions. These devices provide an excellent means of flotation and can support more than one person at one time. Rescue tubes level the playing field by making it possible for a small lifeguard to effectively manage a large drowning victim or for a lifeguard to manage more than one person at a time. In addition to rescue tubes, your aquatic facility should have, at a minimum, the following response equipment on hand:

- Spinal injury board (also known as a backboard) with a head immobilization device (HID) and a minimum of three body straps
- First aid supplies
- Personal protective equipment such as gloves and a barrier mask
- Biohazard cleanup kit
- Functioning telephone or other emergency communication equipment

A variety of additional, or adjunct, emergency response equipment is available for use with an unresponsive drowning casualty. Procedures for using this equipment are described in chapter 11. Your facility's emergency action plan, local health authority regulations, guidance from your responding EMS agency, the equipment's availability, and your level of training determine your use of adjunct equipment. This equipment might include the following:

- Automated external defibrillator (AED)
- Hand-powered suction devices
- Bag-valve mask (BVM)
- Emergency oxygen
- Pulse oximeter (saturometer)

You're now ready to put everything you've learned so far into a system for making an effective rescue. You know how to scan, target, and assess to recognize a distressed swimmer or drowning victim. You have some type of communication device to alert others that you are making a rescue and to activate your facility's emergency action plan. You know how to use the equipment that is available. The next step is to respond and take action.

## Land-Based Assists

If a distressed swimmer is responsive and within reaching distance, it may be faster and just as effective to extend your rescue tube to the person and help from land than to help from the water. The swimmer must be able to

- see or feel the rescue tube as you extend it,
- follow your directions to grab the tube, and
- have the strength to hold onto the rescue tube while being pulled to safety.

When you extend a rescue tube to a person in the water, keep your legs apart to create a stable base (see figure 7.2), and shift your weight back to avoid being pulled in. Be careful not to injure the person with the device as you place it within his reach.

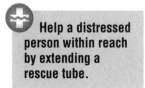
**Help a distressed person within reach by extending a rescue tube.**

**FIGURE 7.2** When using a rescue tube for a land-based assist, keep your legs apart to create a stable base.

# Water Entry

Entering the water to make a rescue is often the most effective way to manage a conscious distressed swimmer or drowning victim. However, before you make a water rescue, follow the steps of the STAAR aquatic rescue model: scan, target, assess, alert, *and then* rescue.

Always use a rescue tube when making a rescue. Wear the strap diagonally around your chest, and keep the tube between you and the person in the water at all times when making a water rescue. To begin a rescue, enter the water using either a compact jump or an ease-in entry (see skill guide on page 79), and then swim toward the person with an approach stroke.

## Compact-Jump Entry

A compact-jump entry is useful in a wide range of water depths and circumstances. Because you enter the water in a compact position, your risk of back, leg, or foot injury is lower than with other techniques.

A compact jump is best performed into water that is at least as deep as the distance from your takeoff point to the surface of the water where you will enter. Depending on the water depth and the height of your lifeguard stand, it might be best to climb down from the lifeguard stand and enter from the deck or another safe point of action.

## SKILL GUIDE

# Entries

### Compact Jump

Hold the rescue tube tightly across the front of your body, with the strap gathered in your hand or tucked behind the tube.

Jump forward and pull your knees up. Lift your toes up so that your body is in a compact position, almost like a "cannonball."

Keep yourself in the compact position until you enter the water. You may submerge momentarily, but the rescue tube will bring you to the surface quickly.

### Ease-In Entry

Sit on the pool edge. Slip into the water feetfirst. Control the speed and depth of your entry by holding onto the side.

### Run-In Entry

Lift your knees high as you run to lift your feet above the waves and water surface.

When you are too deep to run, lean forward onto your stomach and begin to swim.

### Ease-In Entry

If you suspect that a person has a spinal injury, and she is close enough to your entry point that the splash of a compact jump would move the person, use an ease-in entry, which won't create a splash.

## Approach Strokes

Once you are in the water, the objective is to use any combination of arm strokes and leg kicks to make rapid progress toward the person. For example, it may be faster for you to swim using a freestyle arm stroke and kick, or you might prefer a breaststroke or a combination of the two strokes. Swim with your head up to maintain visual contact while you approach.

Keep the rescue tube under your arms and across your chest if the person is responsive and is just a few yards or meters away. This position is safer for you,

### SKILL GUIDE

## Approach Strokes

**Tube Across Chest**

Freestyle kick with freestyle pull.

Freestyle or breaststroke kick with breaststroke pull.

**Trailing Tube** ▶

Keep the strap across your chest. Allow the tube to trail behind. When you are about 10 feet (3 m) from the person, pull the strap to bring the rescue tube into position across your chest.

as it keeps the tube between you and the active person who is in distress or drowning.

Because the position of the rescue tube across your chest creates drag, it is usually faster to swim with the tube trailing behind you. If you anticipate swimming more than a few yards, use this approach stroke. You should also consider swimming with your tube behind you when a victim is unresponsive and time is critical. Your goal in this situation is to get to the person as quickly as possible.

As you swim toward the person you are rescuing, assess the situation to determine which type of water rescue will be best. Depending on the location of and condition of the person, you may decide to use a front, rear, two-guard, or leg-wrap rescue technique. If more than one person needs assistance, you will manage a multiperson rescue.

## Water Rescue on the Surface

The first objective of a water rescue is to minimize body-to-body contact between you and the person being rescued. Other objectives include the following:

- To keep your head and the head of the person you are rescuing above water so you both can breathe
- To make progress toward a safe point of exit, such as a wall, ladder, or zero-depth entry area
- To provide safety instructions before releasing the person from the scene, to reduce the risk of the incident happening again

A responsive person in distress or drowning on or near the surface will either be facing you or facing away from you. Use the front rescue if the person is facing you and the rear rescue if the person is facing away from you or if you feel more comfortable making a rescue from behind. Use the two-guard rescue if you need help with a large or very active person.

### Front Rescue

When making a front rescue you can see the other person's face, which provides you the ability to communicate with him. Also, when you push the rescue tube into the other person's chest, it drives the person backward, minimizing the risk of him grabbing you (see the skill guide on page 82).

Studies of actual rescues involving responsive people who are in distress or drowning show that once a person is holding onto the rescue tube and realizes that it provides flotation, she stops struggling and panic subsides. However, if a person refuses to grab the rescue tube, back away and try the rescue again. If the person still will not grab the rescue tube, swim to a position behind her and use the rear-rescue technique.

> ✚ Use a rescue tube for all water rescues in order to keep your upper body from contacting the victim's upper body.

### Rear Rescue

To perform a rear rescue, you hold the person securely on the rescue tube (see the skill guide on page 82). Approaching from behind minimizes the chance of the person grabbing you. Once the responsive person is secured to the tube, kick to make progress toward the safe point of exit. If the person is calm and secure on the rescue tube, consider maintaining your grasp around the tube and person with one arm and using your other arm to pull. You'll learn how to modify a rear rescue for an unresponsive casualty in chapter 11.

# Front Rescue

Swim to a position about arm's length in front of the casualty.

Push the rescue tube *firmly* and *quickly* into the person's chest by quickly extending your arms and locking your elbows. Encourage the person to grab the tube. Keep your arms straight and extended so the other person is at least an arm's length away from you and on the other side of the rescue tube.

Keep kicking to continue your forward motion. When the person is calm and maintaining contact with the rescue tube, change direction (if needed) toward the closest wall or exit point.

**SKILL GUIDE**

# Rear Rescue

Keep the rescue tube at your chest, and move directly behind the person. Turn your head to the side so that the struggling person's head movements don't hit your face.

Reach under the person's arms and around his chest, and then pull the person slightly back onto the tube. Hold the person securely on the tube.

## Two-Guard Rescue

The two-guard rescue allows you to effectively and safely manage an uncooperative, large, or uncontrollable person. This technique combines the front and rear rescues and requires two rescuers.

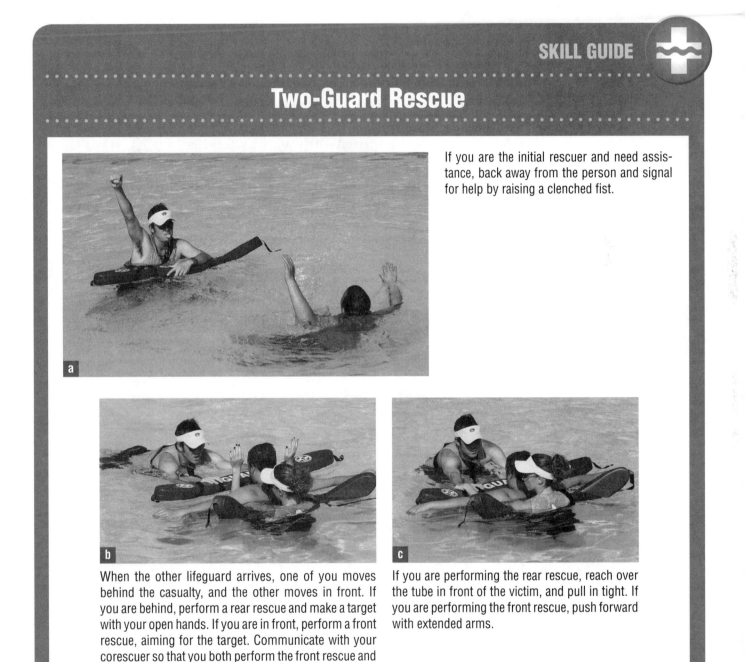

**SKILL GUIDE**

**Two-Guard Rescue**

If you are the initial rescuer and need assistance, back away from the person and signal for help by raising a clenched fist.

**a**

**b**

When the other lifeguard arrives, one of you moves behind the casualty, and the other moves in front. If you are behind, perform a rear rescue and make a target with your open hands. If you are in front, perform a front rescue, aiming for the target. Communicate with your corescuer so that you both perform the front rescue and rear rescue techniques at the same time.

**c**

If you are performing the rear rescue, reach over the tube in front of the victim, and pull in tight. If you are performing the front rescue, push forward with extended arms.

# Water Rescue Under the Surface

Rescues that must be performed while a casualty is submerged under the water can put you in a high risk situation.

## Leg-Wrap Rescue

Use the leg-wrap rescue to reach someone submerged underwater. The benefits of this technique include the following:

- There is no body-to-body contact between you and a drowning casualty.
- If the drowning casualty is struggling and grabs your legs, you can easily escape by pushing the person away using the strength of your legs and feet.
- Because you reach the person with your legs rather than your hands and arms, you don't have to submerge your body as far to make the rescue.
- Your hands are left free, which allows you to maintain contact with the rescue tube. This gives you the ability to use the flotation capability of the tube to bring both you and the casualty to the surface without having to swim up.

## SKILL GUIDE

## Leg-Wrap Rescue

**a** Position yourself behind the drowning casualty. Hold onto the rescue tube, take a breath of air, and submerge. Maintain your grasp on the rescue tube, and extend your arms above your head to lower your body, feetfirst, toward the person.

**b** Use your feet and lower legs to grab the person tightly under his arms. Rotate your feet to provide contact with the person's upper chest. If the drowning casualty is struggling, apply pressure with your lower legs for more control.

**c** Bend your knees, and pull the rescue tube toward your chest. These movements will bring you and the other person up to a position on the surface. Reach over the rescue tube and perform a rear rescue.

Some drowning casualties may be in deep water and are submerged farther than your legs will reach while holding onto the rescue tube body. In this situation you can use the extended leg-wrap rescue or the superextended leg-wrap rescue.

## Extended Leg-Wrap Rescue

If the drowning victim is too deep to be reached with a standard leg wrap, extend your reach by holding onto the tube strap, rather than the tube, when you perform the rescue.

SKILL GUIDE

## Extended Leg Wrap

**a** Let go of the body of the rescue tube, and lightly hold the rescue tube strap so it will slide freely. Maintain a vertical body position with your legs together and your toes pointed. Keep your body as tight and streamlined as possible.

**b** Turn your palms so they face upward, and lift your arms up over your head, pushing the water up toward the surface so your body is propelled downward. Maintain loose contact with the rescue tube strap as you lift your arms.

**c** If you need to descend deeper, reposition your hands at your sides to take another pull. To reposition, bend your elbows and pass your hands and arms in front of your body. Lowering your arms this way will help keep your body streamlined and won't break your momentum.

After you have performed a feetfirst surface dive, position yourself above and behind the victim while maintaining contact with the rescue tube strap. Grasp the victim under the arms and around the upper torso with your feet and lower legs. Extend your arm as far up the tube strap as you can grasp the strap. Pull on the tube strap (hand over hand if needed) to bring yourself and the victim toward the surface. Let the flotation of the tube do the work—it is not necessary to swim to the surface with the victim. As you reach the surface, place the tube across your chest. Bend your knees to bring the victim up to the surface and into a position for a rear rescue.

## Superextended Leg-Wrap Rescue

If further extension is needed, remove the body strap from across your chest. Firmly grasp the end of the wide loop. Holding onto the strap, surface dive (feetfirst or headfirst) to a position just above and behind the victim (see figure 7.3). If you have performed a headfirst surface dive, be sure to reverse yourself before you get within a few feet of the victim so that your legs are positioned downward. Grasp the victim under the armpits and upper torso with your legs and feet. Pull up on the tube strap, hand over hand, to bring yourself and the victim toward the surface. When you reach the surface, position the tube across your chest, and then pull the victim up into a rear-rescue position.

# Special-Situation Rescues

Sometimes more than one person may need to be rescued at a time, or the person being rescued may be injured. You may lose control of your rescue tube, or a struggling person grabs you instead of the rescue tube for support. In these cases, you need to adapt to the circumstances. By understanding the objectives you need to accomplish—from both a water rescue and first aid standpoint—you can modify the skills you already know to make a successful rescue.

**FIGURE 7.3**   The superextended leg-wrap has been successfully used to reach victims submerged in 20 feet (6 meters) of water.

## Rescuing Multiple Victims

If more than one person is in distress or drowning at the same time, you must determine if it is safe to attempt a multiperson rescue. Remember that your primary objective is to maintain your safety by not making body-to-body contact. Your secondary objective is to provide flotation to the people you are rescuing so that everyone, including you, remains on the surface and breathes. A rescue tube can provide flotation for several people at once.

There is no step-by-step method for performing a multiperson rescue. You'll need to keep the objectives in mind and quickly decide on a course of action based on the circumstances.

## Rescuing an Injured Person

Except in the case of a suspected spinal injury, there is no step-by-step method for rescuing an injured person because each situation is different. Your main objective is to place the injured person on the rescue tube so that he remains on the surface and breathes, and then you can progress to a takeout point so you can provide first aid. Minimize movement of an injured area, such as a broken or dislocated arm, as you perform the rescue. When appropriate, begin basic first aid while the person is on the rescue tube on the way to the safe point of exit. For example, you can apply direct pressure to control bleeding or stabilize a broken arm by holding it against the person's body.

Once you have effectively managed an aquatic rescue and are at the pool wall or shoreline, the next steps are to help the person exit the water. Then provide follow-up instructions, and complete the paperwork necessary to document the rescue before releasing the person from the scene.

## Rescuing a Person Having a Seizure in the Water

If a patron experiences a seizure while in the water, she may not have the body control to keep her head above water and breathe. The behaviors associated with seizures range from very subtle changes in responsiveness to evident convulsions. A person having a convulsion may be jerking uncontrollably, with random arm and leg movements. A seizure usually lasts only a minute or so, followed by several minutes of recovery when the person may still be somewhat unresponsive.

When a seizure occurs in the water, the primary goal is to keep the person's head above water to reduce the chance of swallowing water or allowing water to obstruct the airway. This goal is easily achieved by holding the seizing person's head above water. If possible, you may want to place a rescue tube under the person, but you do not want to try to grab around a person having a seizure, such as you would in a rear rescue. Rather, hold the head in a position above the water first, and then place the rescue tube under the person if possible or if needed.

If the seizing person can be safely extricated while the convulsions are occurring, consider doing so and continue with care on deck. You should also extricate immediately if you cannot keep the person's head above water. Otherwise, remove the person from the water after the seizure stops.

## Emergency Escape

A person who is struggling in the water and grabs you instead of a rescue tube or other means of flotation has one objective in mind: to stay on the surface. If you realize that you are about to be grabbed, try to get a quick breath of air and position your head so you will not be choked if someone grabs your neck. Use the phrase "suck, tuck, and duck" to remind you to suck in a breath of air, tuck your chin, and try to duck away from the person's grasp.

If a struggling person does grasp you around your head or neck, submerge under the water, taking the person with you. Often, that action will cause the person to release you, because his objective is to remain on the surface. If the person does not release you, perform an emergency escape, described in the skill guide on page 88.

Suck, tuck, and duck to keep from being grabbed in the water.

## Laryngospasm

When water droplets forcefully hit the flap of skin at the back of the throat (epiglottis), the flap can spasm and close over the windpipe. The person will not be able to breathe. This condition is known as a laryngospasm. When a person forcefully enters the water, such as from a high diving board or down a fast waterslide, or sucks in water quickly through the nose, a laryngospasm can be triggered.

The symptoms of water on the epiglottis are choking or gagging, followed by not being able to breathe. The symptoms may occur immediately while the person is in the water, or even several minutes later. Laryngospasm can be deadly, especially in children, as it has been known to lead to cardiac arrest in under a minute.

## SKILL GUIDE

# Emergency Escape

a Place your hands under the person's upper arms.

b Push firmly up and away.

If you are not released, place your hands on the person's hips and press her away from you while you duck out from her grasp. When you are free of the person's grasp, quickly move backward out of reach. Surface, reposition your rescue tube, and attempt the rescue again.

If a laryngospasm does not release on its own, you will need to intervene and get breathing started as soon as possible. In most instances, opening the airway will create a return of breathing in the casualty. You will learn airway management techniques in chapters 10 and 11.

## After the Rescue

Bringing a casualty successfully to the safe point of exit is not the end of a rescue. There are still several important tasks to complete.

### Remove

When you get to the safe point of exit, help the person you rescued exit the water. Take care not to embarrass or call unnecessary attention to the person, but make sure the person understands what caused the situation, and provide safety instructions to reduce the likelihood of the situation happening again.

Methods for removing a person from the water (extrication) with a suspected spinal injury are explained in chapter 8 and for an unresponsive drowning person are explained in chapter 11. Removal methods useful in a waterfront setting are explained in chapter 16.

**Provide safety instructions to a rescued person, and monitor for laryngospasm.**

## Report and Release

Document water rescues in a rescue report using clear, concise language. Include follow-up instructions, and obtain all the requested information so the report is complete. Avoid stating your opinions of what occurred; stick to the facts. A sample rescue report is included in the web resource in the section for chapter 7.

When the rescue report has been completed, the person can be released from the scene if

- there has not been a loss of consciousness, even for a brief period;
- a serious medical condition or injury is not suspected;
- the person has been observed and has normal rate of breathing, circulation, and skin color; and
- the person is fully responsive (awake and alert) and not coughing or shivering.

Your facility should have a release policy based on the circumstances. For example, children should be released to the parent or caregiver. The conditions of release might include having to wear a life jacket or being restricted to certain areas while at the facility. Be sure to include any release instructions or conditions that you provide on the report form.

> Any casualty who has been submerged even for a short time should be warned to seek medical care immediately if a cough, difficulty breathing, or any other worrysome symptom develops within the 24 hours after the incident.

### ★ Knowledge Into Practice

You will have the opportunity to practice these rescue skills during the in-water portion of your StarGuard training, and you should practice regularly even after you are on the job. Maintaining your skills at rescue-ready levels is an important responsibility of being a lifeguard.

### @ Visit the Web Resource

You can reinforce your learning by visiting the web resource, where you can do the following in the interactive online learning activities for chapter 7:

- ▶ Activity 7.1: Watch video clips of rescue skill demonstrations.
- ▶ Activity 7.2: Evaluate rescue scenarios and decide the course of action.
- ▶ Activity 7.3: Review rescue reports for factual and complete information.
- ▶ Activity 7.4: Chapter quiz. Test your knowledge, receive feedback, and print the quiz page.

### ≋ On the Job

These are the tasks related to water rescue for responsive casualties that you will be expected to competently perform while working as a lifeguard:

- ▶ Perform a reaching-assist rescue (land based).
- ▶ Maintain fitness and strength levels to perform basic water rescues appropriate for your work environment.
- ▶ Perform a basic water rescue in accordance with accepted best practice principles of aquatic rescues for casualties who are on the surface or submerged as well as facing toward or away from you.
- ▶ Be able to avoid or escape the unintended grasp of a casualty.
- ▶ Complete a record of the incident and the action taken using appropriate forms.

PART IV

# Emergency Care

# Managing Aquatic Spinal Injuries

## CHAPTER OBJECTIVES

This chapter

▶ identifies conditions that raise suspicion of spinal injuries,

▶ describes skills for managing spinal injuries on land,

▶ describes the water entry for rescuing someone with a suspected spinal injury,

▶ describes techniques for providing in-line stabilization in the water,

▶ provides objectives of extrication and backboarding, and

▶ considers deep-water constraints and techniques to overcome them.

Spinal injuries do not occur on land, or in the water, unless some sort of trauma causes the injury. Spinal injury can result if a person strikes his head, neck, or back. In an aquatic environment this trauma can come from forcefully hitting the wall, the diving board, a starting block, another person, or the bottom. These events are called the mechanism of injury.

A spinal injury can create permanent paralysis and change a person's life in a matter of seconds. Because you have no way to diagnose the extent of an injury, the objective any time you suspect a spinal injury is to restrict spinal motion while maintaining the person's ability to breathe. You will do this until EMS arrives.

## Mechanisms of Injury and Symptoms

Special precautions are required if you suspect a spinal injury. Activities that might cause a spinal injury include the following:

- Falling from a height greater than the person's height
- Forcefully striking the head on the bottom of the pool
- Suffering a severe blow to the head, neck, or back as a result of a collision with another person, equipment, or hard surface

According to rescue statistics, people who have suffered a spinal injury at a facility with prevention strategies and lifeguards in place are usually responsive and alert. In fact, patrons often get out of the pool on their own and then walk up to the lifeguard or first aid station complaining of pain due to striking the bottom of the pool or slide. Certain symptoms suggest injury. These symptoms can show up immediately or they could be delayed. Suspect spinal injury if a patron exhibits any of the following after experiencing an event with a mechanism of injury:

- Tingling or numbness in hands, fingers, feet, or toes
- Altered consciousness, confusion, slowed thinking
- Pain or headache
- Difficulty breathing
- Impaired vision
- Inability to move a body part
- Vomiting
- Loss of balance

**Suspect spinal injury if you know the circumstances included a mechanism of injury.**

94 ■

## Managing a Spinal Injury on Land

When you suspect a spinal injury, identify yourself to the person and ask her for permission to provide care. Talk to the injured person throughout the process, and tell her what to expect from each step before you perform it. Tell the person to respond to your questions with verbal answers, rather than nodding or shaking her head.

If a person with a suspected spinal injury is on land and is sitting or lying, leave him in that position. Restrict spinal motion by holding the person's head still until EMS arrives. If it is necessary to move the person for safety reasons, minimize the movement of the head, neck, and spine as much as possible.

When a suspected spinal injury occurs on land and the person is standing, you can use the standing takedown technique to lower the person to the ground. This procedure helps prevent additional injury from a fall, should the person become unable to stand. This technique is different from the backboarding procedures described later in the chapter because it does not involve the placement of head immobilization devices or straps required for extrication (removal) from the pool. The intent of the standing takedown technique is to lower the person to a horizontal position and provide manual in-line stabilization until EMS arrives and conducts an assessment.

### Standing Takedown

You must take immediate action if someone walks up to you complaining of pain and symptoms that indicate a spinal injury. If EMS response time is short, you might not need to perform a standing takedown and may simply minimize movement until EMS arrives. However, a person with a spinal injury may begin to have swelling of the brain stem, which could cause the person's legs to be unable to support her body. Lower the person to a horizontal position on the ground to keep her from collapsing and to prevent possible additional injury.

You can also use the standing takedown to extricate a person who is standing in shallow water, such as in a catch pool at the bottom of a waterslide. Use the procedures shown in the skill guide on pages 96-97 to perform a standing takedown.

> ✛ A person who is unresponsive should not be considered to have a spinal injury unless there was some action that causes you to suspect a spinal injury occurred.

> ✛ Signal for help and for a backboard (and consider putting on gloves) before making contact with the injured person because once you begin to stabilize the person's head, you should not let go.

## Managing a Spinal Injury in the Water

When managing a spinal injury in the water, you must do a few things differently than if you were on land.

1. Enter the water using an ease-in entry to prevent unnecessary movement of the water.

2. If the injured person is facedown, turn the person over so he can breathe, while at the same time minimizing the movement of the person's head, neck, and spine to prevent further injury. This technique is called in-line stabilization or restriction of spinal motion.

3. The injured person must be removed from the water. A backboard can be used to further minimize movement during this process. Your facility's emergency action plan (EAP) and protocol for suspected spinal injuries should specify whether lifeguards or EMS personnel perform backboarding. Before rescuing a person in the water who may have a spinal injury, follow the STAAR protocol:

   - **Scan.**
   - **Target.** If you see something happen that could cause a spinal injury or if you recognize symptoms of a spinal injury, focus your attention.

# Standing Takedown

## On Land or In Water

a

Signal for help. Backup rescuers bring the backboard to the scene.

b

Place your open hands on either side of the person's head, and extend your arms down her chest. Position yourself slightly off center in case the person vomits. The other rescuers place the backboard behind the person.

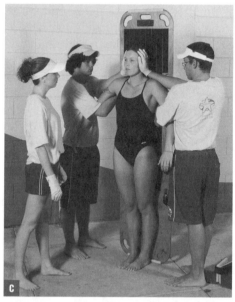

c

The backup rescuers secure the person to the backboard by reaching under his armpits and grasping the backboard handhold. The backup rescuers take control of the person's head by placing the fingers of their free hands between yours. As both rescuers begin to apply even pressure, you begin to slide your hands down and out.

d

Move to the back of the backboard, and grasp the top of the board at the handhold. Make sure there is enough room behind you to lower the backboard. If not, consider having everyone rotate as a unit, maintaining stabilization of the person's head and taking small steps either to the left or right. Turn about three inches (8 cm) at a time until there is room to lower the board.

# Standing Takedown *(continued)*

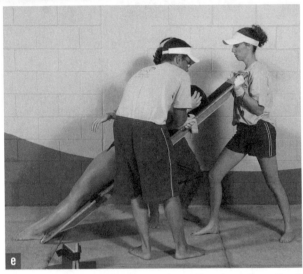

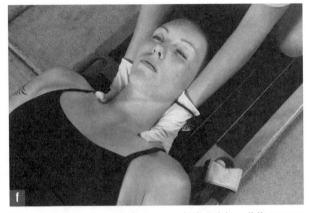

On your count (say, "Ready, on three. One, two, three."), all of you slowly lower the backboard into a horizontal position. You control the descent of the board while the other rescuers walk down into a kneeling position as the board lowers, maintaining even pressure against the person's head.

Now regain control of the person's head by sliding your fingers and palms under the person's shoulders and placing your thumbs over the shoulders. The other rescuers should maintain stabilization of the head. Slide your forearms along the person's head, applying even pressure, as the backup rescuers remove their hands.

Until EMS arrives, maintain this position while monitoring the person's condition.

If the casualty is standing in the water, such as in a catch pool at the end of a water slide, follow the same steps until the person is horizontal with the backboard floating on the surface of the water.

> **Know and practice the spinal injury protocol for your facility.**

- **Assess.** You should suspect a spinal injury if the circumstances could cause an injury. Decide to take action.
- **Alert.** Activate your facility EAP for spinal injury.
- **Rescue.** If you are within a few feet of the person, use an ease-in entry so you do not create excessive water movement around the injured person.

## In-Line Stabilization

If a person with a suspected spinal injury is in the water, your first step is to restrict spinal motion. The objective is to minimize movement of the head, neck, and spine while keeping the person's head above water so that she can breathe.

The best technique depends on the person's position, the water depth, and possibly the person's size or shoulder flexibility. In-line stabilization techniques in the water include the vise grip (if a person is faceup), vise-grip rollover (if a person is facedown), ease-up to vise grip (if the person is submerged), and spinal rollover (if the person has limited shoulder flexibility).

### Vise Grip

Perform a vise grip if a person with a suspected spinal injury is faceup in either shallow or deep water. Then move to the takeout point, preferably in shallow water. Talk to the person to check his level of responsiveness. Wait for EMS, or prepare to place the person on a backboard, depending on the procedures at your facility.

### Vise-Grip Rollover

If a person with a suspected spinal injury is facedown in the water, paralysis may prevent her from rolling over or lifting her head to breathe. Your objective will be to roll her over as quickly as possible while minimizing the movement of the head, neck, and spine. As long as the head is submerged, the person cannot breathe and is a drowning victim, so time is of the essence. After you perform the vise-grip rollover, move to the takeout point, preferably in shallow water. Talk to the person to check her level of consciousness. Wait for EMS, or prepare to place the person on a backboard, depending on the procedures at your facility.

### Ease-Up to Vise Grip

If a person is submerged deeper than your reach, you must slowly ease the person up toward the surface without causing unnatural movement of the head, neck, or spine. As long as a person is submerged, the weightlessness of the water keeps his head and neck in a neutral, nonmoving position, and the surrounding properties of the water cushion and support the head and neck.

The first objective of the ease-up technique is to make just enough contact with the injured person to initiate a weightless rise to the surface. The second objective is to position a rescue tube so that as soon as the person is near the surface and within reach, you can initiate a vise grip in a smooth transition. This transition eliminates the bouncing and bobbing at the surface that is common with other techniques, and it can be performed by one rescuer.

### Change-Up Vise Grip

If you are going to backboard and extricate an injured person from the water, and you have used a vise-grip rollover, you must perform a change-up to move your arm from under the person so you can place him on a backboard.

# Vise Grip

### Vise Grip for Faceup Casualty

Approach the person at his feet, and position yourself next to him. In deep water, position your rescue tube low on your hips; in shallow water the rescue tube may not be necessary.

Reach over the person and place your hands on his upper arms between the elbows and shoulders. Press the person's arms into his head to form a "vise" to minimize movement. Once you make contact and squeeze the arms to the head, do not let go or readjust your hand position.

### Vise-Grip Rollover for Facedown Casualty

Position yourself next to the person so that you both are facing the same direction. In deep water, position your rescue tube low on your hips; in shallow water the rescue tube may not be necessary.

Reach over the person and place your hands on his upper arms between the elbows and shoulders. Press the person's arms into his head to form a "vise" to minimize movement. Once you make contact and squeeze the arms to the head, do not let go or readjust your hand position.

Roll the person over slowly, keeping pressure on his arms. Move forward only if momentum is needed to execute the roll or if you need to move the person into a horizontal position. At this point you do not know if the person's mouth is open or closed, and forward movement could cause the person to swallow water.

# Ease-Up to Vise Grip

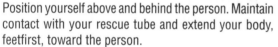

Position yourself above and behind the person. Maintain contact with your rescue tube and extend your body, feetfirst, toward the person.

Secure the person with your legs just under his armpits. Make just enough contact to initiate a rise to the surface.

As he begins to rise to the surface, release your legs and move away from the person. Position yourself to perform a vise grip or vise-grip rollover (if the person is facedown).

Roll the person over, if necessary, to begin performing a rescue. Talk to the person to check his level of consciousness.

# Change-Up Vise Grip

| | |
|---|---|
| **a** | **b** |
| While in the vise-grip position, apply pressure with your outer hand to squeeze the person to your chest. When he is tight against your chest, release the grasp of your hand that is closest to your chest, reach over the person, and place this hand next to your other one. | Keep squeezing the person's body to your chest, and slide your arm that is under the person toward your body. Make contact with the person's upper arm, and apply pressure. When you are applying even pressure to the person's arms with both of your hands, move him away from your chest. |

## Alternative Methods

The vise grip, when performed on a casualty who is either faceup or facedown, is the best method to restrict spinal motion for most in-water rescues. However, there may be instances when alternative methods are the best choice. The skill guide on page 102 provides details about how to perform these techniques.

### Reverse Vise-Grip Rollover

This technique is best for situations in which you will backboard shortly after the rollover. The water should be shallow enough for you to stand. You roll the person away from you, which keeps your arm from being under the person and eliminates the extra step of having to move it before backboarding.

### Spinal Rollover

In some instances, a person's body size or flexibility will not allow her arms to come together enough to form a vise grip around the head. In this case, a front-to-back stabilization method minimizes the movement of the head, neck, and spine. You can perform this technique on a person standing or lying in the water either faceup or facedown. If the person is facedown, she must be rolled over to be able to breathe. The objective of the spinal roll is to have one of your arms along the person's spine and your other arm along the person's chest.

# Alternative Methods

## Reverse Vise-Grip Rollover

Position yourself next to the person. With your arm closest to the person's head, reach under the person and grasp his outside arm between the elbow and shoulder. Place your hand that is closest to the person on his arm between the elbow and the shoulder. Press the person's arms into his head to form a "vise" to minimize movement.

Roll the person over slowly away from you by pushing away with the hand closest to your body.

Keep pressure on the person's arms as you move to a safe point of exit.

## Spinal Rollover

Your goal is to provide equal pressure along both the front and the back of the person before you initiate the roll. Place one of your hands on the back of the person's head, with your arm down along the spine.

At the same time you place your hand and arm along the front of the person, place the fingers of your other hand on the person's cheekbones, with your arm down along the person's chest. Maintain even pressure from the front and back, and avoid covering the person's mouth with your hand. To roll the person, submerge yourself and rise on the other side. The objective of the spinal rollover is to have one of your arms along the person's spine and your other arm along the person's chest.

# Backboarding Equipment

Backboarding is a site-specific technique, dependent on the type of equipment available, water depth, the number of rescuers present, deck and gutter configuration, and other considerations. Backboarding equipment consists of three components: the backboard (also known as a spineboard), the head immobilization device (HID), and the body straps.

Backboards are made out of wood or molded plastic. A backboard suitable for extrication from the water should have numerous handholds at both ends and along the sides. It is also important that the backboard have runners on the bottom or be molded in a way that keeps your fingers away from under the board when it is flat against the deck. Runners also allow you to slide, rather than lift, the board out of the pool and onto the deck, reducing your chance of injury. A HID attaches to the backboard at the place where the injured person's head will be located when placed on the backboard. The purpose of the HID is to keep the injured person's head, neck, and spine in line and prevent movement in instances where manual stabilization cannot be provided (see figure 8.1). The method by which the HID attaches to the backboard and the techniques for applying the devices to an injured person's head vary widely depending on the type of device.

A backboard must have some means of securing an injured person and should be fitted with several body straps. The two most common types of straps are wide strips of Velcro that close up on themselves across the person and thick straps made of webbing with a plastic snap-in clip or seatbelt-style buckle. Some strapping systems are applied straight across. Others crisscross, and some expand from a central point in a "spiderweb" method. Straps that are color coded will help you locate the match more easily in the water. In most circumstances, a backboard with five body straps is sufficient. However, if the pool deck

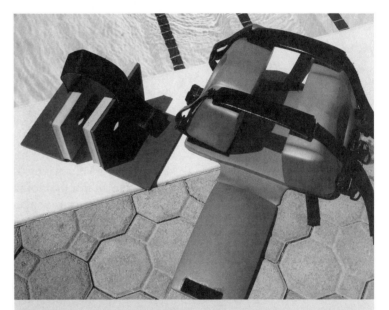

**FIGURE 8.1** Head immobilization devices prevent movement when manual stabilization cannot be provided.

or gutter is much higher than the surface of the water, you may need to place the injured person in an almost vertical position during extrication. In this event, you may need additional straps under the person's feet to keep her from sliding down.

# Preparing to Backboard

If a person with a suspected spinal injury is in the water, at some point he will need to be removed from the water, which is also called extrication. A backboard is usually used for this purpose. It is important to know, practice, and follow the backboarding and extrication protocol established for your facility, which should be determined together with your local EMS.

First aid guidelines recommend that first aid providers restrict spinal motion through manual stabilization rather than devices. In many locations, local health authority or EMS policy requires transport to the hospital of a casualty who has been placed on a backboard with an HID in place, even if the injury was minor and there are no symptoms of spinal injury. Therefore, whenever possible, your facility should coordinate with local EMS to establish a plan that allows you to provide manual stabilization of the head and neck until EMS arrives. EMS personnel can then make the determination on whether to apply stabilizing devices and transport to the hospital.

In instances where it is not feasible to use manual stabilization until EMS arrives, you will need to place the casualty on a backboard and use an HID to restrict spinal movement while you and the other rescuers remove the person from the water.

## Backboarding and Extrication Objectives

The StarGuard course teaches you the objectives for backboarding, which remain the same regardless of the type of facility, equipment, or number of rescuers or bystanders available to help. In chronological sequence, the objectives for backboarding include the following:

**If necessary, reposition the backboard so the person's head is on the HID mounting area. Submerge the backboard slightly, and move it in the direction of the person's feet about three inches (8 cm) at a time.**

1. Minimize water movement around the person during your entry.
2. Provide in-line stabilization; roll the person over if he is facedown.
3. Further restrict spinal movement by placing a backboard under or behind the person and strapping the person's body to the board.
4. Immobilize the head.
5. Remove (extricate) the person from the water.
6. Keep the person warm; monitor the person's airway, breathing, and circulation until EMS arrives. If the person has altered levels of consciousness, reestablish manual stabilization and remove the HID so you are prepared to provide airway management if rescue breathing or CPR is needed. Use a jaw thrust if the airway must be opened. If a jaw thrust will not open the airway, use a head-tilt chin lift.

To illustrate how you might achieve these backboarding objectives in different circumstances, the skill guides on pages 105-107 demonstrate the steps involved when there are two lifeguards and when there are several lifeguards present. These techniques can be modified for use in shallow or deep water. The specific procedure in place at the facility where you work may be different. If your employer requires you to backboard people with suspected spinal injuries, you must receive additional training using the equipment at the facility where you work.

# Two-Guard Backboarding

The initial rescuer provides in-water stabilization and starts moving the person toward the backboard. The backup rescuer grasps the handholds at the top of the backboard and places the board vertically in the water as deep as possible, pressing the bottom of the board against the pool wall to keep it from moving.

The initial rescuer lines up the injured person with the backboard and moves in slowly toward the wall. The backup rescuer positions the backboard to allow it to rise up under the injured person. The goal is to place the person's head on the HID mounting area.

The backup rescuer kneels or lies down on the deck and stabilizes the board with her elbows. With the hands and forearms, she takes control of maintaining the stabilization of the person's head from the initial rescuer.

The initial rescuer first straps the person's chest and then the rest of the body, while the backup rescuer maintains control of the head.

*(continued)*

# Two-Guard Backboarding *(continued)*

The initial rescuer takes over control of the person's head by placing his fingers on the person's cheekbones and his forearm along the person's chest. He places his other arm under the backboard and presses upward for support.

The backup rescuer places both HID pieces at the same time and then applies the head strap. The backup rescuer maintains contact with the backboard and monitors the person's condition.

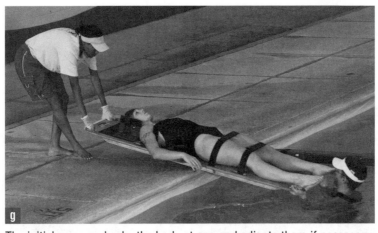

The initial rescuer checks the body straps and adjusts them if necessary; he may need to strap the person's hands to avoid injury during extrication. On count, both rescuers slide the backboard up and out of the pool using the runners, rather than lifting. If needed the initial rescuer can climb out to help from on deck. Keep the person warm, and monitor her condition until EMS arrives.

# Team Backboarding

The initial rescuer signals for help and calls for a backboard before making contact with the injured person. The backup rescuers bring the backboard and place it in the water. The initial rescuer provides in-water stabilization. The backup rescuers place the backboard parallel to the injured person.

The backup rescuers lift the side of the backboard at an angle and then press the board down and under the person.

The injured person's head should be on the HID mounting area, with one rescuer positioned at the head of the board and another rescuer at the foot of the board.

The rescuer at the top of the board takes control of in-line stabilization of the head from the initial rescuer. The initial rescuer then applies the body straps, starting with the chest and followed by the rest of the body. The rescuer at the foot helps stabilize the board.

When strapping is complete, the initial rescuer takes control of the person's head by placing his fingers on her cheekbones and his forearm along her chest. He places his other arm under the backboard and presses upward for support. The rescuer at the head of the board places both of the HID pieces at the same time and then applies the head strap.

The initial rescuer checks the body straps and adjusts them if necessary; he may strap the person's hands to prevent injury during extrication. The rescuer at the head climbs out onto the deck and lifts the board above the pool edge. The other rescuers position themselves at the foot of the backboard and help slide the board onto the deck. Keep the person warm, and monitor her condition until EMS arrives.

## ⭐ Knowledge Into Practice

Understanding the objectives of managing a person with a suspected spinal injury will help you adapt to the site-specific procedures at your workplace.

## @ Visit the Web Resource

You can reinforce your learning by visiting the web resource, where you can do the following in the interactive online learning activities for chapter 8:

▶ Activity 8.1: Identify the rationale for spinal injury management best practices.

▶ Activity 8.2: Sequence the steps of a standing takedown.

▶ Activity 8.3: View photos and identify the appropriate in-water stabilization technique.

▶ Activity 8.4: Simulate correct strap placement to secure a person to a backboard.

▶ Activity 8.5: Listen to descriptions of signs and symptoms and determine the action to take.

▶ Activity 8.6: View video clips of spinal injury management skills and scenarios.

▶ Activity 8.7: Chapter quiz. Test your knowledge, receive feedback, and print the quiz page.

## On the Job

These are the tasks related to managing suspected spinal injuries that you will be expected to competently perform while working as a lifeguard:

▶ If the mechanism of injury indicates a possible spinal injury, provide in-line stabilization and monitor the person's airway until EMS arrives.

▶ If local protocol indicates, backboard and extricate the person while restricting spinal motion.

## CHAPTER 9

# Performing Basic First Aid

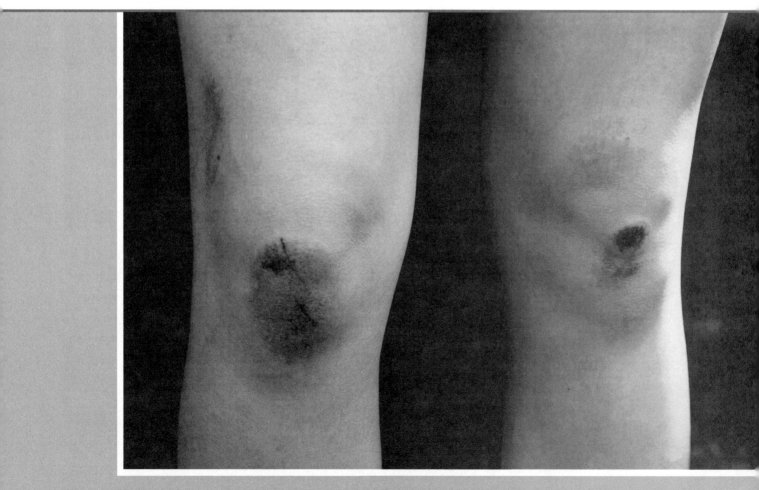

This chapter is reprinted and adapted, by permission, in part from American Safety and Health Institute with Human Kinetics, 2007, *Complete emergency care* (Champaign, IL: Human Kinetics), 19-64.

## CHAPTER OBJECTIVES

This chapter

▸ reinforces the steps of an emergency response and assessment;

▸ identifies how to position a person to protect the airway;

▸ explains how to control bleeding and manage shock;

▸ explains how to identify and provide care for wounds; injuries to the face, bones, joints, and muscles; illness and altered mental status; breathing difficulty and shortness of breath; severe abdominal pain; burns; poisoning; bites and stings; exposure to heat; exposure to cold; and

▸ describes how to triage multiple casualties, and perform emergency moves when the scene is unsafe.

**Always wear personal protective equipment when administering first aid, such as disposable gloves and eye protection, and follow infection-control procedures.**

The more patrons that come through your gates every day, the more likely it is that some will have preexisting medical conditions that could cause them to become ill at your facility. And, despite the best efforts to reduce risk, injuries may still occur. Your role as a lifeguard is to respond appropriately. The first step in providing care is to assess the situation.

*Note to readers:* Because the audience for this course is nonmedical professional rescuers, we have used the term *victim* or *casualty* instead of the typical medically oriented term *patient*. The term *EMS* refers to any system of emergency medical responders, regardless of the name common in your location.

## ⭐ Evidence-Based First Aid

This chapter contains evidence-based first aid recommendations, meaning they are agreed on by members of the International First Aid Science Advisory Board (IFASAB) to be safe, practical, and effective after a thorough evaluation of the medical science and recommendations based on medical literature.

## Primary Assessment

**For a person who appears unresponsive**, perform these steps quickly (a minute or less).

1. Assess scene. If it is safe for you to approach, do so.
2. Assess casualty. Not moving? No response? No regular breathing?
3. Alert. If there is no response, activate EMS or your emergency action plan.
4. Attend to casualty. Provide care based on whether or not there is regular breathing.

If the person does not have regular breathing, begin CPR. Chapter 11 provides more information on how to perform CPR. If the person does have regular breathing, provide this care until EMS arrives:

- Place the person in the recovery position.
- Make sure the airway remains open and breathing remains normal.
- Control bleeding if present.
- Monitor tissue (skin) color and temperature.
- Help maintain normal body temperature.

**For a person who is responsive**, perform these steps quickly (a minute or less).

1. Assess scene. If it is safe for you to approach, do so.
2. Introduce yourself. Let the person know you are trained and there to help, and ask if it's OK to help.
   - Check for an altered mental status.
   - Make sure the casualty is breathing normally.
   - Scan the body for any serious bleeding. If found, control it immediately with direct pressure.
   - Check the skin color of the face. Assess the lips and gums or palms of the hands in a dark-skinned person. Normal tissue color is light pink. Pale skin may indicate blood loss or shock. Blue skin can indicate a problem with an airway, a breathing problem, or shock.
   - Assess skin temperature by touching the forehead with your bare wrist. Normal skin feels warm and dry. Cool, wet skin can be an indication of shock.
3. If the casualty appears to be confused, weak, seriously ill, or seriously injured, quickly activate EMS or your emergency action plan.
4. Provide care until EMS arrives.

> Look for a medical alert bracelet, necklace, wallet card, or other source of medical information.

## Secondary Assessment

If your first, or primary, assessment indicates no life-threatening problems, quickly try to determine the person's chief complaint. Information obtained from performing a secondary assessment can be useful for you and the casualty and should be passed on to EMS providers or other health care professionals. To conduct a secondary assessment:

- Ask the person what happened. If he cannot answer, ask bystanders.
- Clues in the environment, such as the temperature or the presence of medications or containers, may help identify the cause of the chief complaint.
- Physically assess the person. Briefly assess the body in a logical manner (head to toe). Look and feel for the signs of injury. This may be done through simple observation or by gentle touch. If the casualty has been subjected to extreme forces (such as in a car crash) or you suspect head, neck, or spinal injuries, perform a head-to-toe assessment only if another first aid provider is available to hold the casualty's head still. If needed, remove or cut away clothing to get a better look at an affected body part. Compare one side of the body to the other.

Assess the casualty's head, neck, chest, abdomen, pelvis, and all four limbs. If at any time you suspect spinal injury, immediately restrict spinal motion by manually stabilizing the head. The acronym DOTS is helpful for remembering what to look for:

**D**eformities

**O**pen injuries or wounds

**T**enderness

**S**welling

Ask questions to gather information about the casualty's signs and symptoms and medical history. Use the acronym SAMPLE to help you remember what to ask about:

**S**ymptoms: things the person is feeling such as pain, nausea, dizziness, or anything related to the situation

**A**llergies to medications, food, and environmental conditions

**M**edications the ill or injured person is taking

**P**ast medical history that may be related to what is going on

**L**ast oral intake: what the person last ate or drank

**E**vents: what the person was doing just before symptoms began

These same considerations apply when caring for a person with a disability.

## ⭐ Special Concerns for Children, Older Adults, and People With Disabilities

When caring for infants and young children, reverse the head-to-toes assessment sequence so it is toes to head. Infants and young children find it threatening when strangers want to touch their faces. By beginning with the toes and moving upward, you reduce the chance of scaring the child. Try to gain the child's trust as you go. Be calm, friendly, and reassuring. If the child is more comfortable or calm in the parents arms, perform your assessment while the child is supported by the parent. In a critically ill or unresponsive child, you may need additional personnel to care for a distraught parent.

When caring for older adults, keep in mind that communication may be difficult. Elderly people may have trouble seeing, hearing, and talking. Speak face to face at eye level. If the older person seems confused and a relative or friend is available, check with him to see if this difficulty is normal for the older person. Always speak slowly, distinctly, and respectfully. Don't shout.

## Recovery Positions and Protecting the Airway

If the casualty is breathing adequately or starts breathing adequately at any time, consider placing her in the recovery position. Be sure to do this if the casualty is having difficulty with secretions or is vomiting or if you must leave the casualty alone to get help. The recovery position helps to prevent obstruction of the airway by the tongue and allows vomit or secretions to drain from the airway.

The skill guide on page 113 shows positions for an uninjured and injured casualty who is breathing but unresponsive. When you must place an injured person on her side, use a modified recovery position called the HAINES position (see the skill guide). HAINES stands for **h**igh **a**rm **in e**ndangered **s**pine. When you use the HAINES position, there is less neck movement and less risk of spinal cord damage.

# Victim Unresponsive and Breathing—Protecting the Airway, Recovery Position

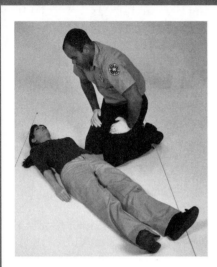

### ◀ Assess Casualty

Pause and assess scene. **_Scene is safe!_** Tap or squeeze shoulder. Ask loudly, "Are you OK? **_No response!_** Look quickly at face and chest for normal breathing. Occasional gasps are _not_ considered normal. **_Normal breathing is present!_** Have someone alert EMS and get an AED.

### Prepare ▶

- Extend the arm nearest to you up alongside the casualty's head.
- Bring the far arm across the chest, and place the back of the hand against the cheek.
- Grasp the far leg just above the knee, and pull it up so the foot is flat on ground.

### ◀ Roll

- Grasp the shoulder and hip, and roll the casualty toward you. Roll in a single motion, keeping the head, shoulders, and torso from twisting.
- Roll far enough for the face to be angled forward.
- Position the elbow and knee to help stabilize the head and body.

### Suspected Injury ▶

- In the case of a serious injury, do not move the casualty unless fluids are collecting in the airway or you are alone and need to leave to get help or if the scene is becoming unsafe.
- During the roll, make sure the head ends up resting on the extended arm and that the head, neck, and torso are in line.

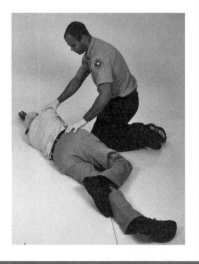

# Control of Bleeding and Managing Shock

Blood vessels are present throughout the body. When tissue is damaged, bleeding occurs. If a major blood vessel is damaged, heavy bleeding occurs. Bleeding reduces the oxygen-carrying capacity of blood. If severe, it can quickly become life threatening.

## Severe Bleeding

Arterial bleeding is bright red and will spurt from a wound. It can be difficult to control because of the pressure created by the heart's contractions. If the blood is dark red and flowing steadily, it is likely coming from a vein. Bleeding from a vein can be heavy but is usually easier to control than arterial bleeding. Clot-forming fibers naturally collect at a wound site to create a patch to stop bleeding. Severe bleeding can overwhelm this process, and the blood continues to flow.

### Direct pressure

Refer to the skill guide on page 115 for severe bleeding and shock procedures for applying direct pressure.

### Using a Tourniquet

When it is clearly not possible to stop heavy bleeding on a limb with direct pressure, the use of a tourniquet is recommended. As a result of armed conflict in the Middle East, there have been significant advances in our understanding of the use of tourniquets. Proper application can stop life threatening bleeding and save lives. All victims to whom a tourniquet is applied should be transported to the nearest hospital. Training to use a tourniquet is important, and its use is guided by the local protocol of your emergency action plan.

Commercial tourniquets have been found to be safer and more reliable than those created from improvised materials. Always follow the manufacturer's directions for use, and practice using the tourniquet as part of your training. Unless directed by qualified medical personnel, do not remove or loosen a tourniquet once it is applied.

## Internal Bleeding

A significant blow can create injury and bleeding inside the body. Organs inside the chest and abdomen are particularly susceptible. Internal bleeding can be difficult to detect and is impossible to control. Because direct access is not possible, surgery may be required to control internal bleeding. Early suspicion, based on the fact that a significant blow occurred to the body, and early activation of EMS are critical for effective treatment and, possibly, survival. Signs of internal bleeding include abdominal pain, nausea and vomiting after abdominal trauma, bruising to the abdomen or sides, or shock without external signs of bleeding.

## Managing Shock

Shock develops when poor blood flow creates a shortage of oxygen to body tissue. Any serious illness or injury has the potential to cause shock. If not treated early, shock can get worse and become life threatening.

Shock is progressive, and serious signs can emerge gradually over time. A person in shock must get to a hospital as quickly as possible in order to survive. Early recognition, treatment, and activation of EMS are essential.

Early signs of shock may be difficult to detect. A person may appear to be any or all of the following:

> Continuous firm and direct pressure applied to the source of bleeding is the best method to control it. It is unlikely that any other treatment will be necessary.

- Uneasy
- Restless
- Worried
- Confused

Other more serious signs can develop over time. Progressive signs of shock may be the earliest evidence that it is occurring:

- Responsiveness may diminish.
- The skin may become pale, cool, and sweaty.

# Severe Bleeding and Shock

### ◀ Assess Casualty

Pause and assess scene. **Scene is safe!** Identify yourself; ask if it's OK to help. **Permission given!** If the casualty appears weak, seriously ill, or injured, direct someone to alert EMS or activate your emergency action plan. Ensure an open airway and normal breathing, and then control bleeding.

### Apply Direct Pressure ▶

Locate the point of bleeding. Rip or cut away the clothing if needed. Place a clean absorbent pad directly over the wound. Apply firm, direct pressure. If a pad is not available, apply direct pressure with your gloved hand. The casualty can apply pressure for himself if he is able.

### ◀ Apply Pressure Bandage

Wrap a roller or elastic bandage snugly over the pad. Wrap with enough pressure to control bleeding but still allow a finger to be slipped under the bandage. If bleeding continues or bandages become soaked, apply more pads or pressure bandages and maintain direct pressure. Do not remove the first pads or bandages.

### Manage Shock ▶

Keep the person lying flat. Monitor for normal breathing. Keep bleeding under control. Prevent chilling or overheating. Keep the person as comfortable and calm as possible.

# Wounds

A wound is a break in the skin. All wounds need first aid, but serious wounds require medical attention. Have a wound evaluated by a health care professional when the wound has the following characteristics:

- Won't stop bleeding with firm direct pressure
- Is deep or longer than half an inch, or about 1 centimeter (these may need closing with stitches or skin glue)
- Is on the face, especially when close to the eye
- Involves injury to underlying structures such as ligaments or tendons
- Was caused by a dirty or rusty object
- Has dirt, stones, or gravel stuck in it
- Was caused by an animal or human bite
- Is extremely painful
- Is infected (warm, red, swollen, or draining)

See table 9.1 for treatment recommendations for major wounds and table 9.2 for minor wounds.

**TABLE 9.1**

## Major Wounds: First Aid Recommendations

| Major wound | First aid (Activate EMS for all major wounds.) |
|---|---|
| **Complete or partial loss of a body part** | ■ Control any severe bleeding.<br>■ Calm, comfort, and reassure the person. Treat for shock.<br>■ Body parts can often be surgically reattached. Once the person is stable, locate the severed part if possible.<br>■ Wrap the severed part in a sterile or clean cloth, and place it in a tightly sealed plastic bag or waterproof container. Place the bag or container on ice.<br>■ Do not soak the severed part in water, and do not put it directly on ice. Give it to EMS providers for transport with the person to the hospital. |
| **Impaled object**<br><br>An impaled object is something that penetrates a body part and remains embedded. | ■ If necessary, remove clothing to confirm the object has penetrated the skin. Look for any serious bleeding, and control it with direct pressure.<br>■ Keep the person still.<br>■ Do not remove the impaled object. It can act like a plug and prevent serious blood loss. An impaled object can also be embedded into body parts below the skin.<br>■ If needed, support the person's weight to relieve pressure on the object. Use padding to provide stability and comfort.<br>■ Reassure the person to keep him calm. Treat for shock. Regularly assess the injury until EMS arrives. |
| **Open chest injury**<br><br>A puncture injury through the chest wall can disrupt the chest's ability to draw air into the lungs. Air movement can be indicated by foamy, bloody air bubbles. You may hear a sucking sound. | ■ Remove any clothing to expose the injury site.<br>■ Check to see if there is an exit injury on the other side of the chest. If there are 2 wounds, treat the more serious first.<br>■ Cover the wound with something airtight. You can start with a gloved hand.<br>■ Consider covering the wound with an airtight dressing material such as plastic wrap or aluminum foil. The covering should be wide enough to extend 2 in (5 cm) or more past the edges of the wound in all directions.<br>■ If available, tape 3 sides of the covering to the chest wall. Leave 1 side of the covering open to allow trapped air to escape.<br>■ If possible, allow the person to find and assume a comfortable position.<br>■ Reassure the person to keep her calm. Treat for shock. Regularly assess the injury until EMS arrives. |
| **Open abdominal injury**<br><br>Injury to the abdomen may result in a condition known as evisceration, in which abdominal organs protrude through an open wound. | ■ The primary treatment is to protect the functioning organs from further injury.<br>■ Cover any organs with a thick, moist dressing. Do not try to push the organs back inside the body.<br>■ Do not apply direct pressure on the wound or exposed internal parts.<br>■ Reassure the person to keep him calm. Treat for shock. Regularly assess the injury until EMS arrives. |

**TABLE 9.2**

## Minor Wounds: First Aid Recommendations

| Minor wound | First aid |
|---|---|
| **Breaks or openings in the skin** including<br>■ abrasions<br>■ lacerations<br>■ punctures<br>■ incisions | ■ If wound is bleeding, apply direct pressure with a clean cloth or absorbent pad.<br>■ Wash with antibacterial soap and clean running tap water for about 5 min or until the wound is clean of foreign matter.<br>■ Apply triple antibiotic lotion or cream to speed healing and reduce infection.<br>■ Cover the area with an adhesive bandage or gauze pad. |
| **Splinter** A splinter is a small piece of foreign material embedded into and just below the skin. Splinters need to be removed to keep the wound from becoming inflamed, leading to possible infection. | ■ Using a pair of tweezers, grab the protruding end of the splinter and pull it out along the direction it entered.<br>■ If the end is not protruding, use a small needle to loosen the splinter in the skin. Once you can grasp the splinter with tweezers, pull it out along the direction it entered.<br>■ If a splinter appears deeply embedded or you have been able to remove only a piece of it, the wound should be seen by a health care professional. |
| **Bruise** A bruise is caused by broken vessels leaking blood under the skin. | ■ Apply ice to the injury to reduce pain, bleeding, and swelling.<br>■ To prevent cold injury, place a thin towel or cloth between the cold source and the skin.<br>■ Limit application to 20 min or less. |

# Facial Injuries

Because they may alter facial appearance and function, traumatic injuries to the eyes, mouth, and face can have significant physical and emotional effects. When a blow to the face or head results in altered mental status, treat it as a possible brain injury (see pages 122-123). Table 9.3 outlines treatment recommendations for facial injuries.

**TABLE 9.3**

## Facial Injuries: First Aid Recommendations

| Facial injury | First aid |
|---|---|
| **Minor irritated eye** | ■ Rinse the affected eye with a saline solution.<br>■ Tap water may be used if no saline solution is available. Use a drinking fountain, faucet, or garden hose running slowly.<br>■ If the casualty continues to have pain or feels that something is still in the eye, or if the object cannot be removed, cover the eye lightly with a gauze pad or a clean cloth and seek medical attention. |
| **Impaled object in the eye** | Stabilize the object, and protect the eye from further injury:<br>■ Activate EMS.<br>■ Do not allow the person to rub the eye, and do not try to remove the object.<br>■ For small objects, cover both eyes with loose gauze pads or a clean cloth.<br>■ Stabilize larger objects with a clean bulky cloth. Cover the uninjured eye with a loose gauze pad. Eyes move together. Covering both eyes prevents movement of the affected eye.<br>■ Since the casualty has both eyes covered, you must become her eyes. Having both eyes covered can be frightening. Calm, comfort, and reassure the person to reduce anxiety. |

*(continued)*

**TABLE 9.3** *(continued)*

| Facial injury | First aid |
|---|---|
| **Chemical burn of the eye**<br><br>Corrosive chemicals splashed into an eye can quickly damage eye tissue and cause pain. Affected eyes will be red and watery. | ▪ Immediately flood the eye with a large amount of water. Use a drinking fountain, faucet, or garden hose. Flush outward from the nose side of the affected eye to prevent contamination of the other eye.<br>▪ Continuously flush for at least 15 min.<br>▪ After you have finished washing the eye, seek immediate medical care.<br>▪ If the person is wearing contact lenses and the lenses did not flush out, have the person try to remove them after the flushing process. |
| **Nosebleed**<br><br>A nosebleed usually involves one nostril. Blood can drip down the throat or into the stomach, causing a casualty to spit or vomit blood. | ▪ Have the casualty sit up straight with the head tilted forward.<br>▪ Pinch the nose with the thumb and index finger for 10 min.<br>▪ Have the casualty spit out any blood that collects in the mouth.<br>▪ If the bleeding does not stop, seek immediate medical care.<br>▪ Do not tilt the casualty's head back or have the casualty lie down. These actions may cause the casualty to swallow blood and vomit.<br>▪ Do not pack gauze in the nose.<br>▪ Applying ice to the casualty's neck is not effective in controlling a nosebleed. |
| **Dislocated or broken tooth** | ▪ If the lips, teeth, or gums are bleeding, have the person gently bite down on an absorbent pad.<br>▪ An ice bag may help reduce pain and swelling.<br>▪ Arrange for the casualty to be seen by a dentist immediately. |
| **Knocked-out tooth**<br><br>Early care can increase the chance that a permanent tooth can be reimplanted. Getting to a dentist within 30 min gives the best chance for success. | ▪ Handle the tooth only by the chewing surface (crown). Do not touch the root, the part of the tooth that embeds in the gum.<br>▪ Keep the tooth moist. Do not allow it to dry. Have the person spit, and place the tooth in the saliva. Avoid putting the tooth in water, which can be harmful to tooth cells.<br>▪ Fresh whole milk can preserve tooth cells for up to 6 hr. Cold low-fat milk, contact lens solution, or Gatorade can serve as an alternative to fresh whole milk for up to an hour. The commercial product Save-A-Tooth is a 24-hr emergency tooth-preserving system<br>▪ Never scrub the tooth or remove any attached tissue fragments. |

# Bone, Joint, and Muscle Injuries

Bones, muscles, and joints give the body shape, allow movement, and protect vital internal organs. Long bones form the upper and lower parts of each limb. Muscles, ligaments, and tendons attach to the bones, allowing for movement where the bones come together. These bones are the most exposed to external forces and injury.

There are four different types of injuries affecting bones, muscles, and joints:

- Strains are stretching or tearing injuries to muscles or tendons.
- Sprains are stretching or tearing injuries to ligaments that hold joints together.
- Dislocations are the separation of bone ends at a joint.
- Fractures are breaks in bones.

Distinguishing between these types of injuries is often difficult. It is best to treat them all as possible fractures (see the skill guide on page 119). **If a painful, deformed, or swollen limb is blue or extremely pale, activate EMS or your emergency action plan immediately.**

Splinting is the most common procedure for limiting limb movement. Apply a splint only in these conditions:

- EMS personnel are delayed or not available (e.g., during a natural disaster or a large scale emergency).

■ You can do so without causing further injury or pain.

Before beginning, gather whatever splinting materials are available. If possible, use at least four ties (two above and two below the fracture) to secure the splints. You can use a variety of materials to improvise a splint:

■ Soft: towels, blankets, or pillows tied with bandaging materials or soft cloths
■ Rigid: cardboard, wood, a folded magazine, a backpacker's sleeping pad

Follow these guidelines when you splint a limb:

■ Immobilize the limb above and below the injury.
■ Splint the limb in the position it was found.
■ Pad the splints where they touch any bony part of the body to help prevent circulation problems.
■ After splinting, check the limb frequently for swelling, paleness, or numbness. If present, loosen the splint.

> Sharp broken bone ends can cut tissue, muscle, blood vessels, and nerves when moved. Assume all painful, swollen, or deformed injuries to a limb include broken bone ends.

## SKILL GUIDE

## Injured Limb

### ◀ Assess Casualty

Pause and assess scene. *Scene is safe!* Identify yourself; ask if it's OK to help. *Permission given!* If the casualty appears weak, seriously ill, or injured, alert someone to alert EMS or activate your emergency action plan.

### Cover Open Wounds ▶

Use a sterile dressing. If a bone is sticking out of the body, control bleeding by applying gentle pressure around it. Gently cut away clothing if necessary. Do not push a bone back under the skin.

### ◀ Apply Ice or Cold Pack

An ice pack will decrease pain, bleeding, and swelling. Limit application to 20 minutes or less. Place a thin towel or cloth between the cold source and the skin.

### Manually Stabilize Injured Limb ▶

Gently place your hands above and below the injury to limit movement while awaiting EMS.

# Illness and Altered Mental Status

A medical emergency can be either an injury or an illness. This section covers illnesses that can suddenly become an emergency and threaten life.

A responsive casualty of sudden illness usually has associated signs and symptoms. A sign is the noticeable evidence of a disease and is something you can observe. A symptom is something the casualty complains about. Major sudden illnesses often cause signs and symptoms of altered mental status, breathing difficulty, or severe pain (such as chest or abdominal pain).

Altered mental status is a sudden or gradual change in personality, behavior, or consciousness that can range from mild anxiety to inability to speak and communicate to complete unconsciousness. **It is a serious warning sign in both adults and children.** The period of altered mental status may be brief or prolonged.

## Stroke

A *stroke*, or brain attack, happens when the blood supply to part of the brain is suddenly interrupted or when a blood vessel in the brain bursts, spilling blood into the spaces surrounding brain cells. Brain cells die when they no longer receive oxygen and nutrients from the blood or there is sudden bleeding into or around the brain.

Limiting the extent of brain damage caused by a stroke depends on rapid diagnosis and treatment in the hospital. This requires the casualty, family members, or bystanders to quickly recognize the signs and symptoms of stroke and activate EMS.

Signs of a stroke tend to show up suddenly. A person may collapse or suddenly appear confused, have difficulty speaking, or understanding simple commands. Sudden numbness or weakness of the face, arm, or leg, especially on one side of the body, may be present. A person experiencing a stroke can become frustrated at being unable to move or communicate clearly. The person may appear confused but still be aware of what is happening. Table 9.4 highlights stroke signs and symptoms and recommendations for stroke first aid.

> Stroke treatments are time sensitive. Alert EMS without delay if you suspect a stroke.

TABLE 9.4

### Stroke: Signs, Symptoms, and First Aid

| Signs and symptoms | First aid |
| --- | --- |
| ■ *Sudden* numbness or weakness of the face, arm, or leg, especially on one side of the body<br>■ *Sudden* confusion, trouble speaking, or trouble understanding<br>■ *Sudden* trouble seeing in one or both eyes<br>■ *Sudden* trouble walking, dizziness, loss of balance, or loss of coordination<br>■ *Sudden* severe headache<br>■ Ministroke (transient ischemic attack, or TIA): same symptoms as a stroke, but it lasts for only a few minutes and may lead to stroke<br>***Note:*** Casualties of stroke are sometimes mistaken for being drunk. | ■ A quick method to determine if someone could be suffering from a stroke is to ask the person to do the following:<br>  1. Smile.<br>  2. Raise both arms.<br>  3. Speak a simple sentence.<br>■ Do not give the person anything to eat or drink.<br>■ Calm, comfort, and reassure the casualty until EMS arrives.<br>■ Be prepared for the possibility of sudden cardiac arrest and the need for CPR and the use of an AED. |

## Acute Coronary Syndrome (ACS)

ACS is commonly known as a heart attack. Blood vessels in the heart and brain can become narrowed over time as a result of heart disease. This narrowing can reduce or even block blood flow and result in significant damage to heart or death. If the blood flow to the heart is cut off, a part of the heart will die, causing disability or death.

There is a wide range of signs and symptoms, from slight to severe. The absence of chest pain, especially in people with diabetes, women, and the elderly, does not mean the victim is not having a heart attack. Women often describe indigestion rather than chest pain. Other unusual symptoms of heart attack include headache, ringing in the ears, dizziness, hiccups, and belching.

Do not downplay the seriousness of the potential problem. Early activation of EMS and early advanced medical care are critical in being able to provide effective treatment and reduce the risk of death from heart attack. A person experiencing chest pain may deny he is having a serious problem. This is a common occurrence. Never let this denial change your approach to care. Table 9.5 lists signs, symptoms, and first aid for ACS (heart attack).

> Encourage a person with heart attack symptoms to chew one noncoated adult or two low-dose aspirin, unless the person is allergic to aspirin or has recently suffered a stroke.

**TABLE 9.5**

### ACS (Heart Attack): Signs, Symptoms, and First Aid

| Signs and symptoms | First aid |
|---|---|
| ▪ Chest pain or a dull discomfort behind the breastbone that may or may not spread to the arms, back, neck, jaw, or stomach<br>▪ Shortness of breath<br>▪ Nausea, dizziness, light-headedness<br>▪ Heavy sweating<br>▪ Fear of impending doom (feeling that something extremely bad is going to happen but not sure what)<br>▪ Uncertainty and embarrassment<br>▪ Denial (victim often refuses to accept or believe she may be having a heart attack, which can delay treatment and increase the risk of death) | ▪ Activate EMS immediately. If an automated external defibrillator (AED) is available, have someone get it.<br>▪ Allow the person to find the most comfortable position in which to breathe. Loosen tight clothing. Calm, comfort, and reassure the person.<br>▪ Ask the person or any bystanders about prior problems or medications being taken. Assist the person in taking nitroglycerine if it is available and prescribed. |

## Diabetic Emergencies

Diabetes is a chronic disease characterized by an imbalance of blood sugar and insulin. A medical emergency occurs when blood sugar becomes very high or very low. Table 9.6 lists signs, symptoms, and first aid for diabetic emergencies.

**TABLE 9.6**

### Diabetic Emergencies: Signs, Symptoms, and First Aid

| Signs and symptoms | | First aid |
|---|---|---|
| Very low blood sugar<br>▪ Pale or sweaty<br>▪ Altered mental status<br>▪ Anxiety or trembling<br>▪ Pounding heart<br>▪ May appear drunk<br>▪ Hungry or weak<br>▪ Fainting<br>▪ Seizure<br>▪ Unconsciousness | Very high blood sugar<br>▪ Altered mental status<br>▪ Nausea or vomiting<br>▪ Flushed, hot, dry skin<br>▪ A strong, fruity breath odor<br>▪ Drowsiness or difficulty waking up<br>▪ Rapid, deep breathing<br>▪ Unconsciousness | If the person is known to have diabetes and is responsive (awake, able to swallow)<br>▪ attempt to raise the casualty's blood sugar level as quickly as possible. Give her about 6 oz (180 ml) of fruit juice.<br>▪ call EMS or activate your emergency action plan if the person does not behave normally within about 15 min.<br>▪ comfort, calm, and reassure the casualty while awaiting EMS.<br><br>If the person is unresponsive or unable to swallow<br>▪ do not give anything by mouth and<br>▪ call EMS immediately. |

Without a medical device called a blood glucose meter, it can be difficult to tell whether the person's blood sugar is very high or very low. When you are uncertain, it is best to give sugar. The immediate effects of low blood sugar can be more harmful than those of high blood sugar. If very low blood sugar is the problem, recovery will usually occur in 10 to 15 minutes. If not, the problem may be very high blood sugar. Prompt medical treatment is required.

## Seizures

A seizure is a sudden attack, usually related to excessive electrical activity in the brain. Seizures can be caused by any of the following conditions:

- Epilepsy
- Head injury
- Brain tumor
- Meningitis
- Stroke
- Very low blood sugar
- Drug use
- Alcohol withdrawal
- Very high fever
- Illness in pregnancy

Seizure signs, symptoms, and first aid are found in table 9.7.

**TABLE 9.7**

### Seizures: Signs, Symptoms, and First Aid

| Signs and symptoms | First aid |
|---|---|
| Simple = no loss of consciousness<br>■ Staring spells<br>■ Confusion<br>■ Wandering aimlessly<br>■ Strange behavior<br>Complex = loss of consciousness<br>■ The casualty suddenly becomes stiff and falls to the ground<br>■ Twitching or shaking of the body (convulsions)<br>■ Recovers quickly, may be confused<br><br>**Note:** Most seizures happen without warning, last only a short time, and stop without any special treatment. People known to have frequent seizures do not usually need to go to the hospital, but even mild seizures should be reported to the casualty's doctor. | Simple<br>■ Do not restrain the casualty.<br>■ Guide the casualty away from dangerous situations.<br>■ Comfort, calm, and stay with the casualty until he has fully recovered.<br>Complex<br>■ Stay calm and note the time.<br>■ Move objects away that the casualty may strike.<br>■ Do not restrain the casualty.<br>■ Allow the seizure to take its course.<br>■ Do not put anything in the casualty's mouth, including your finger. The casualty has no danger of swallowing the tongue.<br>■ When the seizure is over, place the casualty in the recovery position.<br>■ Provide privacy to minimize embarrassment. |

## Brain Injury

A significant blow or force to the head can result in internal injury to the brain within the skull. Injuries to the brain and skull can be closed or open. A typical closed injury is a concussion, in which the brain is bruised from impact against the inside of the skull. An open injury, such as that caused by a bullet, can cause long-lasting functional impairment or death. See table 9.8 for signs, symptoms, and first aid for brain injuries.

**TABLE 9.8**

### Brain Injuries: Signs, Symptoms, and First Aid

| Signs and symptoms | First aid |
| --- | --- |
| Altered mental status after a severe blow to the head | Surgical intervention may be the only treatment.<br>■ Activate EMS, and restrict spinal motion.<br>■ Do not try to stop the flow of blood or fluid from the ears or nose.<br>■ If a bleeding wound is present, place an absorbent pad directly over the area, and gently apply firm, continuous pressure.<br>■ Closely monitor the person's level of responsiveness, and be prepared to manage the airway. Be alert for vomiting. |

## ★ Special Concerns Regarding Concussions

The effects of most minor concussions are usually temporary, but the injury needs rest to heal properly. In other instances a concussion can be serious and fatal brain swelling may occur.

The signs and symptoms of concussion can be subtle and may not start for hours or days. Watch for changes in behavior, especially in children who may not be able to describe symptoms. If a person has experienced a blow to the head and becomes listless, is irritable, experiences change in eating or sleeping habits, vomits more than once or has a loss of balance, seek medical attention.

Medical attention should always be sought if a person is not fully recovered from a previous concussion.

# Breathing Difficulty or Shortness of Breath

Breathing difficulty or shortness of breath is a medical emergency. It is generally caused by an underlying medical illness such as asthma, allergic reaction, heart failure, or lung disease.

At rest, normal breathing is regular and effortless. You may first suspect difficulty when there is a noticeable increase in the effort to breathe and the rate at which breaths are occurring. Unusual breath sounds may occur.

A bluish-purple tissue color, especially in the lips or fingers, is a serious sign indicating a developing lack of oxygen. Do not wait to see if the person's condition will improve. Activate EMS without delay, and if an AED is available, have someone get it.

## Asthma or Reactive Airway Disease

Asthma or reactive airway disease causes the air passages in the lungs to become narrower from swelling, spasm, and extra mucus. This limits airflow into and out of the lungs and causes wheezing or shortness of breath.

Different types and brands of inhalers (e.g., spacers, dry powder inhaler) require different techniques. Assist the casualty with his medication as prescribed. Local health authority regulations and occupational licensing requirements may prescribe specific practices, rules, standards, and other conditions for assisting with prescribed medications. Asthma signs, symptoms, and first aid appear in table 9.9.

**TABLE 9.9**

## Asthma: Signs, Symptoms, and First Aid

| Signs and symptoms | First aid |
| --- | --- |
| *Symptoms vary. They can be very mild to life threatening.*<br>▪ Constant coughing, especially worse at night and early morning<br>▪ Anxiety<br>▪ Sudden onset of wheezing<br>▪ Chest tightness<br>▪ Shortness of breath<br>▪ Extreme difficulty breathing, with the chest and neck pulled in<br>▪ Stooped body posture<br>▪ Bluish color to lips and face<br>▪ Pounding heart<br>▪ Sweating<br>▪ Altered mental status | ▪ Allow the person to find the most comfortable position in which to breathe.<br>▪ Loosen any tight clothing.<br>▪ If the casualty is unable to administer the prescribed medication (using a nebulizer or metered-dose inhaler) without assistance, help her administer it.<br>▪ Alert EMS if the casualty does not improve 15 to 20 min after the initial treatment with medication.<br>▪ Comfort, calm, and reassure the casualty while awaiting EMS. |

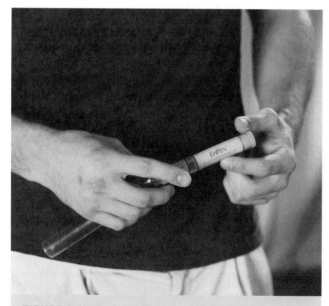

**FIGURE 9.1** People with severe allergies should carry a prescribed EpiPen, which temporarily reverses an allergic reaction, at all times.

## Severe Allergic Reaction (Anaphylaxis)

Anaphylaxis is a sudden, life-threatening severe allergic reaction that involves the whole body. Swelling of the lips, eyelids, throat, and tongue can block the airway. **Anaphylaxis is fatal without prompt treatment** (see table 9.10). Anyone with a history of anaphylaxis should keep an epinephrine auto-injector, or EpiPen, on hand at all times (see figure 9.1). **Waiting for EMS may significantly increase the risk of death.**

An *epinephrine auto-injector* is a device that allows an anaphylaxis casualty to inject herself with epinephrine, a substance that temporarily reverses the allergic reaction. The device is designed to work through clothing.

# Using an Epinephrine Auto-Injector (EpiPen)

To use the auto-injector, do the following:

1. Remove the EpiPen from the storage container. Do not use if the solution is discolored or a red flag appears in the clear window. Do not put your thumb, fingers, or hand over the tip.

2. Form a fist around the injector unit, with the needle tip pointing downward.

3. With your other hand, pull off the safety release cap. Do not pull off the safety release cap until you are ready to administer the medication.

4. Hold the needle tip near the person's outer thigh.

5. Swing and jab the unit firmly against the outer thigh until it clicks so that the unit is at a 90-degree angle to the thigh.

6. Hold the auto-injector firmly against the thigh for approximately 10 seconds. (The injection is now complete. The window on the auto-injector will show red.)

7. Pull the injector straight out. The needle will retract underneath the safety cap. Massage the injection site for about 15 seconds.

8. Carefully place the used auto-injector, needle end first (without bending the needle), into the storage tube of the carrying case. Ask EMS providers for help in proper disposal.

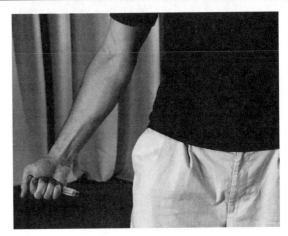

***Note:*** Most of the liquid (about 90 percent) stays in the auto-injector and cannot be reused. However, you will know that a correct dose of the medication has been delivered if the red flag appears in the window. See table 9.10 for signs, symptoms, and first aid for anaphylaxis.

**TABLE 9.10**

## Anaphylaxis: Signs, Symptoms, and First Aid

| Signs and symptoms | First aid |
|---|---|
| Rapid onset of the following:<br>▪ Anxiety<br>▪ Hives or itching<br>▪ Sensation of heart pounding<br>▪ Nausea or vomiting<br>▪ Abdominal pain or cramping<br>▪ Diarrhea<br>▪ Swelling of lips, eyelids, throat, and tongue<br>▪ Extreme difficulty breathing<br>▪ Coughing or wheezing<br>▪ Altered mental status<br>▪ Blueness of skin, lips, nail beds<br>▪ Complete airway obstruction | ▪ If the casualty carries a lifesaving epinephrine auto-injector prescribed by a physician, help him use it. If the casualty is unable to use it, you should administer it. Its beneficial effect is relatively short, so the casualty requires immediate medical assistance.<br>▪ Comfort, calm, and reassure the casualty while awaiting EMS.<br>▪ Do not put your thumb, fingers, or hand over the needle tip when administering the EpiPen.<br>▪ Do not remove the safety release cap until you are ready to administer the medication.<br>▪ Do not use if the solution is discolored or a red flag appears in the clear window. |

# Severe Abdominal Pain

Severe abdominal pain can be a warning sign of serious illness, especially if it appears suddenly or is a new experience for the person. There are a number of important organs in the abdomen. Depending on the body systems involved, many serious problems can occur and cause pain. Early recognition and rapid transport to a hospital may prevent the development of a life-threatening condition. See table 9.11 for signs, symptoms, and first aid for severe abdominal pain.

**TABLE 9.11**

## Severe Abdominal Pain: Signs, Symptoms, and First Aid

| Signs and symptoms | First aid |
|---|---|
| Rapid onset of the following:<br>■ Severe pain<br>■ Rigid abdomen<br>■ Abdomen tender to the touch<br>■ Possible nausea and vomiting | ■ Allow the person to find a position of comfort to try to relieve the pain.<br>■ Do not give the person anything to eat or drink.<br>■ Comfort, calm, and reassure the casualty while awaiting EMS. |

## Emergencies During Pregnancy

Illnesses and problems can occur during pregnancy that have symptoms of severe pain and can put both mother and child in danger. See table 9.12 for signs, symptoms, and first aid for emergencies during pregnancy.

**TABLE 9.12**

## Pregnancy Emergencies: Signs, Symptoms, and First Aid

| Signs and symptoms | First aid |
|---|---|
| Serious warning signs and symptoms:<br>■ Severe abdominal pain<br>■ Persistent vaginal bleeding<br>■ Gushing amniotic fluid<br>■ Sudden severe headache<br>■ Altered mental status<br>■ Seizure<br>■ Fainting or loss of consciousness<br>■ Shock<br><br>*Note:* If the casualty feels faint, has signs or symptoms of shock, or is unresponsive and is more than 3 months pregnant, place her on her left side in the recovery position. When the casualty is lying faceup, the baby puts pressure on a major vein that returns blood to the heart. Placing the woman on her left side reduces this pressure and provides the most blood flow to mother and baby. | ■ Whenever possible, use a female first aid provider.<br>■ Have the woman assume the position that makes her most comfortable.<br>■ Get a SAMPLE history (see description on page 112).<br>■ If the woman is reluctant to discuss problems related to the pregnancy, respect her wishes.<br>■ For significant vaginal bleeding (use of more than two sanitary pads per hour), have the casualty press a sanitary pad or towel to the area.<br>■ Help the casualty maintain a normal temperature, and do not let her become chilled or overheated.<br>■ Comfort, calm, and reassure the casualty while awaiting EMS.<br>■ Do not examine the vagina.<br>■ Do not place dressings inside the vagina. |

# Burns

Burns have several causes:

- *Thermal burns* are caused by the sun, fire, hot liquids or objects, and hot gases.
- *Electrical burns* are caused by contact with electrical wires, currents, or lightning.
- *Chemical burns* are caused by contact with wet or dry chemicals.

**If a casualty is on fire, tell him to stop, drop, and roll. If the casualty is in contact with electricity, shut off the power.** Table 9.13 gives treatment recommendations for burns.

**TABLE 9.13**

## Burns: Signs, Symptoms, and First Aid

| Burn | Signs and symptoms | First aid |
|------|--------------------|-----------|
| **Minor burns**<br>Immediate cooling of minor burns will reduce the swelling, infection, and depth of the injury. It will allow faster healing with less scarring. | ■ Pain<br>■ Redness<br>■ Swelling<br>■ Blisters | ■ Cool heat burns with cold water as quickly as possible, and continue cooling at least until the pain is relieved. Do not directly apply ice to cool a burn.<br>■ Leave blisters intact. Cover the burn with a dry, sterile bandage or a clean dressing.<br>■ Protect the burn from pressure and friction. |
| **Critical burns**<br>■ Burns involving hands, face, eyes, ears, feet, and genitals<br>■ Electrical burns<br>■ Burns involving smoke inhalation, fractures, or other injury | ■ Dry or leathery white skin or blackened, charred skin | ■ Activate EMS.<br>■ Expose the burn. Cut and gently lift away any clothing covering the burned area.<br>■ If clothing is stuck to the burn, do not remove it.<br>■ Remove jewelry, if possible (burns cause swelling).<br>■ Separate fingers or toes with dry, sterile nonadhesive dressings.<br>■ Lightly cover the burn area with a dry, sterile bandage or a clean sheet if the burned area is large. |
| **Chemical burns**<br>Some chemicals can react with and damage the skin tissue on contact. | ■ Burning or itching sensation | ■ The immediate care is to dilute and remove the chemical quickly to minimize the damage.<br>■ Remove contaminated clothing.<br>■ If applicable, brush off any dry powder with a gloved hand or cloth before flushing.<br>■ Flood the affected area with large amounts of water. Continue to flush with water until the burning sensation stops.<br>■ Cover any visible burns loosely with a dry, clean pad and seek further medical attention. |
| **Electrical burns**<br>Turn off the power before touching the affected person. | ■ Possible unresponsiveness<br>■ Visible burns at the places the current entered and exited the body | ■ An electric shock can cause ventricular fibrillation in the heart. If this occurs, activate EMS and have someone get an AED if one is available. Perform CPR until an AED is ready.<br>■ If the person is responsive, treat the burns you can see.<br>■ Seek further medical assessment because the extent of the injury may not be apparent. |

# Poisoning

A poison is any substance that causes injury, illness, or death when swallowed, contacted by skin, or inhaled.

## Possible Swallowed Poisons

Poisons that can enter the body through the mouth include the following:

- Drugs (prescription, illegal, over the counter)
- Alcohol
- Household cleaning products
- Cosmetics
- Pesticides, paints, solvents
- Contaminated foods
- Poisonous plants (plants and plant parts can cause harm)

## Possible Skin-Contact Poisons

Poisons that can enter the body through contact include the following:

- Corrosives (alkalis, acids, hydrocarbons)
- Poisonous plants (poison ivy, oak, sumac)

## Possible Inhaled Poisons

Poisons that may be in the air and enter the body while breathing include the following:

- Chlorine gas
- Natural gas
- Carbon monoxide
- Harmful dusts, fogs, fumes, mists, gases, smokes, sprays, or chemical vapors

See table 9.14 for signs, symptoms, and first aid for poisoning.

**TABLE 9.14**

### Poisoning: Signs, Symptoms, and First Aid

| Signs and symptoms | First aid |
|---|---|
| *Wide ranging and variable. Signs and symptoms of poisoning can copy those of common illnesses.* | Swallowed poison<br>■ Call the Poison Control Center at 800-222-1222 (in the U.S.) to talk to a poison expert.<br>■ Have all medicine bottles, containers, or samples of poisoning substance available. If you go to a hospital's emergency department, take them with you.<br>■ Giving anything by mouth may be harmful.<br>■ Do not give the casualty water or milk unless advised by a Poison Control Center expert.<br>■ Do not induce vomiting.<br>■ Do not administer syrup of ipecac or activated charcoal unless advised by a Poison Control Center expert.<br>Skin-contact poison<br>■ Quickly remove clothing.<br>■ Rinse skin with large amounts of tap water.<br>Inhaled poison<br>■ Assess, alert, and attend to the ABCs.<br>■ Get the casualty to fresh air right away. |

Workplace safety regulations in the United States and other countries require appropriate training and equipment (respirators) for employees who must enter an environment that is immediately dangerous to life or health.

# Bites and Stings

Bites and stings can occur from a wide variety of insects, reptiles, animals, and even humans. Most are not serious and cause only minor swelling, redness, pain, and itching.

Some bites and stings are more serious, especially for people who are very young or old or have existing medical issues. Occasionally, the most important first aid measure is rapid transport to comprehensive medical care. Remove the stinger from a bee sting. All human or animal bites must be referred to a doctor, as many victims will require antibiotics to prevent infection. See table 9.15 for specific recommendations.

**TABLE 9.15**

## Bites and Stings: Signs, Symptoms, and First Aid

| Bite or sting | Signs and symptoms | First aid |
|---|---|---|
| **Venomous snakebite** Your treatment focuses on slowing the absorption of the venom (poison) into the body and quickly getting the person EMS attention for specialized treatment. | ■ Single or double fang marks ■ Intense, burning pain and localized swelling ■ If untreated, the swelling may involve the entire limb within hours ■ Bleeding | For all snakebites: ■ Have the person sit passively, and activate EMS. ■ If the site is bleeding, apply direct pressure with a clean cloth or absorbent pad. ■ Cover the bite with an adhesive bandage or gauze pad. ■ Keep the injured part immobilized below heart level. ■ Keep the casualty warm, reassured, and quiet. ■ Seek medical attention. ■ Do not cut through snakebite wounds or apply suctioning, ice, or tourniquets. These actions are of no proven value and may be dangerous. |
| **Coral snakebite** | ■ Pain and swelling may be minimal or absent. ■ Abdominal pain may occur (within hours of the bite). ■ Whole-body effects (may be delayed up to 6 hr) include nausea, vomiting, sweating, weakness, altered mental status, rapid heartbeat, drooling, difficulty breathing, stoppage of breathing. | Coral snakebite additional first aid: ■ Apply a pressure bandage around the entire length of the bitten extremity to slow the spread of venom. The pressure bandage should be snug but not so tight that you cannot slip a finger under it. |
| **Venomous spider bite** | Initially, venomous spider bites are often difficult to determine. ■ Small puncture marks and bleeding may be seen. ■ Over time, tenderness, swelling, pain, itching, and redness and heat at the bite site can develop. ■ Whole-body effects in a severe reaction may include cramping pain and muscular rigidity in the abdomen or shoulders, back, and chest; fever; chills; rash; anxiety; weakness; nausea or vomiting; difficulty breathing. | ■ Keep the casualty warm, reassured, and quiet. ■ Seek medical attention. |

(continued)

TABLE 9.15 *(continued)*

| Bite or sting | Signs and symptoms | First aid |
|---|---|---|
| **Insect sting** | ▪ Minor reaction: bite site painful, red, swollen, itchy<br>▪ A severe reaction can be fatal, with whole-body effects that may include hives (raised, itchy bumps on skin), itching all over body, swelling of mouth or throat or both, shortness of breath or difficulty breathing, nausea or vomiting, chest pain or palpitations, anxiety or weakness, fainting. | Minor reaction<br>▪ If the stinger is present in the skin, remove it by scraping with a fingernail or the edge of a rigid card (e.g., credit card).<br>▪ Wash the sting site with clean running tap water for several minutes.<br>▪ Cover the area with an adhesive bandage or gauze pad.<br>▪ Apply ice to the injury to reduce pain and swelling. To prevent cold injury, place a thin towel or cloth between the cold source and the skin. Limit application to 20 min or less.<br>▪ Consider using over-the-counter anti-itch medications such as calamine lotion or Benadryl.<br>Severe reaction<br>▪ Activate EMS.<br>▪ If the person carries a prescribed epinephrine auto-injector, help him use it (see pages 124-125). If the casualty is unable to use it, you should administer it. |
| **Tick bite**<br>Ticks are blood-feeding insects that are typically found in tall grass and shrubs. The primary concern with tick bites is the exposure to and transmission of infectious disease. | A tick that has attached itself firmly to the skin should be removed. | ▪ To remove a tick, grasp it close to the skin with tweezers (or use a commercially available tick removal tool). If a tool or tweezers are not available, use your fingers protected by gloves. Pull straight up with a steady, slow motion.<br>▪ If portions of the tick remain embedded in the skin, or symptoms of severe reaction develop, seek medical attention.<br>▪ Do not use fingernail polish, petroleum jelly, a glowing hot match, or alcohol to remove a tick. |
| **Marine animal sting** | ▪ Stings from marine animals such as fire coral, sea anemones, and jellyfish can result in pain at the sting site and a painful, raised, red, itchy rash.<br>▪ Severe reactions can include difficulty breathing, chest palpitations, weakness, and fainting. | ▪ Carefully wipe off stingers or tentacles using forceps or by scraping them with the edge of a rigid card (e.g., credit card).<br>▪ As soon as possible, wash the sting site for at least 30 sec using household vinegar to inactivate the venom and decrease symptoms.<br>▪ Shower or immerse the site in hot water (as hot as the person can tolerate) for at least 20 min or until the pain subsides.<br>▪ If there is a wound from a stingray barb, carefully clean out the wound site.<br>▪ If a severe reaction occurs, activate EMS. |
| **Human or animal bites** | Large animal and human bites can cause significant wounds and severe bleeding. | ▪ If the site is bleeding, apply direct pressure with a clean cloth or absorbent pad.<br>▪ Wash the site with clean running tap water for about 5 min.<br>▪ Cover the area with an adhesive bandage or gauze pad.<br>▪ Apply ice to the injury to reduce pain, bleeding, and swelling.<br>▪ For a severe bite, activate EMS, control severe bleeding, and care for shock. Save any tissue parts that were bitten off. Treat them as you would an amputation. |

# Exposure to Heat

Exposure to hot and humid conditions can lead to heat exhaustion and heatstroke. These are serious conditions that require immediate attention. Do not underestimate the seriousness of heat illness, especially if the person is a child or elderly.

Following are some tips to prevent heat illness:

■ When working in the heat, take rest periods in a cool environment, and drink plenty of fluids.

■ Never leave a child alone in a motor vehicle in the heat, even to run a quick errand. The passenger compartment can quickly turn into a fatal oven.

## Heat Exhaustion

An active body creates heat. Sweating occurs when the body is exposed to hot, humid temperatures. As the sweat evaporates from the skin, it has a cooling effect. Heat exhaustion can develop from the combination of an increased internal temperature and the excessive loss of fluids to the environment. Extended exposure to a hot, humid environment can overwhelm the body's ability to cool itself down.

Although it may not appear serious, treat suspected heat exhaustion without delay. Without immediate treatment it could progress to a life-threatening condition. See table 9.16 for signs, symptoms, and first aid for heat exhaustion.

**TABLE 9.16**

### Heat Exhaustion: Signs, Symptoms, and First Aid

| Signs and symptoms | First aid |
|---|---|
| Heat exhaustion can look like many other common illnesses.<br><br>Early signs and symptoms<br>■ Heavy sweating<br>■ Thirst<br>■ Minor muscle twitches that progress to painful cramping<br><br>Later signs and symptoms<br>■ Pale, cool, and moist skin<br>■ Headache<br>■ Nausea and vomiting<br>■ Weakness, dizziness<br>■ Feels faint or collapses | ■ Stop the person from activity, and move to a cooler place.<br>■ Loosen or remove excess clothing.<br>■ Have the person lie down and raise the legs 6 to 12 in (15 to 30 cm).<br>■ Spray water or apply cool, wet cloths to the person's head and torso. Use a fan if available to speed evaporation.<br>■ Give the casualty cool sport drinks (such as Gatorade) to replace lost fluid, salts, and minerals. If not available, give cool water.<br>■ If the person does not improve or seems to get worse, activate EMS. |

## Heatstroke

Heatstroke is a life-threatening medical emergency. With heatstroke, the body temperature exceeds 105 degrees Fahrenheit (41 °C). This high body temperature can cause permanent damage to organs such as the brain and spinal cord. Heatstroke can result from overexertion in a hot, humid environment or from a breakdown in the body's ability to remove heat. See table 9.17 for signs, symptoms, and first aid for heatstroke.

**TABLE 9.17**

## Heatstroke: Signs, Symptoms, and First Aid

| Signs and symptoms | First aid |
|---|---|
| Heatstroke can have any or all of the symptoms of heat exhaustion, along with the following:<br>■ Altered and decreasing mental status (confusion, hallucinations, bizarre behavior, seizure, unresponsiveness)<br>■ Hot, red, dry skin (however, heavy sweating could be present when exertion is the cause) | ■ Spray or pour water on the casualty, and fan him.<br>■ Apply ice packs to the casualty's neck, groin, and armpits, or cover the casualty with a wet sheet.<br>■ Place the casualty on his side in the recovery position to protect the airway.<br>■ Provide continuous cooling until EMS arrives.<br>■ Do not give the casualty anything by mouth if he is vomiting or unresponsive. |

# Exposure to Cold

Cold, wet temperatures can result in a lowering of the internal body temperature. Hypothermia and frostbite are the most dangerous cold-related conditions.

## Hypothermia

Hypothermia can be a life-threatening medical emergency. In hypothermia, the body temperature has decreased to 95 degrees Fahrenheit (35 °C) or less. Body processes eventually fail, and cardiac arrest may occur. If the casualty is unresponsive or has an altered mental status, alert EMS or follow your emergency action plan immediately.

All deaths from exposure to extreme cold are preventable. Early recognition of the signs and symptoms, along with awareness of risk factors, can help minimize both injury and death. See table 9.18 for signs, symptoms, and first aid for hypothermia.

**TABLE 9.18**

## Hypothermia: Signs, Symptoms, and First Aid

| Signs and symptoms | First aid |
|---|---|
| Early signs and symptoms<br>■ Pale, cold skin<br>■ Uncontrollable shivering<br>■ Difficulty speaking<br>■ Loss of coordination<br>■ Altered mental status<br>Later signs and symptoms<br>■ No shivering<br>■ Slow (or absent) breathing or heartbeat | ■ Get the casualty to a warmer place.<br>■ Remove wet or constricting clothes and replace them with dry ones.<br>■ Cover the casualty with warm blankets.<br>■ Cover the casualty's head and neck to help retain body heat.<br>■ Place the casualty near a heat source, and place containers of warm, but not hot, water in contact with the skin.<br>■ Do not massage limbs, give anything to eat or drink, or allow the person to expend energy.<br>■ Comfort, calm, and reassure the casualty until EMS arrives. |

## Frostbite

Frostbite develops when the skin freezes. Body parts that may be exposed to the cold are the most likely to be affected (fingers, toes, earlobes, cheeks, nose). Affected parts may need to be amputated. See table 9.19 for signs, symptoms, and first aid for frostbite.

**TABLE 9.19**

### Frostbite: Signs, Symptoms, and First Aid

| Signs and symptoms | First aid |
|---|---|
| Early signs and symptoms<br>■ Pins and needles sensation<br>■ Throbbing<br><br>Later signs and symptoms<br>■ Frozen (no feeling)<br>■ Hard, pale, cold, numb skin | If EMS or medical attention is available:<br>■ Move the casualty to a warmer place.<br>■ Remove constricting jewelry and wet clothing.<br>■ Place a sterile dressing between frostbitten fingers and toes.<br>■ Wrap frostbitten area with sterile dressings.<br>■ Comfort, calm, and reassure the casualty until EMS arrives.<br><br>If EMS or medical attention is not available:<br>■ Immerse the frostbitten areas in warm water (not hot) for 20 to 30 min. The recommended water temperature is 100 to 105 °F (38 to 41 °C).<br>■ Severe burning pain, swelling, and color changes may occur.<br>■ Do not rewarm if there is a chance refreezing may occur.<br>■ Do not rub or massage the affected area.<br>■ Do not disturb blisters on frostbitten skin.<br>■ Do not give the casualty alcoholic beverages. Alcohol does not help and may be harmful. |

# Triage for Catastrophic Events

You may face situations in which there is more than one casualty. These situations may range from a few casualties to thousands and result from waterslide or bleacher collapses to catastrophic natural disasters or terrorist attacks. When there are multiple injured victims, you must try to prioritize them by how urgently they need care. This is called *triage*, a French word meaning "to sort." The goal of triage is to do the greatest good for the greatest number. To accomplish this goal, you must have an organized approach to victim management. Remember to activate the EMS system early and convey the expected number of victims so that appropriate resources can be dispatched. There are many different casualty triage systems. Know which is used by your facility and practice it regularly. One such system is described below.

During triage you must efficiently move from casualty to casualty, quickly assessing their condition and sorting them into four basic groups:

1. **Ambulatory** (able to walk). To begin triage, first call out, "If you can walk, come to the sound of my voice." If there are victims who can walk, instruct them to remain at a safe location. Victims who are not ill, uninjured, or have only minor injuries may be able to help provide first aid.

2. **Delayed.** The casualty does not have life-threatening injuries (e.g., responsive casualty with a broken leg). Treatment may be delayed.

3. **Immediate.** The casualty has life-threatening injuries (e.g., profuse bleeding) that can be corrected or slowed down with minimal intervention. Rapid lifesaving treatment is urgent. These victims will require evacuation first.

4. **Dead or expectant.** No signs of life, or death is expected because the nature of the injury cannot be corrected with the resources available.

Use these steps as a guide for triage:

1. Assess for responsiveness.
   - If the casualty is awake and responsive and no immediate life threats are present, such as profuse bleeding, consider her delayed. *Move on to the next casualty. Begin with step 1.*
   - If the casualty is unresponsive, tap or squeeze his shoulder and ask, "Are you OK?" If there is no response, move on to step 2.

2. Open the airway by tilting the head and lifting the chin.
   - If the casualty takes a breath, place him on his side in the appropriate recovery position. This person is considered immediate. Move on to step 3.
   - If the person does not take a breath, reposition his head to make sure the airway is open. If the casualty still does not take a breath, consider him expectant. The time devoted to rescue breathing and chest compressions is not justified when there are multiple people needing first aid. *Move on to the next casualty. Begin with step 1.*

3. Look for profuse bleeding. If present, take immediate action to stop it. If another first aid provider is available, ask her to maintain direct pressure on the wound. Consider this casualty immediate. *Move on to the next casualty. Begin with step 1.*

Remember that victim conditions can change and, depending upon available resources, you may need to reassess and triage all victims again. For example, a person with internal bleeding was "ambulatory", but is now unresponsive and "immediate". Conversely, an initially unresponsive person may now be awake and alert, able to walk without difficulty, changing them from "immediate" to "ambulatory".

# Emergency Moves

Do not move an injured casualty unless it is absolutely necessary, as in the following circumstances:

- When the casualty is lying flat on her back and has debris, blood, or secretions in the mouth that might block the airway
- When you must leave the casualty alone to get help
- The scene becomes unsafe
- When the casualty is lying on a very hot or very cold surface, and you need to get a blanket under him to maintain a normal body temperature

If you decide it is necessary to move someone over a distance, the fastest and easiest move is to use a drag. When using a drag, pull in the direction of the long axis of the body to keep the spine in line. Never pull on a person's head or pull a person's body sideways. Common drags include the following:

- Extremity drag: Grasp and pull on the person's ankles or forearms.
- Clothing drag: Pull on the person's shirt in the neck and shoulder area.
- Blanket drag: Roll the person onto a blanket, and drag the blanket.

When moving someone, use your legs, not your back, and keep the person's weight as close to your body as possible. Avoid twisting. Consider the person's weight, and respect your physical limitations.

Avoid moving injured people from a damaged vehicle unless you believe their lives are clearly in danger. Vehicle fires or explosions in traffic crashes are rare.

## ⭐ Knowledge Into Practice

The need to provide first aid is a common occurrence at aquatic facilities. You need to be prepared to provide care within the scope of responsibility at your workplace.

## @ Visit the Web Resource

You can reinforce your learning by visiting the web resource, where you can do the following in the interactive online learning activities for chapter 9:

▸ Activity 9.1: Reinforce how to perform a secondary assessment, and identify signs of injury and symptoms using the DOTS and SAMPLE memory aids.

▸ Activity 9.2: View a video and order the steps of placing a person in the recovery position.

▸ Activity 9.3: Create a chart to classify wounds.

▸ Activity 9.4: Match signs and symptoms for temperature-related illnesses.

▸ Activity 9.5: Match objects or substances with the type of burn they will cause.

▸ Activity 9.6: Review scenarios and become familiar with providing first aid.

▸ Activity 9.7: Chapter quiz. Test your knowledge, receive feedback, and print the quiz page.

## 🔁 On the Job

These are the tasks related to providing first aid that you will be expected to competently perform while working as a lifeguard:

▸ Recognize the emergency and decide to help.

▸ If the casualty is responsive, get his permission to help.

▸ Quickly assess and care for life-threatening conditions.

▸ Continue care until someone with equal or more training takes over.

▸ Maintain composure. Do no further harm.

▸ Maintain up-to-date knowledge and skills.

▸ With your safety as a priority, make the casualty's needs your next concern.

# Performing CPR and Using an AED for Professional Rescuers

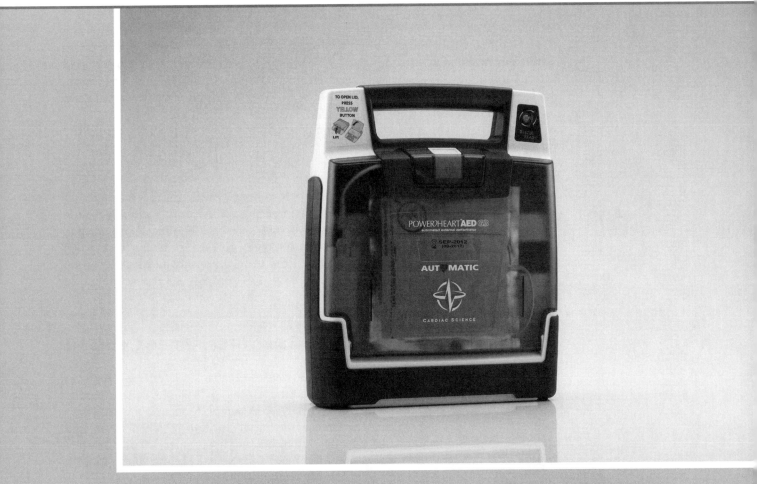

Reprinted and adapted selected text, by permission, from American Safety and Health Institute with Human Kinetics, 2007, *Complete emergency care* (Champaign, IL: Human Kinetics), 99-140.

This chapter

▶ provides cardiopulmonary resuscitation (CPR), basic life support (BLS) and automated external defibrillation (AED) information at the professional rescuer level;

▶ explains how to identify sudden cardiac arrest, check a pulse, and perform effective compressions plus rescue breathing until EMS arrives;

▶ explains how to use an AED;

▶ explains how to perform CPR with two or more rescuers;

▶ identifies how to provide BLS for a person who has a pulse but is not breathing;

▶ considers special conditions for CPR; and

▶ describes how to aid adults, children, and infants who are choking.

*N*ote to readers: Because the audience for this course is nonmedical professional rescuers, we have used the term *victim* or *casualty* instead of the typical medically oriented term *patient*. The term *EMS* refers to any system of emergency medical responders, regardless of the name common in your location.

# Basic Life Support

Basic life support consists of the prehospital techniques used in life-threatening illness or injury that can be provided by trained medical personnel or responders who have received BLS training. BLS treatment recommendations are developed internationally every five years, and then evaluated and published by one representative per country as guidelines. Guidelines in the United States are published by the American Heart Association (AHA). In other countries guidelines are generally published by the local resuscitation council, and may differ slightly from the techniques presented in this chapter.

When you provide rescue breathing or CPR, you help the victim's respiratory and circulatory systems function.

The body cannot survive when circulation stops. Brain tissue is especially sensitive to a lack of oxygen. External chest compressions combined with rescue breathing (CPR) are essential for providing blood flow to vital organs during cardiac arrest and allow a provider to restore some oxygen to the brain. By itself, CPR is only a temporary measure that can buy time until more advanced care can be provided. The algorithm in figure 10.1 on page 139 summarizes the sequence of actions when providing basic life support.

# Treatment for Sudden Cardiac Arrest (SCA)

Sudden cardiac arrest (SCA) occurs when the heart's electrical system malfunctions and the heart abruptly stops working without warning. SCA is one of the leading causes of death among adults in North America. When SCA occurs, most victims have an abnormal heart rhythm known as ventricular fibrillation (VF). The normal electrical impulses in the heart unexpectedly become disorganized. The normally coordinated mechanical contraction of the heart muscle is lost, and replaced with

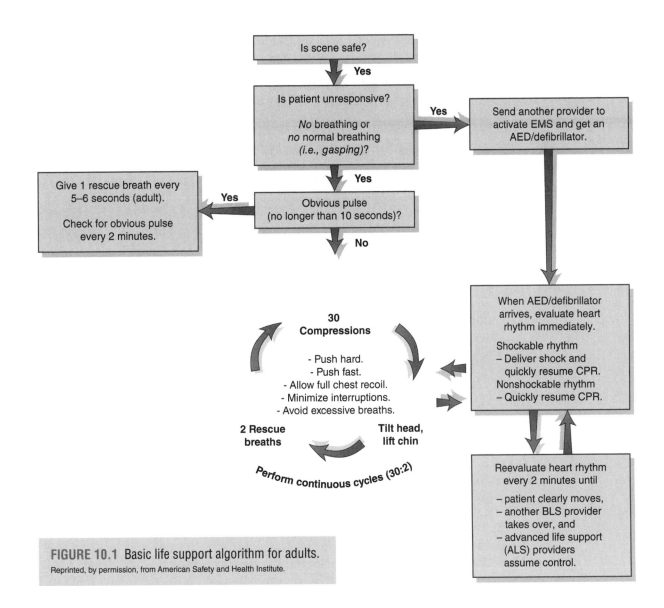

**FIGURE 10.1** Basic life support algorithm for adults.
Reprinted, by permission, from American Safety and Health Institute.

a chaotic, quivering condition. Blood flow to the brain and vital organs abruptly stops. The lack of blood flow and oxygen supply to the brain causes the victim to lose consciousness, collapse, and stop breathing. Without early recognition and care, the person will not survive.

Symptoms of SCA develop rapidly:

- Sudden collapse without warning (some people may have a racing heartbeat or feel dizzy or faint)
- Unconsciousness or unresponsiveness
- Abnormal grunting, gasping, or snoring noises
- Looks dead

SCA often occurs in active, outwardly healthy adults or teens with no known heart disease or other health problems. SCA occurs less frequently in children. The most common causes of SCA in a child are

- a hard blow to the chest, which causes a disruption of the heart's regular rhythm;
- an underlying medical condition that may be undiagnosed; or

■ the loss of an airway or breathing, such as in drowning or choking. Without oxygen, the heart slows and eventually stops.

Sudden cardiac arrest should be treated with CPR and, if available, defibrillation using an AED as soon as possible. The treatment steps include:

1. Primary assessment
2. Chest compressions (C)
3. Airway management (A)
4. Rescue breathing (B)
5. Defibrillation

Use the letters C-A-B to help you remember the sequence.

Procedures differ slightly for adults, children, and infants. Although no single factor can distinguish an infant from a child and a child from an adult, in order to simplify training, CPR guidelines use the age ranges in the following list:

■ Adult = anyone at or beyond puberty. Puberty can be determined by breast development in females and the presence of armpit hair in males.
■ Child = about one year to onset of puberty.
■ Infant = less than about one year.

Determining age can be difficult, and exactness is not necessary.

## Primary Assessment

The first steps in treating SCA are to assess the scene, assess the victim, and alert others, known as a primary assessment. Perform the steps of assessment quickly, in a minute or less.

### Assess the Scene

Assess the scene. If the scene is not safe or at any time becomes unsafe, get out! If the scene is safe, pause for a moment as you approach the victim. What is your first impression? Is the victim lying still or moving around? A person who has just collapsed because of sudden cardiac arrest may convulse for a short time. Do not let this delay your assessment.

### Check for Response

If the person appears unresponsive, tap or squeeze his shoulder and ask loudly, "Are you OK?" For an infant, you may tap the foot. Use the person's name if you know it. If needed, position the person faceup on a firm, flat surface.

### Look for Normal Breathing

Look at the face and chest for breathing. Do this quickly. Normal breathing is effortless, quiet, and regular. Weak, irregular gasping, snorting, or gurgling sounds can occur early in cardiac arrest. These gasps are not normal breathing and do not supply the victim with enough oxygen to sustain life. If you are not *positive* that the victim is breathing adequately, alert others.

### Activate EMS and Get an AED

If the victim is unresponsive, have another person activate EMS so you can begin care. If you are alone with an unresponsive adult, immediately alert EMS yourself. Get an AED, if one is available, and quickly return to the victim. When alone with an unresponsive child or infant, finish your assessment and provide about 2 minutes of care before leaving to call for EMS and getting an AED yourself.

### Feel for a Pulse

If you have determined that the victim is not breathing normally, feel for a pulse to determine whether to administer only rescue breathing (ventilation without compression) or breathing and chest compressions (CPR). Use the carotid pulse (neck) in adults and children. Locate the bony bump at the front of the neck, and slide your fingers into the groove between the windpipe and the muscle on the side of the neck. Compress inward. For infants, use the brachial pulse on the inside of the upper arm. Lay your fingers across the arm and compress inward. If a pulse is absent or not obvious within 10 seconds, perform CPR.

When a pulse is clearly present but less than 60 beats per minute for a child or infant, the heart may not be providing enough blood flow to the body and you should perform CPR, especially if there are signs of reduced blood flow such as poor skin color. (Count for 6 seconds and multiply by 10 to estimate heartbeats per minute. **Do not count for a full minute.**)

> Pulse checks can be difficult in emergency situations, even for experienced providers. If you are not certain that a pulse is present, assume it is absent and perform CPR.

## SKILL GUIDE

# Primary Assessment

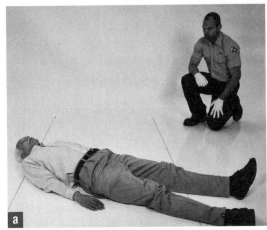

a

### ◀ Assess Scene

Pause and assess scene for safety. If unsafe, or if it becomes unsafe at any time, *get out*! If safe, approach the casualty.

b

**Check for Response ▶**

If casualty appears unresponsive, tap or squeeze shoulder. Ask loudly, "Are you OK?" Use the person's name if you know it.

For infants, try tapping foot and shouting loudly. ▶

c

*(continued)*

# Primary Assessment *(continued)*

### ◀ Look for Normal Breathing

Position the person faceup on a firm, flat surface. Look quickly at face and chest for normal breathing. Normal breathing is effortless, quiet, and regular. Weak and irregular, gasping, snorting, or gurgling is *not* considered normal. If normal breathing is found, place an uninjured person on the side in a recovery position.

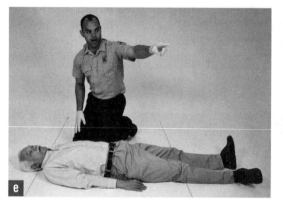

### Activate EMS and Get an AED ▶

If the person is unresponsive, send someone to activate EMS and get an AED. If alone with an adult, place in a recovery position and do this yourself. When alone with a child or infant, provide 2 minutes of care first.

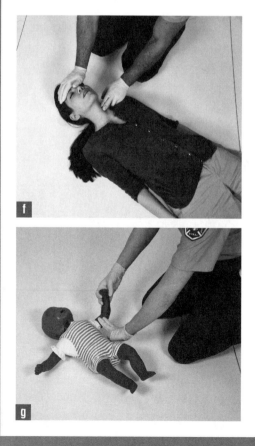

### ◀ Feel for Pulse in Neck

Slide your fingers into the groove between the bump at the front of the neck and the muscle next to it. For an infant, check the brachial pulse in the upper arm. If pulse is not obvious within 10 seconds, assume it is absent. If the casualty is not breathing, or only gasping, and has an obvious pulse, perform rescue breathing. If the casualty is not breathing, or only gasping, and has no pulse, perform CPR.

## Chest Compressions

Chest compressions create blood flow to the heart, brain, and other organs by increasing pressure inside the chest and arteries and by direct compression of the heart. Creating and maintaining this pressure not only keep vital organs alive but also increase the chances that defibrillation will be successful.

Once chest compressions are started, it takes time to build up enough pressure to make blood flow. When chest compressions are stopped, the pressure and blood flow drop quickly. Thus, frequent interruption of chest compressions may contribute to poor survival rates. For that reason, minimize interruptions in chest compressions during CPR.

The most effective chest compressions occur with the rhythmic application of downward pressure on the lower half of the breastbone. It is recommended to push hard and push fast. Blood flow is improved if the chest is allowed to rebound completely between compressions.

Compression techniques are different for infants than they are for adults and children.

### Chest Compression for Adults and Children

To perform effective compressions, the victim needs to be positioned faceup and lying flat on a firm surface. Kneel close to the side of the chest. You may find it helpful to raise the victim's arm overhead to allow your knees to get in close to the body. Place the heel of one hand in the center of the chest. Place the heel of your other hand on top of the first. Your fingers can be straight or interlaced together to help keep them off the chest.

Position your body over the victim's chest so your shoulders are directly over your hands. Straighten your arms and lock your elbows.

Use your upper-body weight to help compress the chest. **For a normal-sized adult,** push straight down on the chest *at least* two inches (5 cm). **For a child,** use either one or two hands to compress the child's chest *at least* one-third to one-half the depth of the chest, or about two inches (5 cm). At the top of each compression, release pressure and completely remove your weight so the chest can fully rebound to its normal position.

Chest compressions and relaxation to allow the chest to fully recoil should be about equal. Give 30 chest compressions at a speed of *at least* 100 per minute. Compressing fast and deep helps create the best blood flow possible. You may find it helpful to count the compressions aloud.

When chest compressions are effective, you might hear an unpleasant sound similar to knuckles cracking, especially in an adult. You might feel the breastbone fall in a bit. This is caused by cartilage or ribs cracking and is normal. Forceful external chest compression is critical if the victim is to survive.

**Push hard and push fast with minimal interruptions.**

### Chest Compressions for Infants

If you are a single rescuer, compress the infant's breastbone with two fingertips placed just below the nipple line. Compress fast and deep. You may place your other hand under the infant's back to create a compression surface. Press down on the breastbone *at least* one-third the depth of the infant's chest. After each compression, completely release the pressure on the breastbone, allowing it to return to its normal position; without pausing, continue into the down stroke of the next compression. Give 30 chest compressions at a speed of *at least* 100 per minute. You may find it helpful to count the compressions aloud.

When two rescuers are present, compress the lower half of the breastbone with both thumb tips and hands encircling the chest and supporting the back, at speed of *at least* 100 per minute. This position allows for more effective compressions while the other rescuer will be providing rescue breaths.

# Chest Compressions

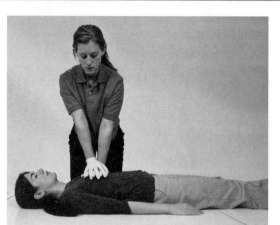

### Adult

- Position the person faceup on a flat, firm surface. Kneel close to the chest. Place the heel of one hand on the center of the chest. Place the heel of the second hand on top of the first. You can interlace your fingers to keep them off the chest.
- Position your shoulders directly above your hands. Lock your elbows, and use upper-body weight to push.
- Push hard, straight down at least two inches (5 cm). Lift hands and allow the chest to fully rebound. Without interruption, push fast at a rate of at least 100 times per minute.

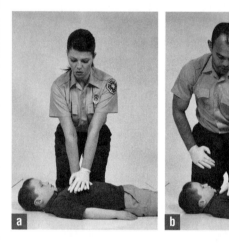

### Child

- Position the child faceup on a flat, firm surface. Place the heel of one hand on the lower half of the breastbone, slightly above where the ribs meet.
- Position your shoulder directly above your hand. Lock your elbow, and use upper-body weight to push.
- Push hard, straight down at least one-third the diameter of the chest, or about two inches (5 cm). Lift the hand and allow the chest to fully rebound. Without interruption, push fast at a rate of at least 100 times per minute. Keep up the force and speed of compressions.
- Compressions can be tiring. If desired, use two hands, as with adults.

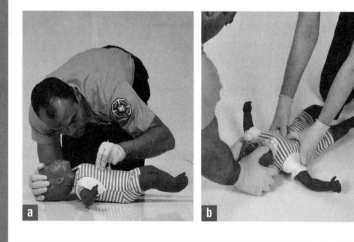

### Infant

- Position the infant faceup on a flat, firm surface. Place two fingertips on the breastbone just below the nipple line.
- Push hard, straight down at least one-third the diameter of the chest, or about one and a half inches (4 cm). Lift the fingers and allow the chest to fully rebound. Without interruption, push fast at a rate of at least 100 times per minute. Keep up the force and speed of compressions.
- When two or more rescuers are present, compress the breastbone using two thumbs, with your fingers encircling the chest.

## Airway Management

The airway is the passageway between the mouth and lungs. It must be open so air can enter and leave the lungs freely. Blockage of the airway in an adult or child is commonly caused by the tongue. The tongue is attached to the lower jaw. Moving the jaw forward lifts the tongue away from the back of the throat and opens the airway.

### Opening the Airway From the Side

If you are by yourself, kneel next to the victim near the head. Place your hand on the victim's forehead. Place the fingers of your other hand under the bony part of the chin. Apply firm, backward pressure on the forehead while lifting the chin upward. Maintain the head tilt with your hand on the forehead. Avoid pressing into the soft tissue of the chin with your fingers, which can obstruct the airway. Leave the victim's mouth slightly open. In an infant, tilt the head and lift the chin only slightly to open and maintain an airway.

If you remove your hands from the head, the airway will close again. You will need to open the airway each time you give rescue breaths.

### Opening the Airway From Behind the Head

If there will be more than one rescuer, position yourself behind the victim's head. This position is a convenient and effective approach, especially if you will be using a CPR mask, bag-valve mask, or AED.

When caring for someone who is seriously injured, establishing an open airway is a higher priority than protecting a possible injury to the spine. Without an airway a person will not survive, regardless of the illness or injury. When the potential for a neck injury exists, you can try to open the airway using a jaw thrust without the head tilt. Position yourself above the victim's head, and place the CPR mask on the victim's face. Place one hand on each side of the victim's head, and use your thumbs and heels of your hands to hold the mask in place. Then place your fingers under the angles of the victim's lower jaw, just below the ear, and lift the jaw forward with both hands. If the jaw thrust does not open the airway, use the head-tilt and chin-lift maneuver.

## Rescue Breathing

If a person is unresponsive, not breathing, or only gasping but has a pulse you can clearly feel, he is in a condition known as respiratory arrest. Without immediate intervention, respiratory arrest can quickly progress to cardiac arrest. The treatment for respiratory arrest is to blow air into the mouth of the victim to inflate the lungs, also called rescue breathing. Your exhaled air still contains 16 to 17 percent oxygen. This exhaled oxygen is enough to support someone's life for a short time.

### Infection Control During Rescue Breathing and CPR

As described in chapter 3, taking universal precautions means handling all blood and other body substances as if they are infectious. While providing care you can be exposed to blood or other potentially infectious bodily fluids.

The risk of contracting a disease while giving CPR or during CPR training is extremely low. Simple infection-control measures, including use of barrier masks, can help you avoid exposure.

Barrier masks come with a replaceable one-way valve or filters to block contaminated fluids. There are many styles, brands, and names of barrier masks used for CPR, depending on your local custom. For purposes of this chapter, we use the term *CPR mask* to refer to any brand or style.

A bag-valve mask device allows rescuers to provide rescue breaths without having to blow into a victim's mouth, offering the best barrier protection.

### Giving Rescue Breaths

Using a barrier device, tilt the head and lift the chin to establish an airway. Give enough air to make the chest visibly rise, but no more than that. Allow the air to exhale completely between breaths. To reduce the risk of inflating the stomach, make each breath last 1 second. If the victim's chest does not rise with the rescue breath, reposition the head, make a better seal, and try again.

Do not take deep breaths when performing rescue breathing. Taking deep breaths is unnecessary and may cause hyperventilation. If you suddenly feel breathless, have tiny prickling sensations, become dizzy, or have muscle spasms in your hands or feet, you are breathing too fast and deep. Slow down or have another rescuer take over for you.

### Rescue Breathing With a CPR Mask

Before giving rescue breaths using a mask, quickly inspect the mask to make sure the one-way valve is in place.

- *If you are alone*, position yourself at the victim's side. Place the mask flat on the victim's face by laying the top of the mask over the bridge of the nose. Use your thumb and forefinger to control the top of the mask. Use the thumb of your hand lifting the chin to control the bottom of the mask. Tilt the head, and lift the chin. Bring the victim's face up into the mask to create an airtight seal and open the airway.

- *If you are with other rescuers*, position yourself above the victim's head. A jaw thrust with head tilt from behind the head can be a convenient and effective method of opening the airway during rescue breathing or CPR with multiple rescuers.

➕ **Breathe with enough air to make the chest visibly rise, but no more than that.**

Take a normal breath, place your mouth around the one-way valve on the mask, and blow through the valve opening. Each breath should be 1 second in length. Remove your mouth from the mask after each rescue breath, and allow the air to exhale. With an infant or small child, it is important to select a mask of the proper size.

### Rescue Breathing With a Bag-Valve Mask

A bag-valve mask has four main components: the bag, an oxygen reservoir, a one-way valve, and a mask. When used alone, a bag-valve mask allows delivery of 21 percent oxygen (room air) to the victim. This oxygen concentration is more than that delivered to a victim when you exhale during rescue breathing (17 percent). A bag-valve mask can be used by a single rescuer but is ideally used by two. It takes significant practice to effectively use this device.

When using a bag-valve mask, place the mask over the victim's mouth and nose. Place your hands on each side of the victim's head. Use your thumbs and the heels of your hands to hold the mask in place. Hook your fingers under the angles of the jaw, just below the ear. Lift and tilt the head backward. Use counterpressure against the cheeks to move the jaw upward. While keeping the airway open, hold the mask tightly against the victim's face. Another rescuer, positioned at the victim's side, will squeeze the bag with both hands to ventilate. Make each breath last 1 second. Give enough air to make the chest visibly rise, but no more than that.

Bag-valve mask rescue breaths for children or infants are done in the same manner as for an adult. It is recommended that the size of the device be appropriate for the age and size of the victim.

# Opening the Airway and Rescue Breathing With a CPR Mask

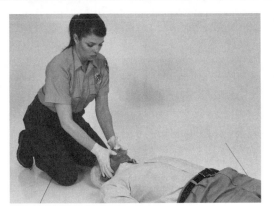

### ◀ Position Mask

Inspect mask to make sure one-way valve is in place. Place mask flat on victim's face by laying top of mask over bridge of nose.

- *From the side:* Use thumb and forefinger to control top of the mask. Use thumb of other hand to control the bottom of the mask.
- *From behind the head:* Place your palms and thumbs on both sides of the mask. Hook your fingers under the angles of the jaw, just behind the ears. Your mask style may differ. Practice regularly with your equipment before an emergency.

### Open Airway ▶

- *From the side:* Tilt the head; lift the chin. Bring the face up into the mask to create an airtight seal and open the airway.
- *From behind the head:* Lift and tilt the head. Use counterpressure against the cheeks to displace the jaw and move it forward.

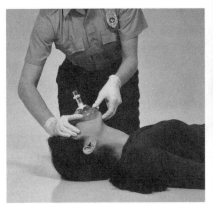

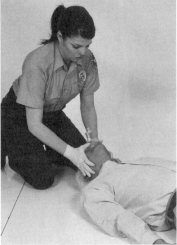

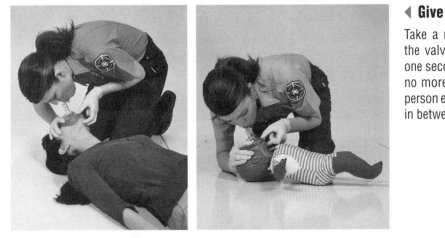

### ◀ Give Breaths

Take a normal breath, and blow through the valve opening. Make each breath last one second. Make the chest visibly rise, but no more. Remove your mouth, and let the person exhale completely. Take a fresh breath in between breaths.

When using a bag-valve mask alone, position yourself above the victim's head. Place the mask over the victim's mouth and nose. Place the thumb and finger of one hand around the valve in a C position to press the mask against the face. Use your remaining three fingers in an E position to lift up the jaw. Tilt the head back to open the airway. Squeeze the bag with your free hand to ventilate. Make each breath last 1 second. Make the chest visibly rise with each breath, but no more than that.

### Rescue Breathing With a Face Shield

Face shields minimize direct contact with a victim but are not the first choice for those who respond at the professional rescuer level. However, in some instances this may be the only barrier available. Begin by placing the breathing port of the shield over or

---

### SKILL GUIDE

# Opening the Airway and Rescue Breathing With a Bag-Valve Mask

### ◀ Prepare Bag-Valve Mask

When possible, two providers should use the bag-valve mask. Provide rescue breaths with a CPR mask until the bag-valve mask is ready. Inspect the bag-valve mask to make sure it is ready for use. If using supplemental oxygen, connect to the bag-valve mask, and allow the reservoir bag to fill completely. Flow rate should be at least 10 liters per minute. Position yourself above the victim's head.

### Position Mask ▶

While a second provider holds the bag with both hands, place the mask flat on the victim's face. Place your palms and thumbs on both sides of the mask. Hook your fingers under the angles of the jaw, just below the ears. If you suspect the possibility of spinal injury in the neck, use jaw-thrust without head-tilt to open the airway. If this does not establish an airway, use head-tilt to do so.

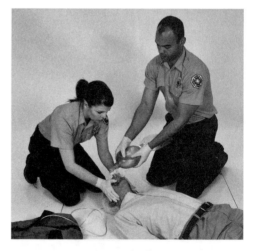

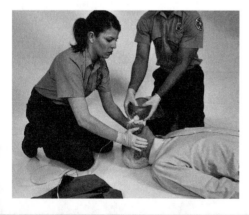

### ◀ Open Airway

Lift and tilt the head. Use counterpressure against the cheeks to displace the jaw and move it forward. If you suspect the possibility of spinal injury in the neck, use jaw-thrust without head-tilt to open the airway. If this does not establish an airway, use head-tilt to do so.

into the victim's mouth. Spread the rest of the shield flat over the victim's face. Tilt the victim's head, and lift the chin to establish an open airway. Pinch the victim's nostrils closed either under or over the shield. Take a normal breath. Open your mouth wide, and press your mouth on the shield over the victim's mouth to create an airtight seal. Blow through the shield to deliver a breath. Each breath should be 1 second in length and have enough air to make the chest visibly rise, but no more than that. Remove your mouth, and let the air exhale from the victim's lungs after each breath. Take a fresh breath in between delivering breaths. See figure 10.2 on page 150.

**The same technique can be used to provide mouth-to-mouth rescue breaths if you elect not to use a barrier device.** Switch to a CPR mask or bag-valve mask device as soon as possible.

## SKILL GUIDE

## Opening the Airway and Rescue Breathing With a Bag-Valve Mask *(continued)*

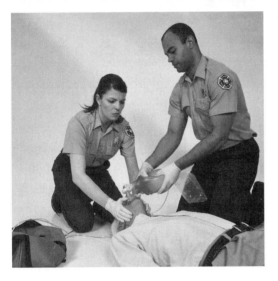

### ◀ Deliver Breaths

Have a second provider squeeze the bag to deliver breaths. Each breath should be 1 second in length. Create a visible rise of the chest, but no more.

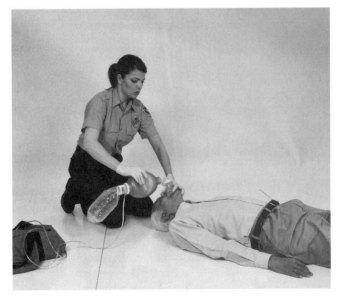

### Using a Bag-Valve Mask by Yourself ▶

Position yourself above the victim. Place the mask flat on the victim's face. Place the thumb and index finger of one hand around the valve in a C shape to press mask against face. Use remaining fingers in an E position to hook the bony part of the chin. Lift and tilt the head. Lift and displace the jaw forward using fingers on chin. Squeeze bag to deliver breaths. Each breath should be 1 second in length. Create a visible rise of the chest, but no more.

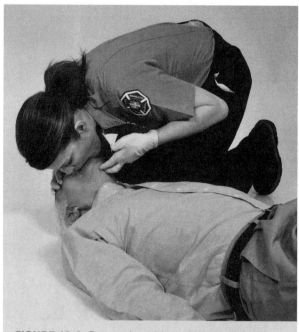

**FIGURE 10.2** Rescue breathing with a face shield.

### *Mouth-to-Nose Rescue Breathing*

When you have difficulty with mouth-to-mouth rescue breathing, you may want to use mouth-to-nose rescue breathing. To give mouth-to-nose rescue breathing, tilt the victim's head back with one hand, and use the other hand to close the victim's mouth. Seal your lips around the victim's nose, and give slow breaths that make the chest rise. If the victim is an infant, place your mouth over the infant's mouth and nose. Because an infant has a small face, covering both is the best way to make a seal.

### CPR Cycles

Effective CPR alternates 30 compressions with two breaths. This cycle should continue, with minimal interruption, until an AED is ready, another provider or the next level of care takes over, the person clearly shows signs of life, or you are too tired.

When two rescuers are present, and the victim is a child or infant, switch the CPR ratio to 15 compressions and two rescue breaths.

## CPR and AED for Multiple Rescuers

It is common for multiple rescuers to respond during a basic life support emergency. Victim management can be adjusted as more rescuers become available.

Begin with single rescuer care. As more people become available, multiple treatment interventions can be done at the same time. It is important to work as a team. When more than one rescuer is present the additional person or persons can help with adjunct equipment such as a bag-valve-mask or an AED. When an AED becomes available, continue CPR if possible, until the AED is ready to analyze the victim's heart.

When more than one person is available to perform CPR, one gives chest compressions while the other keeps the airway open and performs rescue breathing. The rescuer compressing the chest should pause briefly to allow the two breaths to be given by the other rescuer. For adults, the ratio remains at 30 compressions and two breaths. In children and infants switch the CPR ratio to 15 compressions and two breaths.

Studies have shown that rescuers quickly become tired while performing chest compressions. To prevent fatigue and maintain the quality of chest compressions, rescuers should change positions at least every couple of minutes. This should be done quickly, in less than 5 seconds, so there is as little interruption in compression as possible. Rescuers should continually monitor and encourage each other to perform effective chest compressions (hard and fast, with complete recoil and minimal interruption).

### Defibrillation

An automated external defibrillator (AED) is a small, portable computerized device that diagnoses and treats ventricular fibrillation (VF). It is attached with wires and pads to the chest of the victim. It checks the person's heart rhythm, decides if the rhythm is VF, and gives the heart an electric shock. Rapid defibrillation provides the best chance to return the heart to a normal rhythm. More information about how to use an AED is provided later in this chapter.

Rapid defibrillation using an AED along with effective CPR is the best early treatment option for sudden cardiac arrest. The following are the procedures for using the AED on adults and children. Also presented are troubleshooting and maintenance of the AED and how this device fits into an overall program of high-quality care.

### Procedures for AED Use

Automated external defibrillators (AEDs) are designed to be simple to operate. Voice and screen instructions guide an operator using the device. There are many different brands of AEDs, but the same basic steps for operation apply to all. If someone is unresponsive and not breathing, perform CPR until an AED is ready to be attached. Then perform these steps:

1. **Turn on the AED.** This starts voice instructions and readies the device for use. Opening the lid will turn on the power with some AEDs. With others, a power button is pressed.

2. **Adhere the defibrillation pads to the victim's bare chest.** Pads are placed in specific locations to direct the electrical shock through the heart. Most pads are preconnected to the device, but some require you to plug in a connector. Make sure to choose the correct pads (adult or child). **Do not use the child pads or system for an adult.** Remove the self-adhesive backing, and attach the electrodes to the victim's bare chest. Make sure the electrodes attach firmly to the skin. Do not apply the pads over a female's breast because it might decrease the AED's effectiveness.

   *Look at the picture on each pad as a guide for proper placement.*

3. **Allow the AED to analyze the heart rhythm.** An AED automatically starts analyzing once the pads are in place. A voice instruction will state that the analysis is in progress. Movement can interrupt the analysis. Be sure that no one touches the victim while the AED is analyzing the heart rhythm and that the victim is still. If a victim is being moved on a stretcher in an ambulance with an AED attached, stop movement and then analyze. If defibrillation is required, an AED will charge to deliver a shock. A voice instruction will indicate when the AED is ready.

4. **Safely deliver a shock if directed to by the AED.** To prevent accidental shock, keep others clear. Give a verbal warning, and look to make sure no one, including you, is in contact with the victim before delivering the shock. A button is pressed on most AEDs to deliver a shock.

   Immediately after a shock is delivered, resume CPR, starting with chest compressions. Voice instructions and additional analysis by the AED will guide you through further care.

### Considerations for AED Use

Whenever possible, position the AED near the head and next to the rescuer who will be operating it. If feasible, continue CPR while the pads are being applied and until the AED begins to analyze the heart. Listen carefully and follow the machine's instructions.

Before attaching the AED, quickly check for the following situations:

- **Chest hair.** If the victim's chest is covered with hair, it may prevent the electrode pads from making effective contact with the skin. If this is a problem, quickly shave the chest in the area of the pads, and attach another set of electrodes.

- **Water.** Move the victim out of freestanding water before attaching the AED. Water or sweat on the victim's chest may also conduct energy from one electrode pad to the other, reducing the potential for a successful shock. If the victim's chest is wet, sweaty, or dirty, quickly clean and dry it before attaching the AED.

- **Medication patches.** Remove medication patches using a gloved hand, and wipe the skin area clean before attaching the AED electrode pads. Medication patches left in place may block the shock and can cause small burns to the skin.

- **Implanted medical devices.** Pacemakers and other medical devices implanted in the chest can interfere with the use of an AED. A noticeable lump and surgical scar will be visible. Place the electrode pads at least one inch (2.5 cm) away from an implanted device.

- **Oxygen.** Do not use oxygen when delivering shocks with an AED. There have been reports of victims and their bedding being set on fire during defibrillation. Remove the mask and place it at least three feet (1m) from the victim, or shut off the oxygen flow when delivering shocks.

Metal surfaces pose no shock hazard to either you or the victim, however, make sure the pads do not directly touch any metal surface. Cell phones do not interfere with the AED. Always follow the manufacturer's recommended safety precautions.

### AED Use on Children and Infants

Cardiac arrests involving children are primarily caused by the initial loss of the airway or breathing. Well-performed CPR with effective rescue breaths may be the only treatment required for successful resuscitation. However, conditions can occur for which defibrillation of a child or infant is warranted.

After CPR is started and EMS has been notified, attach the AED. If an AED designed for a child or infant is not available, use a standard machine. Most AEDs have specially designed pads, cables, or other mechanisms available that reduce the defibrillation energy to a level more appropriate for a smaller body size. Some AED pads may require that the rescuer place one pad on the child's chest and one on the back. Always look at the pictures on the pads and place them as shown. You may need to use different cables or insert a key or turn a switch to deliver a lower amount of electricity for a child. An AED is used on an infant in the same manner it is used on a child.

### Troubleshooting an AED

If an AED detects a problem with the device during use, a voice or visual prompt, screen message, or lit icon will be displayed to guide you through corrective actions. Stay calm, and do what the AED tells you to do. Here are some examples:

- If a message regarding the pads occurs, the pads are not completely adhered to the skin or there is a poor connection to the AED. Press the pads firmly, especially in the center, to make sure they are adhering well. Make sure the pads' cable connector is firmly connected to the AED. If the chest is wet, remove the pads and wipe the chest dry. Apply a new set of pads. If pads do not stick because of chest hair, pull the pads off and quickly shave the hair. Apply a new set of pads.

- If a message indicating motion occurs, make sure the cables are not being moved around. Stop all sources of movement, such as chest compressions or rescue breaths.

- If a message regarding the battery is displayed, the battery power is probably low. There may be only enough energy for a limited number of shocks. If the AED fails to operate, the depleted battery should be removed and replaced.

### AED Maintenance and Quality Assurance

AEDs perform regular self-tests to make sure they are ready for use. If an AED fails a self-test, it will alert you with an audible or visual prompt. Contact authorized service personnel immediately. Inspect AEDs monthly. If the AED has a visual status indicator, check it to make sure it shows the device is operational. Examine the expiration dates on pad packages and spare batteries, and inspect the AED for obvious damage. Make sure the battery and a replacement battery (or batteries) are fully operational and ready to use.

Store AEDs with the necessary equipment to respond to a cardiac arrest. The equipment should include the following, at a minimum:

- Personal protective equipment (CPR shield or mask and disposable gloves)
- Utility scissors (to cut clothing and expose chest)
- A disposable razor (to shave a hairy chest)
- Disposable towels (to dry the chest)
- A plastic biohazard bag (to dispose of used supplies)

## Rescue Breathing for a Person With a Pulse

When a person is unresponsive, not breathing or only gasping, but has a pulse you can clearly feel, you will need to provide rescue breaths. Without immediate intervention the person's respiratory arrest (lack of breathing) can quickly become worse and require additional care.

- **For adults,** give one breath every 5 to 6 seconds, or about 10 to 12 breaths per minute. Deliver each breath over 1 second and make the chest visibly rise, but no more. Feel for a pulse about every 2 minutes for no more than 10 seconds. If a pulse is absent or you are unsure, begin CPR, starting with compressions.

- **For children and infants,** give one breath every 3 to 5 seconds, or about 12 to 20 breaths per minute. Each breath should make the chest visibly rise. Reassess the pulse every couple of minutes for no more than 10 seconds. If a pulse is absent or you are unsure, begin CPR, starting with compressions.

If a child or infant has a pale or blue tissue color that does not improve with rescue breathing, or has a heart rate under 60 beats per minute, perform CPR.

# Adult CPR and AED for Single or Multiple Rescuers

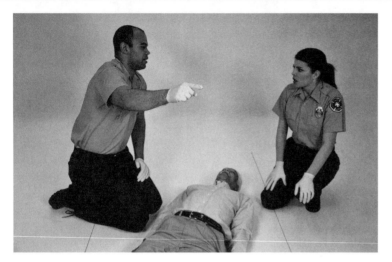

### ◀ Assess

If safe to do so, tap or squeeze shoulder. Ask loudly, "Are you OK?" *No response!* Look quickly at face and chest for normal breathing. Occasional gasps are *not* considered normal. *Normal breathing absent!* Have someone alert EMS and get an AED. If alone, do this yourself. Check for an obvious carotid pulse in neck. *No pulse!*

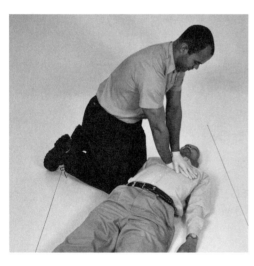

### ◀ Give 30 Compressions

Place one hand on center of chest. Place heel of second hand on top of the first. Position your body so your shoulders are directly over your hands. Using upper-body weight, push hard, at least two inches (5 cm) in depth. Push fast, at a rate of at least 100 compressions per minute. Allow the chest to fully rebound.

**Give two rescue breaths.** Tilt the head and lift the chin to establish an airway. Make the chest visibly rise over one second with each breath, but no more. Take a fresh breath between breaths. Take no longer than 10 seconds to give breaths.

**Repeat cycles of 30 compressions and two breaths.** Don't stop! Continue until an AED is ready, another rescuer or the next level of care takes over, the person clearly shows signs of life, or you are too tired.

### With Multiple Rescuers

One rescuer performs compressions, the other rescue breaths. Quickly switch or change the person doing compressions every 2 minutes.

# Adult CPR and AED for Single or Multiple Rescuers *(continued)*

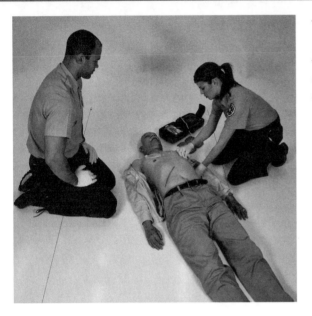

### ◀ When Available, Attach AED

Position the AED close to the victim's head. Turn on power to start voice instructions. Bare the chest. If the chest is wet or sweaty, wipe dry. Remove pads from packaging. Look at pictures on pads for accurate placement. Peel first pad from backing and place below right collarbone, above nipple, and beside breastbone. Place second pad on left side, over ribs, about three inches (8 cm) below armpit.

### If Indicated, Deliver Shock ▶

Allow the AED to analyze the heart. Stop all movement, including CPR. If shock is advised, **clear** everyone from the victim, and press the shock button to deliver shock.

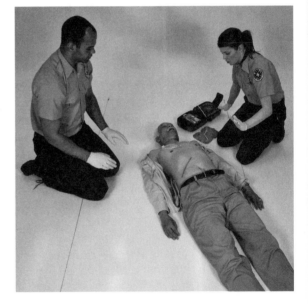

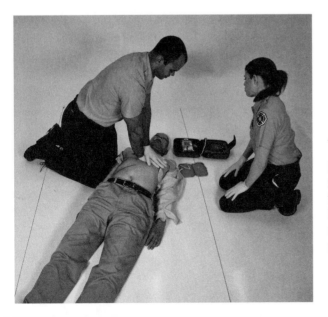

### ◀ Resume CPR

Immediately after delivering shock, **or if a shock is *not* advised**, resume CPR, starting with chest compressions. Follow any additional voice instructions from the AED. Continue with minimal interruption until another provider or the next level of care takes over. If the victim responds, stop CPR and place the victim in recovery position. Leave the AED on and attached.

# Child CPR and AED for Single or Multiple Rescuers

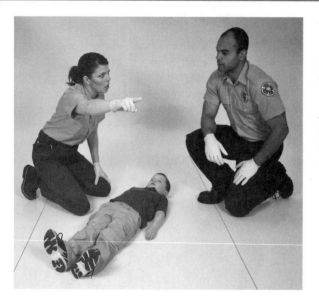

### ◀ Assess

If safe to do so, tap or squeeze shoulder. Ask loudly, "Are you OK?" ***No response!*** Look quickly at face and chest for normal breathing. Occasional gasps are *not* considered normal breathing. ***Normal breathing absent!*** Have someone alert EMS and get an AED. If alone, stay with the child and provide 2 minutes of care before doing this yourself. Check for obvious carotid pulse in the neck. ***No pulse (or less than 60 beats per minute, with pale or blue tissue color)!***

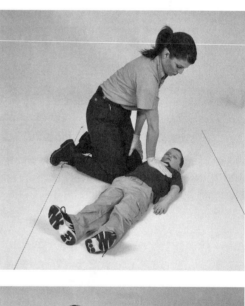

### Give 30 Compressions ▶

Place the heel of one hand on the lower half of the breastbone. Using upper-body weight, push hard, at least one-third the diameter of the chest, or about 2 inches (5 cm). Push fast, at least 100 times per minute. Allow the chest to fully rebound. Compressions are tiring. If desired, use two hands, as with adults.

**Give two rescue breaths.** Tilt the head and lift the chin to establish an airway. Make the chest visibly rise one second with each breath, but no more. Take a fresh breath between breaths. Take no longer than 10 seconds to give breaths.

**Repeat cycles of 30 compressions and two breaths.** Don't stop! Continue until an AED is ready, another provider or the next level of care takes over, the person clearly shows signs of life, or you are too tired.

### With Multiple Rescuers

One rescuer performs compressions, the other rescue breaths, at a rate of **15:2 (15 compressions followed by two breaths)**. Quickly switch or change the person doing compressions every 2 minutes.

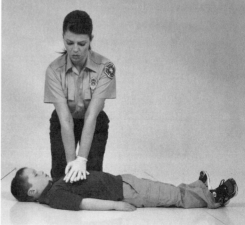

# Child CPR and AED for Single or Multiple Rescuers *(continued)*

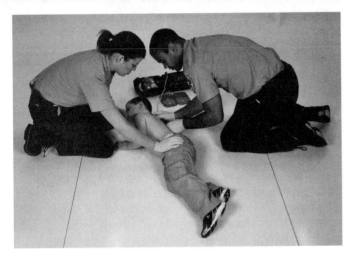

### ◀ When Available, Attach AED

Position the AED close to the victim's head. Turn on power to start voice instructions. Bare the chest. If the chest is wet or sweaty, wipe dry. Remove pads from packaging. Look at pictures on pads for accurate placement. Peel first pad from backing and place in center of chest, just below collarbones. Roll the child and place second pad on center of back between shoulder blades.

### If Indicated, Deliver Shock ▶

Allow the AED to analyze the heart. Stop all movement, including CPR. If shock is advised, **clear** everyone from the child, and press the shock button to deliver shock.

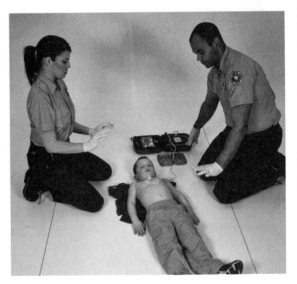

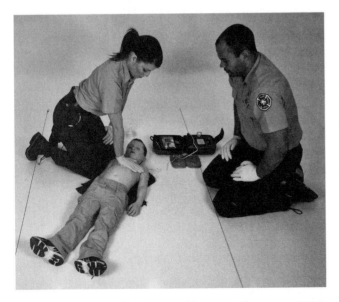

### ◀ Resume CPR

Immediately after delivering shock, **or if a shock is *not* advised**, resume CPR, starting with chest compressions. Follow any additional voice instructions from the AED. Continue until another provider or the next level of care takes over. If the child responds, stop CPR and place the child in recovery position. Leave the AED on and attached.

# Infant CPR and AED for Single or Multiple Rescuers

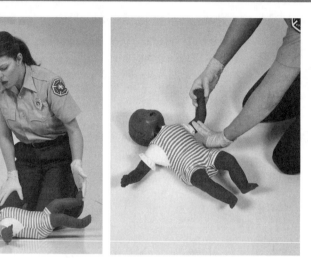

### ◀ Assess

If safe to do so, tap the bottom of the infant's foot and shout loudly. ***No response!*** Look quickly at face and chest for normal breathing. Occasional gasps are *not* considered normal breathing. ***Normal breathing absent!*** Have someone alert EMS and get an AED. If alone, stay with the infant and provide 2 minutes of care before doing this yourself. Check for obvious brachial pulse in the infant's upper arm. ***No pulse (or less than 60 beats per minute, with signs of pale or blue tissue color)!***

### Give 30 Compressions ▶

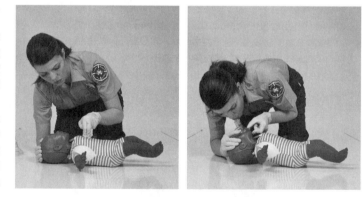

Place two fingertips on the breastbone just below the nipple line. Push hard, straight down at least one-third the diameter of the chest, or about 2 inches (5 cm). Push fast at a rate of at least 100 times per minute. Allow chest to fully rebound.

**Give two breaths.** Tilt the head and lift the chin slightly. Give two rescue breaths (puffs) that make the chest visibly rise over one second with each breath, but no more than that. Take a fresh breath between breaths. Take no longer than 10 seconds to give breaths.

**Repeat cycles of 30 compressions and two breaths.** Don't stop! Continue until an AED is ready, another provider or the next level of care takes over, the person clearly shows signs of life, or you are too tired.

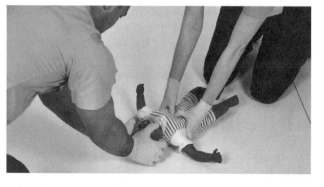

### ◀ With Multiple Rescuers

One rescuer performs compressions, by compressing the breastbone using two thumbs and hands encircling the chest; the other performs rescue breaths, at a rate of **15:2 (15 compressions followed by two breaths)**.

### Use an AED if Available

Use infant pads if available. Otherwise follow the AED pad placement for a child.

# Special Conditions for CPR

The following circumstances may or may not require changes in standard CPR procedures. However, each situation requires some special consideration.

## Pregnancy

Chest compressions may not be effective when a woman who is six months pregnant or more is lying flat on her back. This is because the baby puts pressure on the major vein that returns blood to the heart. If possible, prop up the victim slightly on her left side using a rolled blanket (or something similar) when performing chest compressions. This reduces the pressure and provides the most blood flow to the mother and baby. Perform chest compressions higher on the breastbone, slightly above the center.

## Hypothermia

Get indoors or out of the wind. Prevent additional heat loss by removing wet clothes and insulating the victim from further exposure. If the victim's body is frozen solid, his nose and mouth are blocked with ice, and chest compression is impossible, do not start CPR. If the body is not frozen solid, begin CPR and, if available, use an AED. If a victim does not respond to one shock with an AED, focus on continuing CPR and rewarming the victim to a range of 86 to 89.6 degrees Fahrenheit (30 to 32 °C) before repeating a defibrillation attempt.

## Electric Shock

Consider any fallen or broken wire extremely dangerous. Do not touch (or allow your clothing to touch) a wire, victim, or vehicle that is possibly energized, and do not approach within eight feet (2.4 m). Notify the local utility company, and have trained personnel sent to the scene. Metal or cable guardrails, steel wire fences, and telephone lines may be energized by a fallen wire and may carry the current one mile (1.6 km) or more from the point of contact. Never attempt to handle wires yourself unless you are properly trained and equipped. Start CPR, if indicated, as soon as it is safe to do so.

## Lightning Strike

When multiple victims are struck by lightning at the same time, give the highest priority to those without signs of life. Start BLS or CPR, if indicated, as soon as it is safe to do so. Remove smoldering clothing, shoes, and belts to prevent burns.

## Advanced Airways

When professional rescuers are appropriately trained and authorized, they may use advanced airway and ventilation devices such as the laryngeal mask airway, esophageal tracheal combitube, and endotracheal tube. When an advanced airway is in place, remove the mask from the bag-valve mask device, and attach the bag directly to the airway to ventilate. As with other breaths, provide only enough air to make the chest rise, but no more. If an advanced airway is in place, it is not necessary to stop compressions to give breaths.

## Neck Breather (Stoma)

Some people breathe through a surgically created opening in the neck called a stoma. Use a CPR mask over the stoma to give rescue breaths.

## Cardiac Arrest With Injury

A person in cardiac arrest due to injury is unlikely to survive. If it is clear injury has caused the arrest, do not start CPR.

## Submersion

See chapter 11 for information about CPR for victims of drowning (submersion) incidents.

# Choking (Foreign-Body Airway Obstruction)

Choking can occur when a solid object, such as a piece of food, enters a narrowed part of the airway and becomes stuck. When a person inhales, the object can be drawn tighter into the airway and block air from entering the lungs.

Coughing and gagging are the body's ways of trying to remove a foreign object that has created a mild blockage in the throat. If coughing or gagging does not clear the object, then a severe blockage occurs.

Children are particularly at risk for choking because of the small size of their air passages, inexperience with chewing, and a natural tendency to put objects in their mouths. Since infants do not speak, it may be more difficult to recognize choking. Signs include a sudden onset of weak, ineffective coughs and the lack of sound, even when an infant is clearly attempting to breathe.

> **Give quick inward and upward thrusts until the object is expelled or the victim becomes unresponsive.**

### Treatment for Mild Blockage

With a mild blockage, a person can speak, cough, or gag. You may hear a high-pitched squeaking or whistling noise (wheezing) between strong coughs. Encourage a person with a mild blockage to cough forcefully. Stay close by and be ready to take action if symptoms worsen.

### Treatment for Severe Blockage

The skill guides on pages 161-162 and 163 provide treatment guidelines for dealing with severe-blockage choking in adults, children, and infants.

### Self-Treatment

You can give yourself abdominal thrusts until the object is expelled. If that does not work, forcefully press your abdomen into a firm surface, such as the back of a chair or the side of a table.

# Adult or Child Choking—Severe Blockage

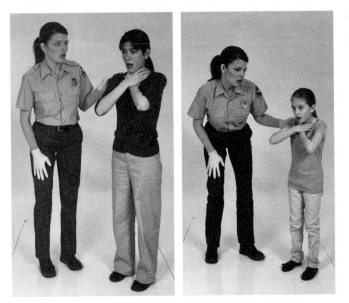

### ◀ Assess the Victim

Ask, "Are you choking?" If the person nods yes or is unable to speak or cough, act quickly! If a bystander is nearby, have her activate EMS.

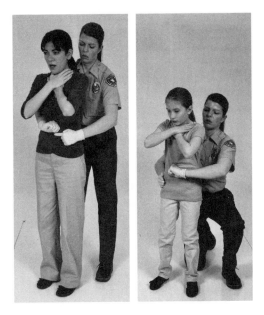

### Position Yourself ▶

Stand or kneel (for a child) behind the person. Reach around and locate the navel with your finger. Make a fist with the other hand, and place it thumb-side down against the abdomen, just above your finger and below the victim's ribs. Grasp your fist with your other hand.

### ◀ Give Thrusts

Quickly thrust inward and upward into the abdomen. Repeat. Each thrust needs to be given with the intent of expelling the object. Continue until the person can breathe normally.

*(continued)*

## Adult or Child Choking—Severe Blockage *(continued)*

### If Person Becomes Unresponsive ▶

Carefully lower to the ground, positioning the person faceup on a firm, flat surface. If not already done, activate EMS. If you are alone with a child, provide at least 2 minutes of CPR before activating EMS.

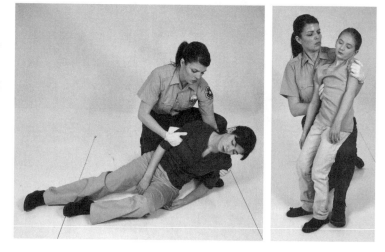

◀ **Perform CPR**

Begin CPR, starting with compressions. Look in the mouth for an object after each set of compressions, before giving rescue breaths. Remove any object if seen. Continue until the person shows obvious signs of life or another provider or the next level of care takes over.

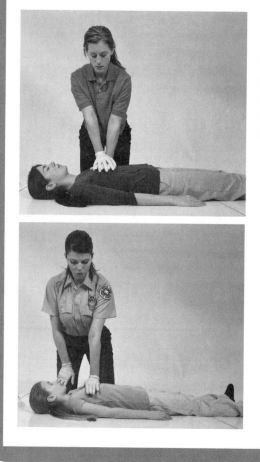

# Infant Choking—Severe Blockage

### ◀ Assess

Look at the infant's face. If the infant is silent; unable to cry; or has blue lips, nails, or skin, act quickly! If a bystander is nearby, have him activate EMS.

### Give Five Back Blows ▶

Straddle the infant facedown over your forearm, with head lower than chest. Support the infant's head by holding the jaw. Using the heel of the other hand, give five back blows between the shoulder blades.

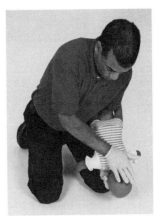

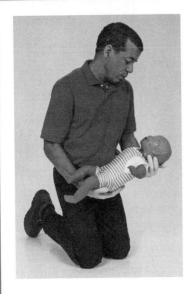

### ◀ Chest Thrusts

Sandwich the infant between your forearms and turn onto back, with legs and arms straddling your other arm. Place two fingers on the breastbone just below the nipple line, and give five chest thrusts. Repeat back blows and chest thrusts until the infant can breathe normally. Back blows and chest thrusts need to be given with the intent of expelling the object.

### If the Infant Becomes Unresponsive

- Place the infant on a firm, flat surface.
- If you are alone, provide at least 2 minutes of CPR before activating EMS.

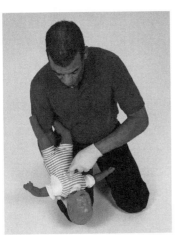

### Perform CPR ▶

Begin CPR, starting with compressions. Look in the mouth for an object after each set of compressions, before giving rescue breaths. Remove any object seen. Continue CPR until the infant shows obvious signs of life or another provider or the next level of care takes over.

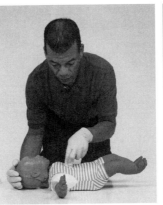
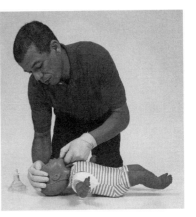

##  Knowledge Into Practice

A person may suffer sudden cardiac arrest (SCA) and collapse without warning and at any time. Choking also requires that you act quickly. You need to be prepared to give care until EMS arrives.

## @ Visit the Web Resource

You can reinforce your learning by visiting the web resource, where you can do the following in the interactive online learning activities for chapter 10:

- ▶ Activity 10.1: View a video clip of how to open the airway and perform rescue breathing.
- ▶ Activity 10.2: Match the age group to the correct location where pulse should be checked.
- ▶ Activity 10.3: View a video clip of how effective compressions maintain circulation.
- ▶ Activity 10.4: View video clips of an adult, child, and infant CPR demonstration.
- ▶ Activity 10.5: Listen to AED voice prompts and decide the course of action.
- ▶ Activity 10.6: View video clips of emergency action steps for choking.
- ▶ Activity 10.7: Evaluate basic life support scenarios, identify symptoms, and determine treatment.
- ▶ Activity 10.8: Chapter quiz. Test your knowledge, receive feedback, and print the quiz page.

## On the Job

These are the tasks related to basic life support that you will be expected to competently perform while working as a lifeguard:

- ▶ Perform basic scene assessment and casualty assessment.
- ▶ Know and apply basic life support techniques for adults, children, and infants, including rescue breathing, one-person CPR, and two-person CPR.
- ▶ Use an AED.
- ▶ Perform emergency treatment for choking.

## CHAPTER 11

# Performing Rescues and Lifeguard CPR for Unresponsive Drowning Victims

## CHAPTER OBJECTIVES

This chapter

▶ describes how to modify rescue skills for an unresponsive drowning victim,

▶ explains how to perform rescue breathing in the water,

▶ describes how to extricate an unresponsive victim from the water,

▶ examines special considerations when caring for drowning victims,

▶ explains how to integrate and use adjunct equipment including suction devices,

▶ discusses the use of emergency oxygen and transfer of care to EMS, and

▶ explains what to do and expect after a drowning incident.

Your goal in managing an unresponsive, nonbreathing drowning victim is simple: Obtain an open airway as quickly as possible so the drowning victim can start breathing spontaneously or so you can begin rescue breathing. This chapter prepares you to begin airway management and rescue breathing while you are still in the water so the drowning victim has the best chance of becoming a drowning survivor. The chapter also explains how to adapt your skills to provide the best care for a drowning victim and establish a framework for response.

## Rescue of an Unresponsive Drowning Victim

When you rescue a person who is facedown on the surface or submerged, you will not know the level of responsiveness until the person's face is lifted out of the water. A responsive person will cough, sputter, move, and begin to regain normal breathing. An unresponsive person will be limp and not respond. Because the person has been without oxygen, the first objective is to get oxygen into the body as quickly as possible. Rescue breaths may be enough to revive the person and cause breathing to resume on its own.

It is important to have a rescue tube and barrier mask available during the rescue. The mask should be capable of making a reasonable seal in the water, and the one-way valve should be made of plastic or a nonabsorbent material (not paper or fiber). The mask should be easily accessible (e.g., kept in a pack either around your waist or attached to your rescue tube).

### Adapting the Rear Rescue

Follow the STAAR aquatic rescue model: scan, target, assess, alert, rescue. When you reach the drowning victim, place him on the rescue tube using a rear rescue. If the person is submerged, use a leg-wrap rescue into a rear rescue.

When you use a rescue tube to perform a rear rescue on an unresponsive drowning victim, you are in an excellent position to provide immediate care. When you place an unresponsive person on the rescue tube, her head will fall back into an open-airway position. From behind the person's head, you can position the mask and begin rescue breathing and still be able to swim and progress toward a safe point of exit.

**Unless there is an obvious mechanism for spinal injury, routine stabilization of the head for an unresponsive drowning victim is not required.**

**Have a pocket mask available to you in the water.**

Because the victim is unresponsive and limp, you'll need to consider controlling the victim's head during placement on the rescue tube. The head-cradle technique is one way you can adapt the rear rescue to provide this control.

SKILL GUIDE

# Head Cradle

In a rear-rescue position, use your hands to cradle the head.

As you pull back, lift your elbows to bring the victim's arms over the tube.

Move to a position behind the victim's head. Look for normal breathing.

If the person is not breathing normally, signal to activate your emergency action plan (EAP) for an unresponsive victim.

Providing rescue breathing as soon as possible, while you're still in the water, can be crucial to a successful rescue outcome—especially when you are not sure how long a drowning victim has been submerged and without oxygen. Let's look at how to perform this technique in more detail.

### Rescue Breathing in the Water

> When managing an unresponsive, nonbreathing drowning victim, open the airway as quickly as possible, and give rescue breaths.

If a drowning victim is not breathing, begin care in the water by opening the airway and providing rescue breathing while moving to a safe point of exit. However, if the rescue occurs very close to an exit point and the victim can be quickly extricated, do so, and start care on land.

Recent research indicates that providing mouth-to-mouth breathing in the water may be just as effective as providing mouth-to-mask breathing. The risk of disease transmission while performing rescue breathing in the water is low, and the chance of saving a life in these cases justifies the action. In instances where the person cannot be immediately brought to deck or land, a mask is not available, or its use would delay care, you may consider the mouth-to-mouth method.

## SKILL GUIDE

# Rescue Breathing in the Water

### ◀ Mouth to Mask

Obtain your pocket mask. Shake out any water. From a position behind the drowning victim's head, place the pocket mask over the person's nose and mouth. Make a good seal. Give two breaths, enough to make the chest rise, but no more. If the person does not respond, continue giving a breath every 4 or 5 seconds while moving toward a safe point of exit and where you can continue care on land.

### Mouth to Mouth ▶

Position yourself beside the victim. Open the airway with a head tilt and chin lift. Placing your arm between the victim's arm and the rescue tube may provide additional support. Pinch the victim's nose shut. Make a seal over the victim's mouth with your mouth.

Give one breath every 4 or 5 seconds, enough to make the chest rise, but no more. Mouth-to-nose rescue breaths can be used as an alternative method. In small children it may be easier to cover the entire nose and mouth.

Keep moving the drowning victim toward the takeout point as you continue rescue breathing. Once you have reached the side of the pool, you must remove the person from the water and place her on the deck so you can continue basic life support care until EMS arrives.

# Extrication

Your objective when removing an unresponsive drowning victim (who does not have a suspected spinal injury) from the water is to do so as quickly as possible and in a way that minimizes the risk of injury to you or the drowning victim. The following factors may affect the type of removal method you choose:

- Size of the deck and gutter. Extrication is much easier if the water and deck are at nearly the same level.
- Size of the drowning victim. You may not need a removal device to lift a small person out of the water.
- Available equipment. A backboard (without using the HID or straps) is ideal for quick extrication.
- Number of people available to assist. Use several helpers if they're available, especially when removing a large or heavy person from the water.

Practice various methods of extrication at the facility where you work, using the equipment available. This practice will help you determine which techniques—the backboard pullout, the backboard walkout, or an alternative method—are effective in meeting the objectives for extrication. Remember, the objective is to remove the person as quickly as possible with the least chance of injury to either the victim or the rescuers.

Regardless of the method you use to extricate, try to move the person several feet from the water's edge so you and other responders will have room to perform CPR. Be sure the person is placed out of standing water if an AED will be applied. Be prepared to encounter circumstances that are unique to providing CPR in the aquatic environment.

> **Extricate using the best method for the circumstances.**

> **Place the person at least 6 feet (2 m) from the pool edge if deck space permits.**

## Backboard Pullout

A backboard, found at most aquatic facilities, is very useful in removing a person quickly from the water. When using a backboard to remove an unresponsive drowning victim who is not suspected of having a spinal injury, **you don't need to place the body straps or headpieces**. The chest strap can be used if the victim is at risk of falling off the board during the pullout, but the time to place the strap **should not delay** the continuance of rescue breathing or the start of CPR.

## Backboard Walkout

Use a backboard walkout extrication where the water is shallow and there are wide stairs or a zero-depth area. This extrication requires at least four rescuers and more if the drowning victim is large or heavy. Follow these steps to perform a backboard walkout:

1. Submerge the backboard, and slide it under the drowning victim.
2. Strap her chest to the backboard.

3. Rescuers position themselves evenly around the board, with at least two on each side, and grasp the handholds.

4. Move toward the exit area while floating the board and victim. The rescuers then lift and support the board as they walk out of the zero-depth area or up the stairs.

## SKILL GUIDE

# Backboard Pullout

Place the backboard vertically in the water. For more stability, push the top of the board out so the bottom of the board is against the wall.

The rescuer in the water lifts the drowning victim's arm up to the rescuer on deck. The rescuer on deck holds the victim's arm with one hand and the top of the board with the other.

The rescuer in the water pulls the rescue tube out from under the victim. Then the rescuer on deck allows the backboard to float up under the victim. The rescuer in the water can move to the end of the board to help push or can climb out to help pull. The chest strap is optional.

The rescuer on deck gives the count ("On my count, ready, one, two, three") and then tilts the head of the board back while sliding and pulling the board up and out onto the deck.

## Lift Out

In a pool or water-park setting, a safe point of exit is often just a few feet away. In this instance, depending on the size of the victim and the height of the deck, lifting the victim out may be the fastest choice for removing the person from the water. With the assistance of other rescuers or bystanders, grasp the victim firmly and lift out onto the deck. Avoid pulling the person over the edge, and take care to keep the head from hitting the edge or deck.

# Special Considerations for Drowning Victims

The American Heart Association (AHA) and European Resuscitation Council (ERC) 2010 CPR guidelines recognize drowning as a special situation because the primary cause of death by drowning is suffocation—a lack of oxygen. In addition to being the cause of unresponsiveness, the immersion in water creates other considerations that can affect emergency care procedures:

- Because of the hypoxic nature of drowning, the recommended BLS treatment sequence is airway (A), breathing (B), circulation/compressions (C).

- The person may have swallowed large quantities of water, making a swollen stomach common and vomiting highly likely. Foam and mucus are also likely to come out of the mouth and nose of an unconscious drowning victim. These circumstances may make it difficult for you to obtain or maintain an open airway. You will need to be prepared to clear the airway of vomit, mucus, or other fluids to maintain an open airway.

- The person may make gasping or snoring noises that may sound like attempts to breathe. However, these sounds are caused by changes occurring in the body. Unless the person is responsive and breathing normally, continue providing rescue breathing or CPR.

- Because you and the drowning victim will both be wet and possibly cold, and you may be breathing heavily from executing the rescue, it will be difficult for you to effectively check the victim's pulse. If possible, have another rescuer check the pulse. Do not try to check the pulse in the water.

- Your hands will be wet, and putting on protective gloves may be difficult and time consuming. Do not delay rescue breathing or CPR to put on gloves. Rescuers who come to assist should put on gloves and be prepared to deal with any bodily fluids.

- Studies show that family members want to be present during a resuscitation attempt. Family presence during resuscitation is a reasonable and potentially desirable option. An experienced staff member should be assigned to the family to answer questions, explain procedures, and offer comfort.

- Bystanders may attempt to become involved. Your facility should have a policy in place regarding bystander involvement, and you should practice how to deal with this situation before it occurs. In many instances, giving a bystander a role in helping you provide care can be a valuable resource, but a bystander should not be allowed to take over the scene.

- The scene will be noisy, and acoustics in an aquatic facility may be bad. If you use an AED, have a designated rescuer or bystander listen closely to the AED prompts and call out the commands.

**Do not delay rescue breathing or CPR to put on gloves or prepare equipment. Integrate these items as others bring them to the scene.**

- If you use emergency oxygen, keep the cylinder in the bag or case—not on the slippery deck—so it does not get knocked over.
- Anyone who has received some form of resuscitation for drowning needs to have follow-up evaluation and care in a hospital, regardless of his condition after the event.

## ⭐ Emergency Oxygen Debate

Health care providers and emergency responders such as EMTs routinely administer supplemental oxygen to ill or injured patients. Although it is believed that first aid use of emergency oxygen is helpful, there is no scientific evidence to prove it. In 2010, members of the International First Aid Science Advisory Board (IFASAB) examined the medical science literature to determine the feasibility and safety of recommending emergency oxygen in first aid. As a result, their treatment recommendations do not include the routine use of supplementary oxygen by first aid providers, with the exception of first aid for divers with a decompression injury.

Scientific evidence either for or against the use of emergency oxygen by lifeguards to supplement resuscitation efforts of an unresponsive drowning victim is lacking. However, because of the hypoxic nature of drowning and the interval between the event and arrival of EMS, emergency use of supplemental oxygen can be lifesaving. The International Life Saving Federation and other national training agencies support its use.

Given the potential benefit to the victim, it is reasonable for properly trained lifeguards to give emergency oxygen when it is available. This text provides information about emergency oxygen (see the appendix on pages 235-242), which should be supplemented with hands-on practice with the equipment at your aquatic facility to constitute appropriate training. In most countries, strict regulations on the use of emergency oxygen are defined. As with any protocol, your local health or regulatory authority guidelines will apply in your situation.

The decision to have and use emergency oxygen should be based on its feasibility at a particular location or in a specific situation. If emergency oxygen is available and you are trained to use it, include it as part of your unresponsive drowning victim protocol.

## Integrating Adjunct Equipment

Bag-valve masks (BVMs), manual suction devices, automated external defibrillators, and emergency oxygen can be useful tools when providing basic life support. However, your critical focus should be on providing basic life support care, not dealing with equipment. If such equipment is available, you can integrate it into your resuscitation efforts at any time in the following ways:

- Begin providing ventilations using your CPR mask. If possible, have another rescuer prepare the bag-valve mask (BVM) and hand it to you when it is ready. You should maintain control of the person's airway, and the other rescuer should squeeze the bag to provide ventilations.
- If a manual suction device is brought to the scene, have another rescuer prepare the device (some have a cap that must be removed or a tube that must be attached) and place it in the ready position. Ideally, the suctioning device and the rescuer responsible for suctioning are located on one side of the victim, with the other equipment, such as oxygen or AED, on the other side. This prevents vomit or other fluids from getting on the other equipment.
- If emergency oxygen is brought to the scene, have another rescuer prepare the mask and tubing and turn on the flow. The rescuer should tell you "oxygen

is flowing" after verifying that the unit is on. You can either switch masks or, if your mask has an oxygen intake port, attach the tubing to the mask you are already using.

■ If an AED is brought to the scene, immediately turn on the unit and apply the pads to the victim's bare chest. Minimize the interruption of compressions to do this. Be sure the chest is as dry as possible. Have a towel available to dry the person's chest before applying AED pads.

You already learned how to use a BVM and AED in chapter 10. Information about emergency oxygen is included in the appendix and is designed as a training module for facilities that will have emergency oxygen on site. Let's now look at how to use a common piece of adjunct equipment: the portable handheld suction device.

Vomiting or the presence of a foamlike mucus occurs during CPR in almost all cases involving a drowning victim. One method of clearing the airway of this content is to roll the victim onto her side to let it drain and then sweeping the mouth with a gloved finger. Another method is to use a portable handheld device to suction out the mouth.

You should become familiar with the manufacturer's instructions for using the specific device at your facility and practice integrating it into your unresponsive drowning protocol and EAP. Follow these basic steps, adapted to your equipment:

1. Prepare the device. Depending on the manufacturer, you may need to remove a protective tip or size and attach a catheter tube.

2. Turn the victim's head to the side, or if possible and necessary, roll the body onto the side.

3. Place the suction end of the device in the victim's mouth, along the side of the cheek and toward the throat.

4. Squeeze the handle or trigger to pull the fluids and secretions into the device. Suction for up to 15 seconds if needed to clear the airway. Resume CPR.

5. Dispose of the collection container according to your facility's policy for potentially infected bodily fluids. Insert a new container so the device is ready for the next event.

**The use of a suction device should not delay or interfere with the priority of providing CPR or rescue breathing.**

## Transferring to EMS

When EMS personnel arrive at the site, have a staff person direct them to the rescue scene. Once they arrive, they will likely tell you to continue your resuscitation efforts as they set up equipment and prepare to take over care. During this transition, follow the directives the emergency medical personnel give you, and be prepared to answer questions about the drowning victim's condition, length of time unresponsive, and other symptoms or circumstances. Someone on your rescue team (usually the supervisor) should do the following:

■ Make a note of the EMS arrival time.

■ Find out which hospital the drowning victim will be transported to.

■ Make a note of the responding EMS unit and the names of the EMS personnel.

■ Obtain replacement equipment from the EMS vehicle if they are taking your equipment (e.g., backboard).

# Unresponsive Drowning Victim Protocol

Place the casualty on the rescue tube in an open-airway position. If the person is unresponsive, activate the EAP.

If extrication is not immediate, begin rescue breathing in the water while moving to the safe point of exit. Backup rescuers bring equipment to the point of exit and prepare to help extricate.

Extricate using the best method for the circumstances.

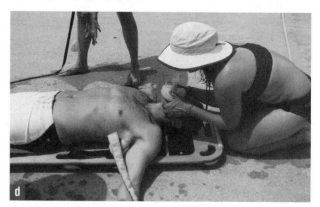

- *If rescue breaths were given in the water;* check for a pulse. *If an obvious pulse is felt* within 10 seconds, open the airway and continue rescue breathing for 2 minutes then reassess. *If a pulse is absent* or not obvious, begin CPR, starting with 30 compressions followed by two breaths.

- *If rescue breaths were not given in the water;* quickly look for normal breathing. If the person is not breathing normally, open the airway (A), and give two breaths (B). Check for a pulse (C). *If an obvious pulse is felt* within 10 seconds, open the airway and continue rescue breathing for 2 minutes, then reassess. *If a pulse is absent or not obvious,* begin CPR, starting with 30 compressions followed by two breaths.

Continue the cycle with minimal interruption. If the chest does not rise during rescue breaths, retilt and try again. If it still does not rise, start or continue CPR.

*(continued)*

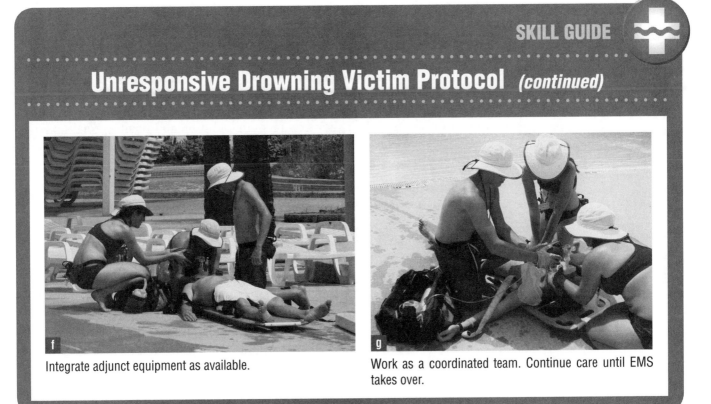

## Unresponsive Drowning Victim Protocol *(continued)*

Integrate adjunct equipment as available.

Work as a coordinated team. Continue care until EMS takes over.

## Coping With Emotional Distress After the Incident

The hours after an unresponsive drowning incident will be challenging, especially emotionally. It is likely you will be questioned by the police (to rule out homicide, suicide, or other criminal behavior). You may not know the condition of the victim or have any way of finding out. Incident reports will need to be completed, the treatment area and equipment cleaned, and other responsibilities taken care of. It is important to take care of yourself and your coworkers both physically and emotionally after the incident. Follow the guidance provided by your employer about how to handle such things as requests from media for interviews or information.

In the days, weeks, or months after the incident it is possible you will be questioned again by insurance company representatives, attorneys, and others. Reports may appear in the media that may disturb you, especially if they contain inaccurate information or do not tell the whole story. You need to be prepared for the symptoms that critical stress can cause, even long after the event.

Everyone involved will suffer some level of emotional distress during or after a drowning incident—you, your coworkers, the victim, the victim's family, and even bystanders. Factors that may make such incidents more distressing include the following:

- If the outcome was fatal
- If the incident involved multiple victims or was caused by a person's actions, such as a suicide, homicide, or other violence
- If the victim was a child
- If the victim was a close friend or relative

Symptoms of a traumatic stress reaction include a pounding heartbeat and fast breathing, which may begin during or within minutes of the traumatic event. Feeling guilty for not having done more, worrying about the safety of loved ones, having nightmares, and repeatedly thinking about the event may follow the incident.

Stress reactions are a normal human response to a traumatic event and are usually temporary. With the help of family and friends, most people gradually feel better as time passes. If you think you need extra help coping after a traumatic event, call your doctor or ask friends if they can recommend a mental health professional. Your workplace may have an employee assistance program available to help you. The following are strategies to help you cope:

- As soon as possible after the incident, relieve the stress by getting physically active. Go for a swim, run, or do another workout activity.
- Get back to your regular patterns of work, school, and social events. The familiarity of day-to-day activities will provide stability in your life.
- Take advantage of the debriefing sessions your facility may schedule to deal with critical-incident stress. These sessions are usually conducted for your benefit within a few days of the incident. Mental health care professionals trained to help emergency care workers deal with stress after a traumatic event will facilitate these group discussions.
- When you start to feel overwhelmed, talk to friends or relatives close to you who will be supportive without being judgmental.

## ⭐ Knowledge Into Practice

A person who is unresponsive due to drowning requires immediate care, and, because it is a special situation, a different CPR response. It is important to understand what needs to be done, and your role as a member of a lifeguard response team at your workplace.

## @ Visit the Web Resource

You can reinforce your learning by visiting the web resource, where you can do the following in the interactive online learning activities for chapter 11:

▶ Activity 11.1: Evaluate unresponsive victim scenarios and identify response steps.
▶ Activity 11.2: View a video clip of a lifeguard describing the legal and emotional repercussions of a drowning incident.
▶ Activity 11.3: View video clips of lifeguards performing the unresponsive drowning victim protocol.
▶ Activity 11.4: Chapter quiz. Test your knowledge, receive feedback, and print the quiz page.

## 〰 On the Job

These are the tasks related to the unresponsive drowning victim protocol that you will be expected to competently perform while working as a lifeguard:

▶ Know and apply appropriate rescue and emergency treatment, including CPR, for an unresponsive drowning casualty.
▶ Extricate a drowning victim from the water.
▶ Learn how to use adjunct equipment available at your facility.

## PART V

# Workplace Environment

## CHAPTER 12

# Facilitating Workplace Safety

## CHAPTER OBJECTIVES

This chapter

- ▶ identifies workplace hazards,
- ▶ describes how to conduct a site safety survey,
- ▶ explains the concept of three points of contact, and
- ▶ explores safety and health considerations important to lifeguards.

Tripping over tools, equipment, or a patron's belongings and falling on wet or slippery surfaces are common causes of injuries. Lifeguards also frequently injure their ankles, knees, or backs after slipping, falling, or jumping from the guard chair. Injuries caused by jumping into shallow water and lifting or twisting during training drills or rescues occur more often than they should. Rounding out the list are injuries that occur when a lifeguard comes in contact with machinery, equipment, or chemicals. Factors that often contribute to injuries include being in a hurry, talking with coworkers or patrons, wet or slippery surfaces or equipment, carrying equipment, failing to use appropriate personal protective equipment, or failing to maintain three points of contact with ladders on guard chairs.

Although your focus as a lifeguard is on the safety of patrons, your personal safety in and around an aquatic environment is also important. Many of your work-related tasks seem to carry little or no risk for injury. However, even the simplest of activities can cause injury when performed improperly or prudent precautions are not taken. It is important to know how to manage some of the workplace safety risks of your profession:

- Sun exposure
- Slips, trips, and falls
- Lifting, twisting, reaching, and bending during rescues
- Using tools or equipment
- Prolonged standing or sitting
- Site-specific concerns such as chemicals, confined spaces, weather, illness

> **Pause and conduct a 30-second site safety survey before beginning a task.**

## Minimizing the Risk of Workplace Injury

Your participation in minimizing the risk of injury is essential for a safe and healthful workplace. Take the time to conduct a 30-second site safety survey before beginning a job task to reflect on the potential job safety hazards or concerns that relate to the specific work site or task.

### 30-Second Site Safety Survey

1. Pause before you approach: Are there any obvious potential safety hazards? Generally, your first impression will be correct.
2. Observe your surroundings: Is there something about the location, depth of water, or surface that could create a hazard or injury?
3. Ask yourself about traffic: Will the amount of pedestrian traffic cause a safety hazard or concern?

4. Protect yourself! Should you be wearing personal protective equipment? Are you wearing the appropriate footwear to safely perform the job? What are safe lifting techniques? Do you have your sunscreen, sunglasses, umbrella? Do you have drinking water to keep hydrated?

5. Consider the unknown: What is unique about the site that may cause a safety concern? Will the equipment, materials, or job task introduce safety concerns?

## Workplace Hazards

In addition to the 30-second site safety survey for specific job tasks, there are other considerations you should reflect on throughout your workday, including equipment and machinery hazards; slip, trip, and fall hazards; lifting hazards; and site-specific hazards.

### Equipment and Machinery Hazards

- Do I have the right equipment for the job?
- Is the equipment in good repair and operating correctly?
- Do I have the proper personal protective equipment?

### Slip, Trip, and Fall Hazards

- Are there potential tripping hazards?
- Is the ground or surface slippery or wet?
- Will I need to step over or around equipment?
- Should I use three points of contact?
- Do I have the proper footwear?

### Lifting Hazards

- What are the proper body mechanics or lifting plan for the job?
- Do I need to get help?

### Site-Specific Hazards

- Are there job-specific hazards to consider?
- Do chemicals, electricity, or severe weather pose a hazard?
- Do I know the guidelines for chemicals and hazardous materials? If you must handle chemicals or hazardous materials, follow the established guidelines and precautions as detailed in the material safety data sheets (MSDSs; see figure 12.1 on page 182) your employer will provide you. You have a legal right to know about any risks associated with chemical products, and an MSDS provides this information. In addition, your employer should provide training for safe handling of these chemicals and hazardous materials.
- In the event of a toxic spill, either of a known or unknown chemical, clear the area immediately. Do not attempt to clean up a spill or enter a confined space without specific training and protective gear. If hazardous chemicals are used or stored at your facility, there should be emergency action plans (EAPs) to handle a chemical spill.

**FIGURE 12.1** Material safety data sheets provide guidelines and precautions for handling chemicals and hazardous materials.

## Practical Guidelines for Workplace Safety

■ Know and practice the emergency action plans at your facility for fires and emergency evacuations, know and practice procedures for performing rescues or first aid duties, and be familiar with alarm system requirements.

■ Walk, don't run, on the pool deck—even during emergencies. You cannot provide care to someone else if you are injured on the way to the scene.

■ Keep floors cleared of obstructions, and keep guardrails and covers to pits or vats in place.

■ When possible, avoid closing or opening your facility when you are alone. If you are alone, consider carrying a cell phone or a personal defense device such as pepper spray, and have your whistle ready in case you need to signal for help.

■ Follow all the rules and policies of your facility at all times, even when you are using the facility for after-hours training or staff events.

■ If you work outdoors, carry insect repellant.

■ Obtain practical (hands-on) instruction for equipment you will be authorized to use such as a pool vacuum, lawn tools, or motor-powered watercraft.

■ Notify your supervisor immediately or call your local emergency number (e.g., 9-1-1) if a patron physically threatens you or if violent behavior breaks out or appears likely at your facility.

## Three Points of Contact

Information courtesy of Park District Risk Management Agency (PDRMA).

Injuries occur because entering and exiting pools, or mounting and dismounting lifeguard chairs, include the potentially hazardous activities of reaching, twisting, pulling, and climbing. The three-points-of-contact method will help you reduce or eliminate many of the injuries associated with these on-the-job activities (see figure 12.2). The one exception to using the three-points-of-contact method is when you are performing a compact jump while training or performing a rescue.

To perform three points of contact:

■ Wear appropriate water shoes when possible and feasible for the lifeguard station.

■ Get a firm grip on the ladder or chair, and maintain three points of contact. Two hands and one foot or two feet and one hand should be on the equipment at all times.

■ Break three points of contact only when you reach the ground or lifeguard chair platform.

■ Mount and dismount facing the ladder or chair.

Don't climb with the rescue tube in your free hand. Either set the tube down on the deck or lifeguard chair when climbing out of the pool and climbing or descending the lifeguard chair. After you are firmly standing on the pool deck or seated in the guard chair, then strap the rescue tube in position. You may also have another guard hand you the tube.

Never jump from the lifeguard chair or platform down to the deck.

**FIGURE 12.2** Three points of contact: *(a)* Get a firm grip on the ladder or chair, and maintain three points of contact. Two hands and one foot or two feet and one hand should be on the equipment at all times. *(b)* Keep your back straight and lift or lower using your legs during extrication.

## Using Safe Lifting Techniques

Injuries occur because moving people or equipment include the potentially hazardous activities of lifting, reaching, and pulling. Use these techniques when performing extrication, or any type of lifting:

1. Clear a path before lifting. Know what may be behind you if you will be moving.
2. Have a firm hold. Keep the object close to your body for stability.
3. Have a solid base of support. Keep your feet about shoulder-width apart. When moving, take small steps.
4. Raise and lower by bending your knees and lifting with your legs. Keep your back straight.

Using safe lifting techniques will help you reduce or eliminate many of the injuries associated with strain on the back.

# Health Considerations

In addition to safety risks in the workplace, there are also health considerations while working as a lifeguard, including skin damage, skin cancer, eye injuries, and illnesses.

## Skin Cancer Awareness

If you lifeguard outdoors, you will be exposed to the elements, including sunlight. The sun emits ultraviolet radiation, which is the primary cause of skin cancer, and chronic exposure to the sun's ultraviolet rays can also cause skin damage, premature aging, and eye damage. If you work outdoors, you are at risk. The good news is that skin cancer is preventable, but before we talk about protection and screening, here are some sobering facts from the World Health Organization and the Skin Cancer Foundation:

- Between two and three million skin cancers occur globally each year.
- In the United States, one person dies every hour from skin cancer, primarily melanoma.

■ Melanoma is the most common form of cancer for young adults 25 to 29 years old and the second most common form of cancer for young people 15 to 24 years old.

■ More than 90 percent of all skin cancers are caused by sun exposure, yet fewer than 33 percent of adults, adolescents, and children routinely use sun protection.

■ One blistering sunburn in childhood or adolescence more than double a person's chances of developing melanoma later in life.

■ The effects of skin aging caused by ultraviolet radiation can be seen as early as in one's 20s.

■ Putting proven cancer prevention and early detection techniques into action could eliminate thousands of cases and deaths each year.

**Shade yourself from the sun with a shirt, hat, umbrella, or all three. Apply sunscreen with an SPF value of at least 30 (see figure 12.3).**

The sun emits many wavelengths of light, but UVA and UVB are those that can have the most effects on your skin due to overexposure. UVA rays penetrate through glass and clouds and penetrates the skin to its deep layers. UVA is responsible for tanning and contributes to two types of skin cancer. UVB rays only penetrate the superficial layers of skin and are responsible for the reddening and blistering of sunburns. UVB rays are most prominent in the heat of the day from 10 a.m. to 4 p.m. and can be reflected. This property of UVB rays makes them dangerous around water, snow, and ice.

The global solar UV index has been developed to indicate the strength of the solar UV radiation on a scale from 1 (low) to 11-plus (extremely high). The ozone layer, which shields the earth from UV radiation, can be affected by depletion and seasonal weather changes. Weather services around the world predict the UV index for the next day and issue the UV index forecast. If the level of solar UV radiation is predicted to be unusually high, you should take appropriate sun-protective precautions and avoid overexposure.

Your lifeguarding job should not be an excuse to get a suntan. You must take personal responsibility to protect yourself, and the best way to accomplish this is to use skin protection products and to cover up.

■ *Always* use sunscreen and lip coat rated at SPF 30 or higher. Apply sunscreen at least 30 minutes before exposure. Reapply every two or three hours or more often if you have been sweating or swimming. Lifeguard staff should use a sunscreen log for documenting application.

■ In addition to sunscreen, use sun shade. Have at least one physical barrier, such as a hat, shirt, or umbrella, between you and the sun. Wide-brim hats and tightly woven clothing designed for sun protection are best.

**FIGURE 12.3** Lifeguard following sun protection best practices.

### ★ Facts About Sunscreen in the United States

▶ In order to clarify confusing labeling, the FDA released new guidelines and regulations for sunscreen. Sunscreens may be labeled "**broad-spectrum**" if they provide protection against ultraviolet A (UVA) and ultraviolet B (UVB) radiation.

▶ Only broad-spectrum sunscreens with a Sun Protection Factor (SPF) of 15 or higher can state that they protect against skin cancer if used as directed with other sun protection measures.

▶ Sunscreens with an SPF of 2-14 will be required to have a warning stating that the product has not been shown to help prevent skin cancer or early skin aging.

▶ The terms "**sunblock**", "**sweatproof**", and "**waterproof**" are no longer allowed on sunscreen labels.

▶ A sunscreen may claim to be "**water resistant**"; however, the product must specify if it offers 40 minutes or 80 minutes of protection while swimming or sweating, based on standard testing. Sunscreens that are not water resistant must include a direction instructing consumers to use a water resistant sunscreen if swimming or sweating.

▶ Sunscreens cannot claim to provide sun protection for **more than two hours** without reapplication.

▶ The FDA reiterated that sunscreen alone is not enough, and should be used in conjunction with a complete **sun protection** regimen, including seeking shade, wearing long pants, long-sleeved shirts, hats, and sunglasses.

■ Examine your skin regularly, and seek a physician's opinion if you have suspicious-looking moles or dark areas on your skin. You should have a skin cancer check performed by a physician yearly.

## Eye Care

Your eyes are one of your most important lifeguarding tools. Most of your time is spent scanning for visual indications of problems. Adequate eyesight is critical for your success. Follow these tips to protect your vision:

■ Shield your eyes from the effects of the sun, wind, water, and dust by wearing sunglasses that are both ultraviolet protective and physically protective.

■ Wear sunglasses with lenses that filter 100 percent of UV rays. Glasses with side protection that do not obscure your peripheral vision are best.

■ Have your eyes tested at least once a year to screen for vision problems.

■ If you wear glasses or contact lenses to correct your vision, wear them at all times when you are on duty. If you wear contact lenses, close your eyes briefly when you enter the water in order to avoid losing your lenses. If you know you will be swimming with lenses in or may have to get in the water during a rescue, consider wearing disposable lenses so that if the lenses do come out, they are easily replaced.

■ Keep your lenses clean, and replace them as needed. Chlorine and other pool contaminants may remain on a contact lens and cause eye inflammation.

## Illness

Following are methods to reduce work-related illnesses:

- Minimize your risk of dehydration, heat exhaustion, or heatstroke by drinking lots of water. Keep a water bottle on the stand, and make sure you have protection from the sun.
- Obtain a hepatitis B vaccination if you have not been immunized.
- Use personal protective equipment (PPE), and follow universal precautions when in contact with blood, bodily fluids, or other potentially infected material.
- Do not swallow recreational water.
- Always use your personal protective equipment when cleaning up bodily substances.
- Remove wet swimwear frequently to avoid skin chafing and urinary tract infections.
- Wear aquatic footwear to prevent exposure to fungus or bacteria and to protect feet from cuts.
- If you work at an indoor aquatic venue, especially those with waterfalls or sprays, you may become exposed to chlorine-resistant bacteria in small water particles that have become airborne. Lifeguards who work long shifts in this type of environment appear to be at higher risk. Seek medical attention if you develop chronic respiratory symptoms such as a cough or difficulty breathing.

**Stay hydrated by drinking water.**

## ★ Knowledge Into Practice

Your safety is as important as that of the guests at your facility. You cannot effectively perform your job if you are ill or injured. Additionally, without reasonable precautions, exposures you may have on the job could have long-term effects on your health.

## @ Visit the Web Resource

You can reinforce your learning by visiting the web resource, where you can do the following in the interactive online learning activities for chapter 12:

- ▶ Activity 12.1: Identify ways to minimize personal risk and review scenarios about workplace risk.
- ▶ Activity 12.2: Look up the UV index for your location or download tools to check the index on your mobile phone.
- ▶ Activity 12.3: Read case studies of incidents involving pool chemical accidents.
- ▶ Activity 12.4: Chapter quiz. Test your knowledge, receive feedback, and print the quiz page.

## ⊕ On the Job

These are the tasks related to workplace safety that you will be expected to competently perform while working as a lifeguard:

▶ Contribute to maintaining a safe and secure workplace environment.

▶ Protect yourself from job-related health risks.

## CHAPTER 13

# Meeting Workplace Expectations

This chapter

- ▶ explains components of professionalism and how these traits relate to your performance as a lifeguard;
- ▶ explains the need for ongoing and site-specific training;
- ▶ reinforces the need for responsibility, accountability, and good judgment;
- ▶ identifies what to expect from your employer; and
- ▶ identifies what your employer will expect from you.

Professionalism is one of the most important components of the StarGuard course because it carries through to everything you do. Even something as simple as the way you sit in the lifeguard stand can affect the professional image you project. Note the differences in figure 13.1 on page 191 between a very professional posture and a less professional posture.

Professionalism can be expressed in many ways; the most common is the opinion others have of you based on the way you act, talk, dress, or perform your duties. This chapter explores how to maintain a high level of professionalism in your workplace.

## Projecting a Professional Image

To perform your job at a high level, you must instill confidence in the patrons you serve. Because they may know nothing about you, the only way they can evaluate your ability is through what they see. If you slouch in the lifeguard stand looking bored and twirling your whistle, they will assume you are bored and don't care about the safety of those in your care. If you seem to be more interested in goofing around with your coworkers or kids at the pool than doing your job, this image will affect the opinion others have of both you and the facility you represent. Your actions speak louder than your words. There are two kinds of behaviors you can project: (1) those that enhance your image and (2) those that demean your image.

### Professional Behaviors

There are several things you can do every day to build up your professional image, including the following:

- Wear a clean, neat uniform that distinguishes you from the crowd.
- Maintain excellent posture. When sitting this includes having your feet flat, shoulders forward, and rescue tube across your lap, with strap gathered.
- Keep focused, and follow StarGuard best practices.
- Behave as you expect others to behave.
- Speak to others as you wish to be spoken to.

### Unprofessional Behaviors

Some behaviors are not appropriate for lifeguards, harm your professional image, and may place patrons at risk. Make a conscious effort to eliminate any of these behaviors while **on the stand or in view of patrons:**

**Display behaviors that build up your professional image; eliminate behaviors that harm your professional image.**

- Slouching
- Whistle twirling
- Looking bored (e.g., frequently looking at watch)
- Sitting with legs crossed or leaning your head on your hand or hands
- Socializing
- Talking on the phone
- Texting
- Reading, smoking, chewing gum, grooming, or eating
- Talking in a belittling manner, gossiping, or using profanity
- Participating in pranks or encouraging unsafe patron behavior
- Appearing to be unfocused or tired
- Using the rescue tube as a backrest or footrest
- Playing with rescue equipment
- Diving or cannonballing from the lifeguard stand
- Wearing sloppy or inappropriate clothing or personal attire

However, professionalism goes beyond your actions. It involves your commitment to performing at a high level. This commitment requires ongoing training to maintain your skills and fitness at rescue-ready levels, the ability to take responsibility for your performance, and good judgment.

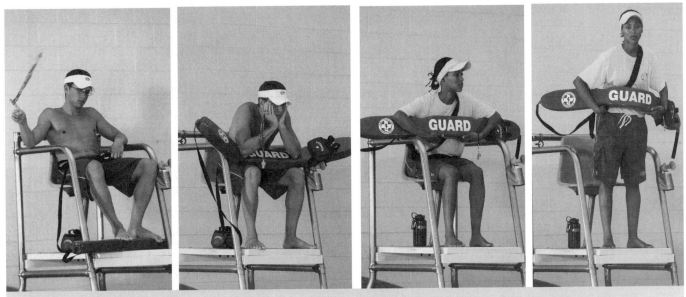

FIGURE 13.1 The first two photos exhibit unprofessional behavior, while the last two photos exhibit professional behavior.

# In-Service Training and Fitness

In-service training is an important part of your professional development. Depending on the requirements of your facility, you can expect to spend several hours per month in site-specific training sessions. Topics should be geared toward maintaining your rescue and basic life support skills, using the rescue equipment at your facility, practicing surveillance skills, and reviewing other information related to your responsibilities. In-service training conducted where you work enhances your development in the following ways:

- Validating that you can perform and helping you gain confidence (this will be evident not only to your employer but also to yourself)
- Allowing you to practice skills on the equipment available at your facility while following the facility's emergency action plan (EAP)
- Strengthening teamwork with your coworkers
- Identifying areas of concern and developing more effective EAPs
- Building endurance and stamina, especially in regard to physical conditioning
- Reinforcing your knowledge of workplace safety standards

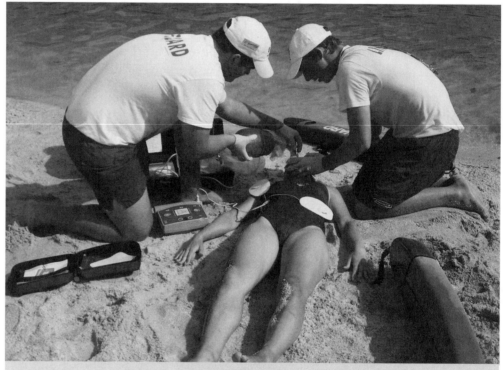

Ongoing in-service training is an important workplace expectation.

Physical conditioning to maintain rescue-ready fitness levels is also important. Your fitness training schedule should be appropriate for the physical response and rescue demands of the lifeguarding position you hold at your workplace. In most instances this will include, at a minimum, maintaining the physical ability to perform effective CPR compressions, to descend to the deepest area you are assigned, and to swim to the farthest point in the area you are assigned.

## Accountability

Expect to be involved in an evaluation system such as a lifeguard audit or review that measures your ability to perform your prevention, surveillance, response and rescue, emergency care, and professional skills. Whether your supervisors or an outside agency conducts this evaluation, it will provide you with an accurate picture of how well you focus on the important objectives of your job.

The first part of a lifeguard review, which is usually conducted without your knowledge that you are being watched, documents your level of professionalism, the prevention strategies you are using, and the level of surveillance you are providing. The second part usually consists of an aquatic rescue and emergency care scenario to evaluate your ability to manage an emergency situation. The objectives of an audit or review are as follows:

- Document your ability and the operational procedures in place to support you.
- Identify any areas that need improvement so remediation and education can be conducted.
- Recognize and award you for outstanding performance.

Reviews are valuable competency assessment and motivational tools.

For those facilities that utilize the Star-Review system, awards and recognition are given to the lifeguards who are part of the review as well as an overall facility award based on operational and management evaluation. Awards are based on earning a rating of three, four, or five stars. Lifeguards and facilities earning awards are set apart by actions, appearance, attitude, and workplace culture. This distinction validates consistent planning, training, and risk management practices that exceed standards.

## Judgment Skills

When you are on the job, you will often face choices that determine how you act. Your ability to use sound judgment to make decisions will mean the difference between being valued at your workplace or not, and it may mean the difference between saving a life or not. What types of decisions might you have to make? What would you decide if the following thoughts were going through your head?

- *I wonder if that is a shadow on the bottom or if I'm just seeing things. Should I go check it out or wait to see if it moves or goes away?*
- *The water is a bit cloudy, and I can't see the bottom. Should I close the pool even though I know people will be upset?*
- *Should I put on sunscreen or get a tan?*
- *My replacement didn't show up on time, and I have to be somewhere. Should I leave?*
- *My friends want me to go with them to a baseball game. Should I call in sick even though I know the pool will be short a lifeguard?*

■ *I partied late last night, hardly got any sleep, and feel terrible. Should I let my supervisor know and reassign my duties, or should I go on the stand and fake being alert?*

■ *It will be slow at the pool today, and I know my supervisor won't be around. Should I call some friends to come hang out with me while I work?*

These are just a few of the types of decisions you will make every day. Depending on the choice you make, there could be devastating long-term consequences. Your decisions should be based on the principles that value life, including yours, above all else. The decisions you make outside of the workplace can also have serious consequences. You might think that what you do on your own time doesn't matter, but the effects of substances such as alcohol or drugs, or lack of sleep, can carry over into your working hours even though the activity occurred on your personal time.

## What to Expect From Your Employer

The StarGuard course provides the information you need to understand the objectives of lifeguarding, teaches you the required physical skills, and suggests best practices as methods to help you perform. However, each aquatic facility is different, with different types of rescue equipment and procedures. Therefore, it is your responsibility to make sure your employer provides you the necessary equipment and supplemental training and support to do your job. At a minimum, your employer should provide the following:

■ Personal protective equipment, such as gloves and a barrier mask

■ Rescue tube

■ Umbrella or shade for outdoor venues

■ Drinking water

■ Lifeguard identification, such as a uniform

■ Communication or signal device

■ Telephone to call EMS

■ First aid supplies

■ A break from scanning at least every hour

■ Ability to change position so you can stay alert and can scan the bottom

■ Orientation to and practice of the facility's emergency action plan (EAP)

■ Training in how to safely handle chemicals and hazardous materials if you are responsible for using them

■ Orientation to and practice with the rescue equipment present at your facility

■ Orientation to facility operating procedures

■ Ongoing in-service training

■ Ongoing performance assessment

■ Coverage under a liability insurance policy or immunity from liability

**Understand what your employer should provide for you in order to do your job.**

If your employer does not provide this support, you may be in a position in which it is impossible for you to perform at minimum standards.

# What Your Employer Will Expect From You

A big part of being professional is being a good employee. You may just be entering the workforce, and this may be your first job. It is important to know what will be expected so you don't make mistakes that could jeopardize your job or ruin opportunities in the future. Just as you need support from your employer to do your job, your employer needs support from you to operate a safe facility. Your employer should require you to do the following:

- Provide proof of certification or authorization for lifeguard, CPR, first aid, and other required emergency care courses.
- Provide proof, through skills assessment, that you can perform rescue skills, including testing to see if you can descend to the deepest area of the pool to which you will be assigned.
- Uphold employment agreements, whether written or verbal. If you are hired with the understanding that you will work certain dates, such as through the summer, it is very important that you honor this agreement.
- Find approved substitutes if you cannot work an assigned shift, or follow the procedure set up at your facility. Calling in at the last minute or not showing up for a shift compromises the safety of everyone at the facility.
- Participate in a drug-testing program. Depending on the regulations in your location, this program may include preemployment screening, random testing, or postincident testing.
- Exhibit a high level of professionalism, and follow StarGuard best practices.

**Fulfill the expectations of your employer.**

## Knowledge Into Practice

How you are perceived by your guests, coworkers, and employer can have a significant impact on your success as a lifeguard. Your positive actions define you as a professional. Your unprofessional actions can place patrons at risk.

## Visit the Web Resource

You can reinforce your learning by visiting the web resource, where you can do the following in the interactive online learning activities for chapter 13:

- ▶ Activity 13.1: Select ways to improve a lifeguard's professional image.
- ▶ Activity 13.2: Evaluate scenarios and identify professional responsibilities such as using sound judgment and decision making.
- ▶ Activity 13.3: Watch video of lifeguards performing 5-star award professional behavior while on the job.
- ▶ Activity 13.4: Chapter quiz. Test your knowledge, receive feedback, and print the quiz page.

## On the Job

These are the tasks related to workplace expectations that you will be expected to competently perform while working as a lifeguard:

▶ Project a positive image.

▶ Be committed to improvement and accountability.

▶ Develop the ability to be a responsible employee and make responsible decisions.

## CHAPTER 14

# Considering Site- and Situation-Specific Circumstances

The basic concepts and skills of lifeguarding apply to any aquatic environment: Everyone is at risk of drowning, and it is your job to perform preventive interventions, look for distress and drowning, and respond in an emergency. However, aquatic environments—and how patrons use them—vary, and you may need to consider additional strategies to be effective. As explained in chapter 2, the management of the facility where you work, or those who hire you for special events, will set the policies and operating procedures that guide your day-to-day actions. The goal of this chapter is to provide an overview and awareness of the need for site- and situation-specific considerations. The suggestions may or may not be feasible or relevant in your situation, and the information does not cover all possible circumstances. Chapter 15 provides additional site-specific information for the water-park environment and chapter 16 for waterfronts. The most common situation requiring site-specific considerations is when a single lifeguard is on duty.

## Single-Lifeguard Facilities

Having more than one lifeguard on duty has many advantages but is often not feasible, particularly for small venues that are used infrequently. Economic or logistic limitations may mean choosing between having one lifeguard or none. If you work at a single-guard facility you need to be aware of how to adapt the StarGuard Risk Management Model to your circumstances.

### Prevention Considerations

Most single-guard facilities are not open to the general public, meaning those who attend do so through a residence, membership, or guest relationship. This relationship allows patrons to be informed in advance of policies; rules; and their responsibility in preventing illness, injury, or drowning at the facility.

When you are by yourself, your primary responsibility and attention will need to be on patron surveillance. You'll need to perform prevention and other responsibilities at times when you are not responsible for scanning so these tasks don't intrude on your ability to provide constant and dedicated surveillance. You may be responsible for multiple duties at a single guard facility such as cleaning, administrative tasks, and customer service. You must manage these duties in a way not to interfere with your lifeguard responsibilities, the ability to enforce rules, as well as see the entire pool—including the ability to frequently scan the bottom.

## Surveillance Considerations

When you are the only lifeguard, the entire water area is your zone, 100 percent of the time. Your scanning strategies and responsibilities do not change, but since there is no one to rotate in for you, consider the following:

■ How will you work in breaks from surveillance? It may be that you have periods when there are no patrons at the facility, followed by periods of high use. Or your facility may have patrons in the water for your entire hours-long shift. One method is to clear the water for 10 minutes every hour so you can break from surveillance, perform prevention tasks, and care for yourself. Everyone should clear the water—including adults, who are at risk of having a medical emergency while swimming that would require your immediate attention.

■ Most single-guard facilities require that patrons check in or provide proof of membership or use privileges. How can this process be managed so it does not interfere with your ability to provide surveillance?

■ Is the lifeguard station located in a position where you can see the entire zone, including the access point into the facility? It is important for you to see when patrons arrive and when they leave.

■ Lifeguards at single-guard facilities have more personal interaction with the patrons and are often expected to be social and accommodating. What strategies will you employ to deal with patrons who request attention that takes away from your ability to provide surveillance?

## Response and Rescue Considerations

When you are the only lifeguard, being able to alert others that you need help is critically important. You will need to know the system at your facility for summoning others and for contacting EMS. The most effective communication system is an alert button so you can quickly activate the emergency response of coworkers, such as front desk personnel, who have been instructed on how to help you and who know the facility's emergency action plan. The alert button is wired directly to a place where someone is always present to hear it. The button should be close to you, ideally on your person, so you don't have to travel to the button before assisting a distressed or drowning victim, thereby losing valuable time (see figure 14.1).

A secondary method is to use whistle or air horn signals. You should practice to be sure the signals can be heard by those who will respond, in a variety of noise conditions. In cases where it is not possible to alert coworkers that you need help, you will have to rely on bystanders. Tell bystanders what you need them to do. Use clear and concise directions.

**FIGURE 14.1** Wireless alert buttons (shown attached to the rescue tube) allow for manual activation of the alarm by the lifeguard.
Reprinted, by permission, from Safety Turtle.

Some ways to use support personnel or bystanders include the following:

- Calling EMS. Be sure the calling instructions and facility address are clearly identified near the phone.
- Meeting EMS to direct them to the scene.
- Clearing the pool and crowd control.
- Bringing equipment.
- Helping you extricate the victim.
- Helping you perform CPR compressions.
- Helping you perform rescue breaths if the person is trained to do so.
- Locating family members if they are not present.
- Calling for the assistance of others within your facility's chain of response.

## Emergency Care Considerations

During an emergency, bystanders can also be used to help you provide CPR if they are willing. Research has shown that bystanders can perform effective chest compressions with minimal instruction. While you manage the airway and provide rescue breaths in between sets of compressions, direct the bystander to

- place the heels of her hands on the center of the victim's chest, and
- keeping her arms straight, push as hard and fast as she can, letting the chest recoil after each push.

You can monitor the count of compressions and let the bystander know when to stop so that you can provide rescue breaths.

## Workplace Considerations

The single-lifeguard workplace can be one of the most challenging. It is easy to perform well at multiguard facilities when there is always something going on and supervisors are constantly monitoring your performance. It requires a high level of personal responsibility and accountability to maintain best practices and a high level of vigilance when you are by yourself. A true measure of your professionalism is what you do when no one is watching. You should always follow best practices that are appropriate for the situation, and avoid behaviors that take away from your professional image. When patrons are present there is no place for socializing, texting, talking on your phone, reading, sleeping or other behaviors that would not be allowed if you were being directly supervised.

# Lifeguarding People With Disabilities

Most people know someone with a disability or may even have one themselves. A disability occurs when a health condition or disorder results in an inability to perform typical functions, such as walking, learning, working, eating, grooming, and enjoying recreation. A disability can be caused by conditions at birth, genetic reasons, trauma, or illness later in life.

Some people who come to your facility may have disabling conditions that cause them to function differently. These people might visit an aquatic facility alone or accompanied by family members or a caregiver. As medical science continues to advance, you can expect more and more people with disabilities to be active in the community. Your professional responsibility should be to help people with disabilities enjoy the aquatic recreation environment with dignity. Because a person with a disability may function differently from a person without a disability, you may have to communicate with him in a different manner and consider additional safety issues.

## Communication

Do not make assumptions about the abilities of a person with a disability. When you talk with a person with a disability, the following guidelines will help you communicate effectively:

Your responsibility is to help swimmers with disabilities safely enjoy the water with dignity.

- Use person-first language, such as "person with a disability" instead of "disabled person."
- Don't raise your voice; speak in a normal tone.
- When providing assistance to people with disabilities, first ask if they want help, and if so, ask how they would like to be helped. Ask the person directly rather than speaking to the caregiver about the person.
- Make certain that assistive features of the facility, such as pool lifts, are clean and in working order.
- Talk to the patron the same way you would want someone else to talk to a member of your family, or how you would want to be talked to.

## Safety

When enforcing safety regulations, keep in mind that the rules are meant to keep all patrons safe, including people with disabilities. However, you can be flexible about rules for a patron with a disability as long as being flexible doesn't create a safety hazard. To keep all pool patrons safe, follow these guidelines:

- When a person with a disability enters the pool, note whether she is alone or accompanied by a family member or caregiver.
- If a patron with a disability breaks a pool rule, warn him and explain the rule.
- Watch a person with a disability when she is in the water. Some of the person's normal movements may look like distress but are not. Watch for changes in the disabled person's movement patterns. If you notice something different or unusual, target the person, assess the situation, and decide whether you need to take action.
- Some people with disabilities will be accompanied by assistive animals, such as dogs, cats, or even monkeys. These are well-trained assistants that are allowed on the pool deck but not in the water in most circumstances.

Let's now look at some strategies to consider when lifeguarding at events such as parties or during programs and competitions.

## Lifeguarding Special Events and Programs

Chapter 2 identifies the high-risk nature of birthday parties and other group outings at an aquatic facility (see page 12). These same risks can be present at events your facility hosts, such as "dive-in" movies, concerts, and staff events, whether held during or after hours.

Understand the situation- and site-specific risk factors for activities taking place while you lifeguard.

## Movies, Concerts, and After-Hours Parties

Special events bring a higher level of excitement to an aquatic facility. Consider these situations:

- If events are held after dark, consider ways you will have to adapt your surveillance strategies. If patrons are watching movies from within the water, one method is to require that everyone float on the surface on a tube or raft—no swimming—so that when you scan you are looking for empty floats as a sign to target and assess. The presence of the floats could also obscure your view of the bottom, making it difficult to scan. Other strategies include requiring that everyone wear a life jacket and having a pair of scuba divers providing surveillance from under the water.

- If music or movies are loud, you may need to adapt your emergency communication signals so they can be heard over the noise, or develop a system of visual signals if feasible.

- If alcohol is served at special events, remember that patrons who are drinking are at higher risk of drowning and making poor decisions about their ability in the water.

- The same level of surveillance needs to be provided when staff are using the facility, and staff should follow the same rules and expectations required of patrons.

## Swim Classes and Teams

The role of the instructor or coach is to teach and focus on her students. Safety practices should be a part of any program, but your role is to provide dedicated surveillance of the entire zone. Consider these situations:

- Young children who are nonswimmers or weak swimmers can very quickly and silently slip off the edge and immediately submerge to the bottom. Pay particular attention to the areas along the wall during your scan. If parents are allowed on deck during programs, other siblings often accompany them. The adults may get distracted, allowing children to wander off—often toward the pool.

Children in swim lessons can quickly and silently slip off the edge and into the pool.

- Participants in water fitness or therapy classes may lose their footing, tipping into a floating position on or just under the surface, and be unable to right themselves to breathe. This situation is even more likely if the person is wearing flotation or resistance devices on the ankles or lower body.

- If scuba training is conducted in your facility, coordinate with the instructor to determine communication signals and your role in rescuing a submerged diver. Dive instructors are trained in the techniques to use in a scuba emergency, but there may be a situation in which the instructor is the person in need of care.

- If military training is conducted at your facility, coordinate with the commanding officer to determine communication signals and your role in rescuing a submerged soldier. Military training often involves activities that would not normally be allowed, and clear understanding by all involved about expectations, assumption of risk, and the EAP is important.

■ Lifeguarding a team of highly skilled swimmers, divers, water polo players, or synchronized swimmers seems unnecessary at first thought. However, instances of death and drowning during practice occur more often than you may think. Skilled athletes are not immune to medical emergencies such as seizures, heart attacks, asthma, dehydration, or shallow-water blackout occurring suddenly and silently in the water. Collision injuries can also occur.

## Swim Meets

Most aquatic sport competitions are held under the sanction of a governing organization that sets safety guidelines and rules. Sanctioned competitive swim meets usually have a person designated as a safety marshal who will help enforce rules, such as feetfirst entries during warm-up and designated lanes for supervised practice of dives off the starting platforms. It is helpful to communicate with the safety marshal ahead of time so that everyone understands the EAP for the event and to ensure it does not conflict with the EAP for the facility.

Medical emergencies that occur in the water are a risk during team practices or competitions.

## Open-Water Swims and Triathlons

Consider these challenges of open-water swims and triathlons:

■ Swimmers can get kicked or pushed under by crowd crush during a mass start.
■ A person who experiences a medical emergency while in the middle of the pack will be hard to spot and get to.

**Obtain event-specific orientation before lifeguarding meets, open-water swims, and triathlons.**

- The course may be spread over a long distance, so visual communication between spotters may be hard to see and whistles may be hard to hear, especially if it is windy.
- Swimming against waves, currents, or tides may cause swimmers to expend more energy than expected or to become seasick.
- With the growing popularity of triathlons, more novice and inexperienced athletes are participating. Do not assume that all participants in a triathlon are strong swimmers.
- In an open-water swim, the final decision of whether or not to conduct the race may rest upon your assessment of the safety of the conditions.

Prerace training and orientation should include practice scenarios with the rescue team.

If you are assigned to lifeguard at one of these events, you will likely be a part of a rescue team that includes spotters in kayaks or on watercraft, along with support personnel such as EMS, rescue divers, and event managers such as the race director, safety officer, and race referee. You should receive race-specific orientation and training before the event that provides information about

- course layout and expected conditions,
- the type of start,
- communication signals,
- the safety and surveillance plan,
- the EAP for responsive and unresponsive victim incidents, and
- the evacuation plan.

## The Fran Crippen Tragedy

United States National Team member Fran Crippen, age 26, died on October 23, 2010, while swimming the last race of FINA's 10K series in Fujairah, UAE. He had won the penultimate race in Cancun, Mexico, the weekend before. Fran failed to finish the race and his body was discovered two hours later near the last bouy on the course. Fran was an advocate for safe competitive environments and his untimely death has resulted in a push for improved safety protocols, precautions, and procedures in open-water swimming events.

## Lifeguarding Outside the Workplace

You may be asked by friends, family, or acquaintances to lifeguard outside of your workplace, such as for special events or parties at private homes. Often in these situations, the host does not expect you to enforce rules because they don't want to spoil the fun, and they also do not understand the risks. Rescue equipment may not be available, and you may not be familiar with emergency procedures for that location.

Absolutely do not drink alcohol and avoid distractions like food and games with guests. If you need to take a restroom or food break from scanning, appoint a sober, responsible individual to watch the water. Give them your whistle, rescue tube, or some other token to remind them that they are watching the water. There are numerous case reports of children drowning at crowded backyard parties because everyone "thought someone else was watching the pool".

Unless you are representing, and being paid by, your employer in an after-hours situations, you will not be covered by liability insurance unless you have your own policy. In these situations, make sure the host clearly defines what is expected of you, and get these expectations and a release from liability in writing.

## Lifeguarding in Wilderness Settings

Many organized groups visit remote places and find themselves swimming in rivers, creeks, springs, and lakes. Lifeguarding in wilderness environments requires strategies and adaptations different from traditional lifeguard training. The Wilderness StarGuard program is a specialty certification offered to wilderness-based youth programs and camps, backcountry guide services, paddling schools, and other outdoor leadership organizations, delivered through a partnership with Landmark Learning.

Visit www.landmarklearning.org for more information about Wilderness StarGuard.

**Knowledge Into Practice**

While the basic concepts and skills of lifeguarding apply in most situations, there are unique demands during different activities. You will need to understand how to adapt your skills to meet varying needs.

## @ Visit the Web Resource

You can reinforce your learning by visiting the web resource, where you can do the following in the interactive online learning activities for chapter 14:

- ▶ Activity 14.1: Evaluate real-life scenarios about assisting people with disabilities and build your decision-making skills.
- ▶ Activity 14.2: Evaluate real-life scenarios that could occur at an aquatic facility and build your decision-making skills.
- ▶ Activity 14.3: Learn more about water watcher programs for water safety enhancement during special events, safety protocols in open-water swimming events, and the Wilderness StarGuard program.
- ▶ Activity 14.4: Evaluate situations and identify the best course of action in the poolside challenge activity.
- ▶ Activity 14.5: Chapter quiz. Test your knowledge, receive feedback, and print the quiz page.

## On the Job

These are the tasks related to site- and situation-specific circumstances that you will be expected to competently perform while working as a lifeguard:

- ▶ Be aware that skills and strategies may need to be adapted to meet the needs of a specific activity, situation, or site (e.g., a wilderness setting or a swim meet).
- ▶ Follow the operating policies and procedure in place at your workplace.
- ▶ Understand how to interact effectively with people with disabilities.

## CHAPTER 15

# Lifeguarding at Water Parks and Similar Spaces

## CHAPTER OBJECTIVES

This chapter

▶ identifies features of a water park;

▶ identifies additional prevention, surveillance, response, rescue, and emergency care strategies for the water-park setting; and

▶ reinforces workplace safety and performance expectations for the water-park setting.

If you will work at a water park or a facility with play features such as slides or moving water, you must complete the water-park training module in addition to the basic StarGuard course. The water-park module may be taught at the same time as your StarGuard course or presented as a separate training session. Each section of this chapter covers a StarGuard risk management model component as it applies to lifeguarding in water parks. *Note:* The material presented in this chapter supplements the other chapters in this text.

# Water-Park Features

The unique features at water parks or at aquatic facilities with attractions like those at a water park require additional prevention, surveillance, and response strategies. Let's look at the most common attractions and features you will find at a water park.

## Waterslides

There are several types of waterslides:

■ **Body and tube slides.** These are fiberglass flumes that might be open (with high, curved walls) or enclosed to form a tube through which the rider slides. Some slides have a combination of open and closed areas. The end of the flume is about even with the water surface, and the flow of the water pushes riders into a catch pool about three to four feet (.9 to 1.2 m) deep. Wider flumes are designed to hold an inner tube on which the rider sits. Tubes might be single for one rider or double for two riders at a time. Another type of body slide is called a drop or shotgun slide because instead of pushing the rider into a catch pool at water level, the slide ends several feet (about a meter) above the surface, and the rider drops the distance from the slide to the water. Catch pools for drop slides are deeper.

■ **Speed slides.** Speed slides are narrow, steep, and straight slides that start from a high tower. They are body slides, but they don't push the rider into a catch pool. Instead, when the slide reaches the ground, the rider is pushed down a long flume until the movement stops. The flume run-out area usually contains just a few inches (several centimeters) of water.

■ **Kiddie slides.** Kiddie slides are not very high and are usually attached to a play structure, although some are stand-alone attractions. These slides usually send a rider into a few inches (several centimeters) of water at the bottom of the slide.

■ **Multilane slides.** Multilane slides are similar to speed slides but are usually not as tall, and several riders participate at once. Often multilane slides are designed to be used with a foam mat for the rider to sit or lie on.

■ **Raft rides.** Raft rides are usually a combination of wide, closed and open flumes that can accommodate a raft holding several people. These slides push the raft into a catch pool, usually three to four feet (.9 to 1.2 m) deep, at the end of the ride. Blaster raft rides are similar to family raft rides but have rollercoaster-like features that allow the raft to go both uphill and downhill throughout the ride.

## Wave Pools

A wave pool creates an experience similar to the water action of an open-water surf environment. A wave pool is usually fan shaped, with a wide zero-depth "beach-front" entry area where the water meets the "shore" and then a narrow, deeper area where the waves are generated and pushed out to the zero depth. Swimmers are usually not allowed access along the back wall of the wave pool where the waves are created.

## Flowing Currents

A lazy river is a long, narrow, shallow pool with slow-moving water. Patrons usually float on inner tubes as they are pushed by the current, although some attractions allow patrons without tubes to be in the water as well. A lazy river usually has several points along the route where patrons can enter or exit the water. A wave river or torrent river uses wave action to move riders faster along the route.

## Play Structures

Play structures are usually located in shallow water and have multiple levels that include waterslides, interactive water features, and tipping beakers.

## Specialty Rides and Attractions

Other popular water-park attractions include those that create an ocean-like wave for surfing, flumes that enter into a vortex with a drop into water below, climbing walls, and in-water areas for basketball or volleyball. New types of attractions are always being designed and introduced to the water-park industry, and that trend is likely to continue.

## Facilities Similar to Water Parks

A water park is not the only place where you might find waterslides, interactive water features, and other water attractions. A sprayground or spraypark or splashpad consists of a variety of water-play elements without any standing water. Because there is no standing water, lifeguards may not be

This type of leisure pool has many features similar to a water park.

required. Leisure pools combine a variety of design features such as lap swimming lanes, a small lazy river, a zero-depth entry, waterslides, and possibly other water elements in one area, rather than being spread out like a larger water park. This type of facility is becoming common in both indoor and outdoor community recreation and resort settings. Waterslides are often added to older swimming pools as part of a renovation. You will use the same water-park strategies and considerations for lifeguarding these attractions, adapted for the site-specific location.

## Prevention Strategy at Water Parks

The water-park industry has an overall excellent track record of providing safe recreation. The most effective way to reduce the risk of injury to patrons enjoying water-park attractions is to consistently enforce the rules for proper usage and regularly inspect the attraction.

### Safety and Use Instructions

Each area or attraction should have safety and use instructions clearly posted for patrons. These instructions should answer the following questions for each attraction:

- Must patrons be a maximum or minimum height before using this attraction?
- Must patrons be a maximum or minimum weight before using this attraction?
- Are certain types of apparel prohibited?
- Must patrons use a certain body position with this attraction? Are certain body positions prohibited?
- Is there a time or distance requirement between users?
- Is equipment such as tubes or mats required for use of this attraction? Is equipment prohibited from use on this attraction?

**Enforce rules specific to each attraction.**

The attraction manufacturer usually provides guidelines for use that answer these questions, and then site-specific facility rules support these guidelines. It is important that you know the restrictions and rules for each area or attraction that you lifeguard and enforce these rules with all patrons.

### Mandatory Use of Life Jackets

Many water parks require that children under a certain age or height, as well as all nonswimmers, wear life jackets in wave pools, lazy rivers, and deep-water areas. There are also laws in some locations that require life jacket use. If you work at a facil-

Mandatory life jacket use can be an effective prevention strategy.

ity with a life jacket requirement, you will need to be trained in the site-specific policy and procedure for life jacket sizing and distribution.

## Inspections

The facility where you work should have checklist forms for you to use if you are responsible for inspecting a water attraction. Inspections are usually conducted each morning before opening. Even if you know that the attraction has been inspected, stay alert for problems that may develop during the day. Look for and report to your supervisor any of the following:

- Cracks
- Loose bolts
- Missing or broken pieces
- Nonfunctioning parts
- Unusual noises
- Increased frequency of injury or patron complaints
- Anything different or unusual

Besides knowing the rules for using water-park attractions and inspecting them, you must also adjust your surveillance techniques when guarding in a water park.

> **Notify your supervisor if you identify attraction hazards.**

# Surveillance Strategy at Water Parks

The specific features of a water attraction may affect your scanning pattern or posture. For example, the waterfalls and sprays of a children's play area may block your view from a stationary chair and make it necessary for you to walk or stand within the zone to scan. A sitting position at a wave pool may be adequate when the waves are off, but when the waves begin, a standing position may offer you a better view of the zone. The curves of a river-current attraction may make it necessary for you to walk the zone in order to cover all areas. Let's look at four common kinds of water attractions and how you should plan to guard them: slides, river-current features, wave pools, and other types of features.

## Waterslide Considerations

Injury trends indicate that the large majority of injuries at water parks happen on waterslides. The most common are impact injuries that involve any of the following:

- A patron's body hitting against a slide terminus
- A patron colliding with another person
- A patron's tube flipping, causing the rider to hit the slide

When lifeguarding at a waterslide, your zone will usually be the catch pool or run-out. However, some waterslides have sections of catch pools where riders briefly stop the descent until the flow pushes them into the next section of the ride. Depending on the manufacturer's recommendations, lifeguards may need to be placed at these catch pool areas.

### Slide Terminus

Your responsibilities in a slide catch pool, run-out, or splashdown area may include the following:

- Helping patrons regain balance or stand up after landing
- Scanning for distress or drowning symptoms
- Helping patrons manage tubes as they make their way to the exit
- Directing patrons out of the slide path
- Enforcing rules and reminding patrons of ride procedures
- Keeping nonriders out of the splashdown or catch pool area
- Communicating, via hand or flag signals, with the dispatch lifeguard or attendant

If you are assigned to the catch pool, you are responsible for watching sliders enter the water and then following their path all the way to the exit. You are also responsible for scanning the catch pool to make sure someone has not entered the water from the side or stairs rather than by coming down the slide.

The procedure at your facility will determine whether you guard from an in-water or on-deck position at a slide catch pool (see figure 15.1). Many slide catch pools can be effectively covered from a seated or standing position on the deck.

To provide surveillance for the zone, you must be positioned so you can see the entire area, including the stairs and exit points. The amount of head turn necessary to allow you to see the entire zone will vary depending on your position and the size of the catch pool, but generally it will be less than that needed for scanning a traditional pool. You will also deal with only a few patrons at a time, depending

**FIGURE 15.1** This lifeguard is at an in-water catch pool position.

on how many sliders enter the catch pool, and for only the few seconds it takes them to exit the area.

If you are in the catch pool, your additional duties would include communicating with the dispatch lifeguard or attendant, enforcing slide rules and procedures, and keeping nonriders out of the catch pool.

Remember that your safety is always a consideration. If you stand too close to the direct slide path, you could suffer an injury from a collision with a slider. The current in the direct slide path is likely to be strong and could cause you to lose your balance or footing.

### Slide Dispatch

The length of time it takes patrons to ride down the slide and then move out of the slide path determines dispatch (controlling and timing riders). Usually, a lifeguard or attendant at the top of the slide who can see the lifeguard monitoring the catch pool or run-out area controls when riders start down the slide (see figure 15.2). If you are in charge of dispatch, your responsibilities may include the following:

- Monitoring riders for height, size, age, ability, or other rider criteria that the slide manufacturer or your facility has set (height sticks, signs marked with the minimum requirement, and prescreening guests to identify eligible riders with wrist bands help with this task)
- Helping riders get into position on tubes or mats
- Scanning for distress or drowning symptoms
- Instructing riders in proper body position for the slide
- Issuing "go" commands when it is safe to dispatch

FIGURE 15.2 A lifeguard in a slide dispatch position.

Modify your scanning strategy and communication signals for the needs of the attraction.

- Controlling the emergency stop (E-stop) to shut off water flow during an emergency
- Monitoring severe weather conditions
- Clearing patrons from the slide tower in the event of severe weather or other emergencies
- Communicating, via hand or flag signals, with the catch pool lifeguard

## Flowing Current Considerations

A zone on a lazy river or torrent river usually includes a length of the river, with the lifeguard located in the middle so half the zone is upriver and half the zone is downriver. Because the river attraction is narrow, your scanning pattern will be from side to side. Even though the river is shallow, you should still scan the bottom and use changes in posture such as alternating sitting, standing, and strolling to help you stay alert (see figure 15.3).

The presence of tubes in a river-current attraction may limit your ability to see under the surface of the water. Pay particular attention to the entry and exit areas of the river where tubes may get jammed and could possibly trap small children underneath. Keep these areas free of tubes. Your responsibilities at a river-current attraction may include the following:

**FIGURE 15.3** Surveillance on a flowing current attraction.

- Directing patrons to enter and exit at designated points along the river (multiple or controlled entry and exit areas minimize patron and tube congestion)
- Helping patrons get in or out of tubes
- Enforcing rules and reminding patrons of ride procedures
- Pulling out unused tubes

## Wave Pool Considerations

A wave pool is essentially a flat-water pool part of the time and a flat-water pool with water movement when the waves are on. When lifeguarding in either condition, you will be assigned a specific zone that is your area of coverage. This area should be small enough that you can get to the farthest point in about 20 seconds and small enough and without obstructions so you can scan the area within 10 seconds.

One difference between wave pools and regular pools is the sudden shift in patron use. Most wave pools are equipped with a signal that gives a 15- to 30-second warning before the wave action starts. When the signal for the wave action begins, patrons who do not want to be in the water when the waves are on will leave the wave pool, and patrons who have been waiting for the waves to start will enter if they are not already in the pool. You need to be extra vigilant during these times.

The size of the wave pool, the crowded conditions, patrons moving in and out of the water, and the wave action all combine to make scanning, targeting, and rescuing more difficult than at traditional pools (see figure 15.4).

Wave pools provide various types of waves depending on the equipment used. Some wave machines create a back-and-forth water movement on the surface; others create a series of realistic cresting waves that patrons can surf. Your facility orientation should include a description of the types of waves your machinery generates, the water depth in the wave pool during waves and during calm, the timing of wave sequences, and the locations and use of the E-stop buttons that shut down the wave action.

Your wave pool responsibilities may include the following:

- Scanning for distress or drowning symptoms
- Monitoring the entrance and exit to the wave pool and restricting entrance and exit to the beach area only, not from the sides
- Monitoring and restricting use around or near wave chamber outlets or intakes
- Enforcing rules

FIGURE 15.4 A wave pool rescue and carry.

### Other Attractions

Inflatable slides, cable drops, rope challenges, climbing walls, and children's play structures are some of the common attractions found in aquatic facilities. Each of these attractions comes with the manufacturer's guidelines for use. Your facility may add its own specific rules or procedures. Learn the rules and prevention strategies for all the attraction areas at the facility where you lifeguard.

Your main priority will always be to scan for distress or drowning symptoms, target when you see symptoms, assess the situation, and decide to act. Let's now discuss how to adapt your response, rescue, and emergency care skills in a water park setting.

# Response, Rescue, and Emergency Care at Water Parks

The currents, waves, noise, large spaces, and crowded conditions at aquatic attractions can all affect your response. This is why you must practice rescue scenarios in a variety of conditions at the facility where you work. The more familiar you are with the conditions, the easier it will be for you to adapt your emergency care and rescue skills to meet the objective of the rescue.

**Practice your emergency action plan at each attraction.**

### Communication Systems for Water-Park Lifeguards

Hand or flag signals work best when communicating between a catch pool and the top of the slide. At some facilities visual signals are combined with whistle commands. However, signals that rely only on sound can become difficult to hear when the facility is crowded or when the water is rushing out of the slide. For these reasons, a visual signal is preferred—which means the dispatch guard and the catch pool guard must be positioned so they can see each other.

You also must be aware of the location and use of emergency stop buttons that will quickly shut off water flow or wave action. Your facility's emergency action plans detail how and when to activate the E-stop.

**Know the location of the E-stop device to shut down water flow or wave action.**

### STAAR at Water Parks

The StarGuard aquatic rescue model (STAAR) can be used to illustrate what might need to be adapted at a water park or facility with play features so you can effectively see and respond to an emergency.

■ **Scan.** You should be aware of how the attraction affects your ability to see your zone. For example, when waves are on in a wave pool, scanning in a standing position might be necessary. The long, narrow zone of a river current will require a lot of head turning to scan the zone, whereas the catch pool of a slide might not require much head turning at all because the zone is small and right in front of you. The obstructions created by a play feature may require that you stroll the zone to see all areas. As you become familiar with each attraction at your facility, you will be able to identify positions and scanning patterns that work best.

■ **Target.** To help you target potential emergency situations, you should be aware of behaviors that might be unique to various attractions. For example, in a wave pool you might notice a patron get knocked over by an oncoming wave or get a mouthful of water when submerged by a wave. In a river current, you might notice a patron fall off a tube, be struggling with a tube, or be completely motionless. In a slide catch pool you might hear a person cough after getting a nose-full of water or notice the person struggling to stand. These are examples of behaviors that could catch your eye and cause you to assess the situation. As you become familiar with each attraction at the facility where you work, you will notice patterns in patron behavior that will help you target unusual situations.

■ **Assess.** You should be aware of what information must be determined when you scan. When you assess the condition of patrons at various water-play attractions, you are in essence asking yourself questions about the situation and deciding whether you need to act. For example, if you target a woman who gets knocked over by a wave or is unable to initially get her footing after exiting a slide, the question you ask yourself might be *Can the woman get up on her own?* If you assess that she cannot, then you decide to act. In a river-current attraction, the question you ask yourself might be *Is this man relaxing and asleep as he floats by, or is he unresponsive?* If you suspect he is unresponsive, then you decide to act. As you become familiar with each attraction at the facility where you work, you will develop the ability to assess the conditions of patrons based on the circumstances.

■ **Alert.** You should be aware of any additional actions needed at an attraction when you alert others that you have identified a distressed or drowning person. For example, at a wave pool you may need to push an E-stop button to stop the waves, or at a slide you may need to signal to the dispatch person to stop the flow of riders. As you become familiar with each attraction at the facility where you work, you will know the procedure for alerting others and activating the emergency action plan.

■ **Rescue.** You should be aware of how the conditions at an attraction might affect your ability to make a rescue and provide emergency care. For example, making a rescue in a wave pool when the waves are off may be different from making a rescue when the waves are on. Currents created at the bottom of slides may make in-water rescues more difficult. The only way to obtain this information is to practice rescue scenarios at each attraction at the facility where you work.

Let's look at some strategies that will be helpful in the various types of water park attractions.

## Waterslide Considerations

- If your facility protocol calls for backboarding patrons with a suspected spinal injury, it may be necessary to backboard or provide other emergency care in a slide run-out, in a catch pool, at the top of a slide, in a moving current, or in another situation. Using the objectives of spinal injury management as your foundation, adapt the backboarding procedures to the conditions at the attraction.
- Signal the dispatch guard or attendant to push the E-stop to prevent other patrons from sliding into your rescue scene.
- Keep hold of the rescue tube, and remember to keep it between you and the other person at all times; it is likely that you will lose your balance and footing if you are in the path of the slide run-out.
- Spinal injury or sudden illness can occur inside the slide trough as well as on or at the base of the slide tower; practice rescue scenarios in these locations (see figure 15.5).
- Practice performing scenarios with unresponsive victims in the catch pool and run-out area as well as at the top of the tower.

FIGURE 15.5 Spinal injury management in a slide trough.

## Flowing Current Considerations

- The pull of the current may complicate a rescue in a river-current attraction. Enter the water upstream of the distressed swimmer or drowning victim, and let the current move you to the person; if you jump in downstream, you will have to fight your way back against the current.

- The water depth in river attractions is usually shallow; always enter feet-first with an ease-in entry or compact jump from the side.

- When you make contact with the person, don't try to fight the current, but rather move with the water flow to a takeout point.

- For a suspected spinal injury or to perform rescue breathing in the water, hit the E-stop to turn off the water flow, and position yourself with your back to the current and the injured person so the water is flowing from head to toe to help support her body.

- If the current is too strong, stop trying to stand on the bottom; float with the person while performing rescue breathing.

- If possible, your backup team should be prepared to follow you to an appropriate takeout point rather than making you fight the current to get to a designated spot.

## Wave Pool Considerations

- Push the E-stop button as part of your alert response, and point toward the intended location of your rescue.

- Because the wave action of the water may not stop right away, time your compact jump so you enter the water at the height of the wave where the water is deepest rather than at the trough where the water may be shallow.

- Be prepared to swim around and through a crowd of swimmers and tubes.

- Be prepared for longer extrication times in a wave pool because of the large size of the area, crowded conditions, wave action, and other factors. When rescuing an unresponsive victim in the deeper area of the wave pool, farthest from the entry point, you will probably not be able to extricate the person to the beach entry or deck within 30 seconds. Therefore, you should be prepared to begin rescue breathing in the water while you make progress to the safe point of exit.

- When placing the ventilation mask on the drowning victim, make a good seal to prevent the wave action from pushing water into the victim's nose and mouth.

- Because the wave action may not stop right away, practice rescues with the waves on to become comfortable with the movement and the effort required to perform rescue breathing in the waves.

■ Practice extrication methods that are practical for the zero-depth beachfront area, such as those described in chapter 16. Usually, the safest and most effective way to extricate a person from a wave pool is to exit at the beachfront zero-depth entry. The sides of a wave pool are usually very high, with the deck several feet from the water surface. Stairs may or may not be built into the side walls, but when side-wall stairs are present, they tend to be narrow and steep.

## Emergency Care Considerations

Many large water parks have supervisory or EMS personnel on site who respond to a call for emergency care such as CPR or spinal injury management. In these situations, your role would be one of the support team. This is why it is important to practice emergency care scenarios with the personnel who would respond if it were a real situation, so you can work together as a team and know your responsibilities before an incident occurs.

Now let's consider what you can expect, and what will be expected of you, at the water-park workplace.

# Water-Park Workplace Expectations

The crowds that attend water parks spotlight your need to present a professional image and be a role model to the guests in your care. Set a good example whenever you enjoy the water attractions at your facility. If you use the attractions, either during or outside of operating hours, follow the rules and regulations as though you were a patron.

A water-park lifeguard team dressed in their professional attire.

In some ways, lifeguarding at a facility with play features or water-park attractions is easier than lifeguarding at a traditional pool. It's easier to maintain a high level of anticipation and vigilance when there is a lot of action. In other ways, lifeguarding at a water park is more difficult. There are many more distractions in a water-park environment. The noise of the crowd, the noise created by the slides or waves, and the activity level can all entice you to watch the fun rather than your zone. Be prepared to deal with and tune out these distractions.

Water parks usually have a large number of lifeguards on duty at any given time, and you will operate as part of a team. Because there are so many attractions, in-service training will likely be on a continual basis and include site-specific operational procedures, customer service training, vigilance and scanning drills, rescue scenarios, and physical conditioning. It is also likely that you will participate in frequent reviews (audits) of your performance while you are on the job.

## ★ Knowledge Into Practice

While the basic concepts and skills of lifeguarding apply in most situations, there are unique demands at water parks and water-park-like features in similar spaces. You will need to understand how to adapt your skills to meet varying needs.

## @ Visit the Web Resource

You can reinforce your learning by visiting the web resource, where you can do the following in the interactive online learning activities for chapter 15:

▶ Activity 15.1: Respond to simulated scenarios at a waterslide, a wave pool, and a flowing current attraction.
▶ Activity 15.2: View videos of lifeguards scanning various water-park features.
▶ Activity 15.3: View videos of lifeguards performing rescue scenarios at water parks.
▶ Activity 15.4: Chapter quiz. Test your knowledge, receive feedback, and print the quiz page.

## ✚ On the Job

These are the tasks related to lifeguarding at water parks that you will be expected to competently perform while working as a lifeguard:

▶ Adapt prevention strategy.
▶ Modify surveillance methods.
▶ Adjust aquatic rescue and emergency care.
▶ Identify best practices to meet the site-specific needs of a water park or facility with similar features.

## CHAPTER 16

# Lifeguarding at Nonsurf Waterfronts

## CHAPTER OBJECTIVES

This chapter

- ▶ identifies features of a nonsurf waterfront;
- ▶ identifies additional prevention, surveillance, response, rescue, and emergency care procedures for the waterfront setting; and
- ▶ reinforces workplace safety and performance expectations for the waterfront setting.

If you will work at a waterfront, you must complete the waterfront training module in addition to the basic StarGuard course. The waterfront module may be taught at the same time as your StarGuard course or presented as a separate training session. Each section of this chapter covers a StarGuard risk management model component as it applies to lifeguarding at waterfronts. *Note:* The material presented in this chapter supplements the other chapters in this text.

## Waterfront Features

A waterfront, for purposes of the StarGuard lifeguard training program, is a restricted swimming area enclosed by lines, docks, or piers within an open body of water and the accompanying beach. The waterfront designation applies to non-surf bodies of water such as lakes, ponds, and rivers and does not include ocean lifeguarding.

Lifeguards who work at a surf or nonrestricted waterfront, such as an ocean beach with no enclosed swim area, must have additional open-water and surf rescue skills that are outside the scope of the StarGuard training program. Open-water or surf rescue training for beach lifeguards usually is conducted by the agency responsible for providing protection at the beach and should follow the guidelines of the International Life Saving Federation (ILS) or the ILS-affiliated organization in your area, such as the United States Lifesaving Association (USLA) or the Royal Life Saving Society of Australia (RLS). Many agencies that operate surf beaches use StarGuard training as a prerequisite and then provide additional USLA-accredited or other surf rescue training as the operating standard of care. If you work at a surf or nonrestricted waterfront, you must obtain this site-specific training from your employer.

Each waterfront will have its own natural characteristics, but common features include the following:

- ■ Turbid (dark) water that prevents being able to see or identify anything under the surface
- ■ Uncontrollable environmental conditions such as weather, temperature, wildlife, moving and turbulent water, varying water depths from tides or dams, unstable bottom conditions, and rocks and other submerged hazards
- ■ Locations that may have long EMS response times

The unique features at a nonsurf waterfront require additional site-specific skills. Let's start by looking at ways to reduce risk at a waterfront setting.

# Prevention Strategy at Waterfronts

Waterfront areas present unique risks that you must manage in order to provide a safe environment for swimmers. Some ways to manage risks are inspecting sites frequently and choosing appropriate areas for aquatic activities. Other prevention strategies include preparing participants for waterfront aquatic activities.

## Site Inspections

Because hazards at outdoor water areas often change over time, you must check frequently for hazards. Depending on your location, your responsibilities for a site inspection may include the following:

- Clear the beach or swim area of debris, such as glass, cans, branches, hooks, food and drink containers, and human or animal waste.
- Check that appropriate rescue equipment is available, which for protected waterfronts may include rescue watercraft, masks, fins, snorkels, scuba gear, waterproof flashlights, search nets, and binoculars.
- Place equipment in a rescue-ready position. Determine the best rescue-ready position by conducting rescue scenarios. After each scenario, evaluate how long it took the rescue equipment to reach the scene and how practical it is to keep equipment in various locations.
- Check that appropriate communication equipment is available, which for protected waterfronts may include two-way radios, a bullhorn, a public address system, flags, cell phones (if service is available), or other means to communicate with patrons across open spaces.
- Make sure you can receive cell phone and radio signals before you need them in an emergency. Keep in mind that when dialing 9-1-1 from a cell phone in the United States, you may reach an emergency dispatch service in a different county than you expected.
- Monitor the environment. Post or announce weather and water conditions along with warnings about restricted areas.
- Swim and walk the area to identify holes, drop-offs, rocks, or other hazards.
- Identify currents.
- Identify underwater obstructions.
- Check the water level and depth.
- Check the depth under floating docks; the water depth at lakes linked to dam systems can change significantly from day to day.

> Frequently inspect waterfront swimming areas for hazards.

## Screening Swimmers and Mandatory Life Jacket Use

When it is necessary to assign people to swimming areas, you must first assess their swimming abilities by screening them. You should also assess swimming ability during group outings to a water area before allowing people to participate in water activities in which the water is more than waist deep. Don't rely on a swimmer's assessment of his own swimming ability before testing. The purpose of the skills screening is to identify participants who do not have the endurance or ability to comfortably keep their heads above water without a life jacket.

A skills test must reflect the skills needed for the activity and conditions. As an example of a general skills screening, consider asking participants to swim approximately 25 yards (or meters) and to tread water without using their hands for 1 minute. Your objective is to have each participant demonstrate to you in a measurable way a swimming ability appropriate for the activity. To conduct a skills screening in a waterfront setting, follow these guidelines:

- Choose specific screening activities appropriate for your environment. Your test must reflect the skills needed for the activity and conditions.
- Choose a screening area in which the water is no more than waist deep for the participants.
- The screening area should be free of sudden drop-offs or submerged objects such as logs or other debris.
- Conduct screenings near the shoreline or along a dock.
- Participants should enter the water feetfirst.

Assign the swimmers, based on the results of the screening, to either a swimming area or a nonswimming area. You might also require that nonswimmers use a life jacket. Document the results of the swim tests. Include the date, time, and each swimmer's name, age, and skills assessment outcome.

When managing large groups, consider using some type of identification that shows which people belong in which areas. In restricted waterfront settings, one way to do this is to provide a wristband or breakaway necklace to each patron who has completed skills screening. Use one color to designate a swimmer and another to designate a nonswimmer.

## Buddy System and Buddy Check

Another useful surveillance strategy is using a buddy system and calling for frequent safety breaks, during which all patrons get out of the water for a short time. In a buddy system, pair swimmers by ability. If the pair's ability is not equal, the less skilled swimmer defines the swim area for that pair. Buddy swimmers must stay within sight of each other at all times. To identify which buddies are swimming and which have left the swim area, use one of the following methods:

- Keep a buddy board or swimmer chart on a notepad; buddy pairs must check in and check out with the specified staff person in charge of the chart.
- Designate two ball caps as "in" and "out"; swimmers place their names in the hat that designates their swimming status.
- Have each swimmer leave a similar article of clothing, such as a shirt or cap, in a designated area to indicate to staff which swimmers are in and out.

Besides using a buddy system, you may want to use a buddy check (also called a safety break) as well. Simply signal a check after a set amount of time, asking all participants to get out of the water. A buddy check takes less than 1 minute to implement and allows you to make sure all participants are present and accounted for. Preassigned buddies or small groups account for each other.

## Surveillance Strategy at Waterfronts

In most waterfront settings, you cannot scan the bottom because the water is turbid, so it becomes even more important to keep nonswimmers in shallow water, wearing life jackets if feasible, and to keep track of all swimmers. Setting up clear boundaries for safe swimming and nonswimming areas, screening people to assess their swimming skills, and conducting buddy checks and safety breaks will help you accomplish this. In waterfront settings, it may also be helpful for someone to provide surveillance from a watercraft, floating dock, or platform.

Depending on the layout of your waterfront, swimming areas and nonswimming areas may be marked using buoy lines or a combination of piers, docks, and lines. When possible, divide the water into areas for specific uses, such as swimming, diving, and sliding. Communicate to participants through signs, visual markings, and verbal safety briefings the clear boundaries between the swimming areas and nonswimming areas.

When you guard in a waterfront area, keep track of patrons by doing the following:

- Maintain a constant count of patrons in your zone with each scan or sweep.
- Visually follow the path of patrons swimming to or from floating platforms.
- Allow only one diver or slider to enter the water at a time. Allow subsequent divers or sliders to enter only after you have seen the preceding diver or slider return to the surface and move out of the entry area.
- If it helps you, mentally sort swimmers into groups according to ability, age, or risk factors during successive scans.
- Do not allow prolonged underwater swimming or breath-holding games.
- If flotation devices such as rafts or noodles are allowed, pay particular attention to those using these devices, and restrict their use to people who have passed the skills screening.

> **Restrict non-swimmers to water that is less than waist deep, or require them to wear life jackets.**

## Guarding From a Rescue Watercraft

Guarding the area from a watercraft in the water is another way to keep track of swimmers at a waterfront. You can use watercraft at a waterfront to patrol the perimeter of a swim area or to serve as an anchored surveillance position. Watercraft can be human powered, such as a paddleboard, kayak, canoe, or rowboat, or motor powered, such as a personal watercraft (e.g., Jet Ski), inflatable boat, or small motorboat (see figure 16.1). Your facility should provide you with an orientation

**FIGURE 16.1** Guarding from a sit-on kayak.

and instruction in safety practices for the specific watercraft you might use. You should also practice rescue scenarios using the watercraft.

For motor-powered watercraft, it is ideal to have two lifeguards on each craft: one serving as an operator and one providing surveillance. When this is not possible and the operator also provides surveillance, it is important to have a good communication device, such as an air horn or radio. Rescue watercraft should carry the following equipment:

- Life jackets for each occupant and at least one extra life jacket for a potential passenger
- Oars or paddles
- Lines (ropes)
- Flotation devices that can be thrown
- A rescue tube
- A bailer (except for a paddleboard, sit-on kayak, or Jet-Ski)
- A waist pack or kit with a ventilation mask, gloves, and first aid supplies
- Water or fluids for hydration
- Communication devices (e.g., whistle, air horn, radio, signal flags)

Depending on the size of the craft, the U.S. Coast Guard might require motor-powered craft to carry additional equipment such as an anchor and line and a fire extinguisher.

## Guarding From a Floating Dock or Platform

Many waterfronts have floating docks or platforms that are for use by patrons and also serve as a lifeguard station (see figure 16.2). A means of effective communication from this position to other lifeguards is important, especially if you need help managing unruly or threatening behavior or need to enter the water to

FIGURE 16.2 Guarding from a floating dock.

make a rescue. Practice your emergency whistle or air horn signals during times of peak use to be sure others on the waterfront can hear you. When feasible, a set of first aid, emergency response, and search equipment should be present on the station for quick access.

Be sure to prohibit patrons from swimming under the dock or platform or into areas where you cannot see them.

# Response, Rescue, and Emergency Care at Waterfronts

Providing response, rescue, and emergency care may be more difficult at waterfronts than at pools because of the natural environment and the distance between the site and emergency help. However, by preparing for rescues, developing emergency action plans and methods for search and rescue (and search and recover), and determining safe ways to perform rescues, your organization should be ready to deal with these circumstances.

At waterfronts, preparation should include training on the communication system that is in place and how to use underwater search equipment such as a mask or goggles, fins, and a snorkel.

## Communication System for Waterfront Lifeguards

Waterfront swimming areas can become noisy. You need some means besides yelling to communicate with participants and other lifeguards or rescuers. Systems include hand or whistle signals or a combination of the two, megaphones, and other signaling devices such as flags, air horns, two-way radios, and cell phones. You and the other lifeguards or rescuers must agree on what the signals mean before allowing participants to enter the water.

## Mask, Fins, and Snorkel

Wearing a swim mask will let you see better under the water when performing a rescue or conducting an underwater search. Here are some tips for using a mask:

- Be sure the mask fits correctly, forming a watertight seal around your eyes to prevent leaking. If a mask is not available, goggles can help if you will be swimming underwater in shallow depths (under 10 feet, or 3 m) and for short periods of time. If you will be deeper, the water pressure against goggles may become uncomfortable, and you should consider using a mask.

- To prevent fogging, wipe the interior surface with an antifog agent or a small amount of saliva.

- To remove water from a leaking mask, tilt your head back slightly. Press the top of the mask faceplate toward your forehead; the bottom of the mask will move slightly away from your face. Exhale strongly through your nose to push the water out of the mask.

- To prevent or relieve mask squeeze (an uncomfortable pressure against your face and eyes when you descend) exhale small bursts of air from your nose. This air will equalize the pressure in the mask to that of the pressure in the water.

- To prevent or relieve pressure in your ears when you descend, you must equalize your ears. Choose a method that works for you: Blow gently against a pinched nose, pinch your nose and swallow, or pinch your nose and yawn.

Using a snorkel allows you to keep your face submerged as you search (see figure 16.3). Use a snorkel keeper to secure the snorkel to the head strap of your mask or goggles. Place the mouthpiece in your mouth, and hold it in place lightly with your lips and teeth. Breathe slowly and deeply. When you are ready to submerge completely and swim deeper, take a relaxed, deep breath and hold it, and pull yourself down under the water. Do not hyperventilate (caused by breathing rapidly several times and then holding your breath) before submerging.

When you surface, clear your snorkel by exhaling strongly with a short burst of air to force the water from the tube. Exhale to clear the tube only when you are sure you are at the surface and the top of the snorkel is no longer submerged. When the water has been expelled, inhale through your mouth and continue relaxed breathing.

Wearing fins will increase your propulsion through the water. Fins come in two styles: full heel and open heel, which usually requires you to wear booties. Whenever possible, put on your fins when you are in the water or at the water's edge. If you have to walk with fins on, move sideways or backward to prevent tripping. When you swim, kick with slow, smooth kicks. The movement should come from your hips, and your knees should have a slight to moderate bend, depending on the style of fin.

**FIGURE 16.3** Search swimming with a mask, a snorkel, and fins.

While swimming with a mask, a snorkel, and fins, keep your arms either in front or in a relaxed position along your sides. If you are performing a bottom search, keep your hands forward, and sweep them toward the sides to feel for the victim. To surface dive while wearing a mask, a snorkel, and fins, do the following:

1. Tuck your chin to your chest, and press your head and shoulders forward.
2. Bend your hips to roll into a pike or tuck position.
3. Lift your legs to extend your body; this movement allows you to descend headfirst. Move your hands in front of your body into the search position, which will also protect you from submerged hazards.

## Missing-Person Emergency Action Plan

A waterfront should have a specific emergency action plan (EAP) in place in case someone is reported missing. Until the person is found, there is no way to know if she is on land or submerged under the water. Customize the emergency action plan based on the site-specific waterfront, and consider these factors:

■ Number of staff available
■ Number of bystanders that are likely to be present
■ Response time of EMS or search and rescue or recover teams
■ Water depth
■ Water temperature

- Water clarity
- In-water hazards
- Search methods appropriate for the waterfront setting
- Equipment or watercraft available

Regardless of the circumstances, a missing-person EAP should include these elements:

- A specific communication signal to indicate a missing-person situation
- A designated staging area for all staff and bystanders
- Two groups of searchers: one water based and one land based; begin the water search immediately

Those searching on land should gather information about the person, including name, age, and description, and start the search in the immediate area, including the bathhouse, campsite, and parking lot. The search should then extend to the surrounding area, including woods, cabins, and outbuildings.

## Search and Rescue Versus Search and Recover

Search and rescue refers to situations in which it is likely that a missing person will be found quickly enough that survival is possible. Search and recover refers to situations in which so much time has passed that survival is unlikely.

At a waterfront, enough lifeguards and other rescuers should be available that search and rescue is your initial protocol. Search the bottom of the swim area first because your window for performing search and rescue is relatively short. For this reason, it should take no more than 5 minutes to completely search the swim area. The specific conditions at your facility—including the number of staff, equipment, water depth, availability of bystanders, and search techniques—determine how large an area you can search within this time frame and should help in establishing appropriate swim area size.

Search and rescue efforts should begin near the place where the person was last seen. If possible, visually mark the spot where the person was known to have submerged by sighting, or lining up, the spot with a stationary object on the shore. Sighting from several positions and vantage points further helps pinpoint the area. If currents are present, begin the search downstream because it is likely that the person has been pushed to a different location by the moving water.

Search and rescue efforts by lifeguards and bystanders should continue until the person is found or until a search and recover dive team (usually EMS, fire, or police professionals) arrives. When EMS arrives, continue your search until the person directing the EMS effort directs you to stop or gives other instructions. Search strategies for restricted waterfront areas may include the following:

- Dragnet search. Use a weighted net which is pulled by two rescuers along the search area. One method of constructing a dragnet is to string a weighted net on a section of PVC. The rescuers use the PVC as a handle to pull the net. Another option is for rescuers to hold the top of the net at each end. Begin the search near the person's last known location, and follow a predetermined pattern to quickly move the net across the bottom of the swimming area. You may walk or move the net while swimming as long as the net reaches the bottom.

- Grid system. Some waterfronts may have lines or markers anchored along the bottom to help when conducting an underwater search. The search team, wearing

> **If a person is missing, conduct a bottom search first.**

> **Plan and then practice search and rescue drills to determine the methods best suited to the physical conditions at your waterfront.**

masks, snorkels, and fins (or scuba gear, if trained to use such equipment), line up along each grid mark and move forward along the designated path.

■ Swimming search line. This search method is similar to the grid system but without the benefit of physical markings on the bottom. In shallow water where the bottom can be clearly seen, the search team should swim in a line, shoulder to shoulder. In deeper water, the search team should combine short surface dives to look and feel for a victim on the bottom. Surface dive to the bottom, swim and sweep with the arms for 10 to 15 feet (3 to 4.5 m), surface, back up approximately 3 to 5 feet (1 to 1.5 m), and repeat the process.

■ Walking search line. The search team forms a line, facing the direction in which the search will begin, and hooks elbows. The line of rescuers moves forward while rescuers sweep the area in front and to the side with the feet and legs.

For all search strategies, if contact with the missing person is made, the rescuer immediately stops and signals to initiate the emergency action plan.

Performing search and recovery in a setting with murky water and moving currents may be more difficult, as these conditions make a "point last seen" indistinguishable from the surrounding area. Using quick dives, you and other rescuers must rapidly search where the victim was last seen. After these first few minutes have passed, the chances of a successful recovery and resuscitation decline. However, drowning in cold water may be the exception to this case, so continue recovery attempts for up to one hour or until the situation becomes unsafe for rescuers. When someone is reported missing in conditions of murky water or currents, follow these steps:

■ Activate the emergency action plan.

■ Ask people on shore to help fix the point last seen.

■ Pick out a landmark on an opposing shore in line with the point last seen to help identify the appropriate search area.

■ Identify the time of submersion.

■ Initially search the point last seen with either an in-water search by wading and swimming; a surface search by surface swimming or using a watercraft; or an underwater search with goggles or a mask, fins, and a snorkel.

■ In turbid water conditions, using a waterproof flashlight while performing underwater swim search procedures may increase visibility.

## Rescue Approach and Entry Considerations

At a waterfront, you may need to swim a greater distance to make a rescue than in a pool. To save time, you may want to run down the shoreline to a position in line with the person and then enter the water. If the person is more than 30 feet (9 m) from you, it may be faster to swim trailing the rescue tube than holding it. Stop about 10 feet (3 m) from the person, pull your rescue tube into position, and then complete the rescue.

Depending on the circumstances and equipment available, a swimming water rescue may be your last choice. The phrase "reach, throw, row, and go" identifies water rescue options in order of preference:

1. **Reach.** Extend a rope, flotation device, or pole to the person.

2. **Throw.** Throw a rope or flotation device to the person.

3. **Row.** Use a rescue watercraft to row or motor to the person, and use the boat as a rescue platform.

4. **Go.** Swim out, and perform an in-water rescue.

Throwing a buoy or rope can be effective, but often it is difficult for the person to find and maintain contact with a thrown object. There is also the chance of injury if you hit the person with the device. When throwing an object, aim behind and upwind of the person (and upstream in moving water). Then pull the object toward the person. If you aim in front and fall short, you will waste valuable time pulling in the line and rethrowing.

When making a water rescue, you must decide how to enter the water based on your distance from the person and his condition. Use a compact jump when you are jumping from a height into water of any depth where there may be underwater obstructions. Use a protected water entry when entering from water level (see figure 16.4).

The protected water entry is a modified bellyflop, which will help you stay on the surface and protect your face and neck from possible injury. To perform this entry, do the following:

FIGURE 16.4 Protected water entry.

1. When you are about knee deep, push off with your legs and lean forward.

2. Arch your back and cross your arms in front of your face.

3. Your chest and abdomen should enter the water first. The more you are able to stay on the surface, the better you will be able to maintain a constant view of the person's position in the water.

## Shoreline Extrication

Injured, ill, or unconscious people may need to be removed from the water or moved to another location away from the water's edge. Always lift with your legs, keeping your back straight and bending your knees. Keep your center of gravity low and the weight of the victim close to your body. Factors that may affect the type of extrication method you choose include the following:

- Presence and size of waterfront obstructions, such as rocks and trees
- Size of the victim
- Whether or not you will use spinal injury precautions
- Height from the water to the shore
- Equipment available
- Number of people available to assist

# Shoreline Extrication (Nonspinal)

### ◀ One-Rescuer Assist

Use this method if a person is responsive and can walk. Place the person's arm around your shoulders and your arm around his waist. Provide support and assistance as needed as you walk out. A second rescuer can move to the other side of the injured person to provide additional support.

### Seat Carry ▶

This method requires two or three rescuers. Use it if a person is conscious but cannot walk. Two rescuers are at the person's upper body and place the person's arms around their shoulders. If there are only two rescuers and the injured person's size allows, rescuers can create a "seat" by joining hands under the person's upper legs and lifting. If a third rescuer is available, he can hold the person's legs and help carry the person out.

### ◀ Cradle Carry

Use for a small responsive or unresponsive person. Hold the person just above the knees. Cradle your arm around the middle of her back.

### Two-Person Extremity Carry ▶

Use for a responsive or unresponsive person. One rescuer gets behind the person and prepares to lift by grasping under the person's arms. The second rescuer stands at the person's feet, between the legs, facing away from the person. This rescuer grasps the person's ankles and pulls them into her body for support. For a larger person, back up and hold under the knees. Both rescuers lift the person at the same time and walk forward, with the rescuer at the feet leading the way.

### ◀ Beach Drag

One or more rescuers use this extrication method if a person is unresponsive. Hold the person under the armpits. Walk backward out of the water and up onto the beach.

Do the following after you reach the shoreline:

- On a sloping beach, kneel with your back to the water for better evaluation and so you do not fall over the victim.
- Pull the victim far enough on shore to avoid incoming waves.
- Place the victim parallel to the waterline, with the head the same level as the rest of the body. This position reduces the risk of vomiting.

## Emergency Care Considerations

Conditions specific to waterfront areas may affect how you manage an unresponsive drowning victim. You must be prepared for a potentially long EMS response time and to extricate an unresponsive drowning victim at a shoreline. The equipment you have available and the number of rescuers or bystanders you have to help will determine the techniques you use to get an unresponsive drowning victim onto land to begin emergency care.

In rural waterfront areas where delayed emergency medical system response times can be expected, you must plan your emergency procedures accordingly. For example, if your emergency oxygen equipment is capable of administering 15 minutes of oxygen and you can expect a 20-minute response, you should have an extra tank or two on site.

Here are additional considerations to take into account when working in a waterfront setting:

- Consider the effects the shoreline may have on rescue equipment. For example, sand will stick to a CPR mask placed on the ground and will be difficult to remove quickly.
- Continue CPR as long as possible for a victim who has drowned in cold water. Survival, even after long submersion times, is more likely if the water is cold.
- Continue CPR and rescue breathing as long as possible for people who have been struck by lightning.
- Collect a sample of the water from all drowning events that require resuscitation. The water may be needed to determine if contamination was present, which can be helpful for postresuscitative care.
- Monitor drowning survivors closely until EMS arrives because complications can occur after resuscitation, especially when a victim has been submerged in saltwater.

# Waterfront Workplace Expectations

Be aware of how cold water, which is often present in waterfront areas, can affect your endurance and swimming skills. Wear a wetsuit during training activities to prevent hypothermia, and maintain your physical conditioning through regular exercise.

If the waterfront workplace is remote, you may have certain times during the day when there are no guests present. It will be important to remain vigilant and perform best practices, even if you and other lifeguards are the only people present.

## ⭐ Knowledge Into Practice

While the basic concepts and skills of lifeguarding apply in most situations, there are unique demands at waterfronts. You will need to understand how to adapt your skills to meet varying needs.

## @ Visit the Web Resource

You can reinforce your learning by visiting the web resource, where you can do the following in the interactive online learning activities for chapter 16:

- ▶ Activity 16.1: Click on a waterfront setting and identify hazards and zone problems.
- ▶ Activity 16.2: Equip the lifeguard with items needed to conduct a search, make a rescue, and provide emergency care in a waterfront setting.
- ▶ Activity 16.3: Evaluate scenarios and identify how to adapt skills to the waterfront setting.
- ▶ Activity 16.4: Chapter quiz. Test your knowledge, receive feedback, and print the quiz page.

## On the Job

These are the tasks related to lifeguarding at waterfronts that you will be expected to competently perform while working as a lifeguard:

- ▶ Adapt prevention strategy.
- ▶ Modify surveillance methods.
- ▶ Adjust aquatic rescue and emergency care.
- ▶ Identify best practices to meet the site-specific needs of a waterfront.

······························································

# Emergency Oxygen

······························································

**D**rowning causes a forced respiratory arrest (breathing stops). With each heartbeat, oxygen is removed from the blood until it is essentially zero, at which time cardiac arrest occurs (heart stops), and eventually irreversible brain damage develops.

In drowning casualties, especially children, the primary cause of cardiac arrest is hypoxic respiratory arrest. Therefore, when available, treatment should be to treat this underlying cause with emergency supplemental oxygen. The use of emergency supplemental oxygen is not recommended for routine use in other first aid situations.

It is reasonable to provide emergency oxygen for a responsive drowning victim who has been pulled from the water before going into cardiac arrest, but has symptoms from hypoxia. Symptoms of hypoxia include:

- cough,
- foam at the mouth or nose,
- low oxygen saturation (as measured by a pulse oximeter), and
- altered mental status.

For the drowning victim who is not breathing, emergency oxygen fed into a barrier mask during CPR enriches the oxygen concentration of the breath being blown into the victim by the rescuer. In either case, the amount of oxygen available to the victim is greatly increased.

## Oxygen in Emergency Care Versus Medical Care

Over the years there has been confusion about the legal regulations in the United States con-cerning the use of emergency oxygen and the need for a prescription. All oxygen cylinders are filled with what is known as medical-grade oxygen, as established by the United States Pharmacopeia (USP). The type of equipment that is attached to the cylinder and the intended use determine any restrictions or prescription requirements.

Oxygen equipment intended for emergency use (see figure A.1) can be purchased over the counter (OTC) without a prescription, and anyone properly instructed in the use of emergency

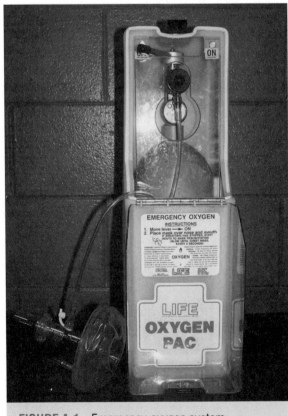

**FIGURE A.1** Emergency oxygen system.

Reprinted and adapted selected text, by permission, from American Safety and Health Institute with Human Kinetics, 2007, *Complete emergency care* (Champaign, IL: Human Kinetics), 141-155.

oxygen can administer it. Requirements for emergency-use equipment are as follows:

■ Emergency oxygen is in a portable cylinder with a regulator that provides oxygen for a minimum of 15 minutes.

■ The device has a constant fixed-flow rate of not less than 6 liters per minute.

■ A content indicator gauge is present to determine how much oxygen is in the cylinder.

■ The device is labeled "emergency" and has operation instructions.

■ A mask with a connection for oxygen tubing is supplied for oxygen administration.

The U.S. Food and Drug Administration (FDA), the regulatory agency for medical gases, requires that labeling for all oxygen equipment bear the following statement: "WARNING: For emergency use only when administered by properly trained personnel for oxygen deficiency and resuscitation. For all other applications: CAUTION: Federal law prohibits dispensing without prescription."

Even though the regulations at the federal level in the United States allow the use of emergency oxygen without a prescription, your local requirements may vary. Check the regulations that govern oxygen equipment or use in your location.

If oxygen equipment is not intended for emergency use and is capable of providing less than 6 liters per minute, it requires a prescription. The Food and Drug Administration requires a doctor's prescription for use of oxygen in medical applications, such as for people with chronic lung disease or other conditions that require a varied flow and dosage of oxygen supply under the direction of a medical professional. The physician's staff or other personnel (e.g., EMS) may administer it as prescribed by the physician. Oxygen for medical use has a flow rate of 0 to 25 liters per minute that is controlled at the discretion of the operator.

The training you receive as part of lifeguard training is general in nature. To be considered properly trained to administer emergency oxygen, you must also have specific knowledge of the equipment you will use. You will need to become familiar with the manufacturer's directions and instructional materials provided with your system.

## Components of an Emergency Oxygen System

An emergency oxygen system consists of these main components (see figure A.2):

■ The *cylinder* holds the oxygen under pressure.

■ The *regulator* controls how fast the oxygen flows from the cylinder.

■ The *gauge* indicates how much oxygen is in the cylinder.

■ The *tubing* carries the oxygen to the delivery point.

■ The *delivery mask* is placed on the person's face so that oxygen can enter the person through the mouth, nose, or both.

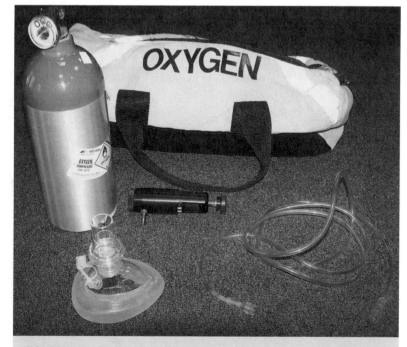

FIGURE A.2 Components of an oxygen system.

■ The *case* safely secures the cylinder and other components.

## Cylinder

The cylinder is constructed of steel or aluminum and is painted green for easy identification. Cylinders come in various sizes, identified by a letter such as C, D, or E. The size determines how much oxygen the cylinder can hold. Most emergency systems use a C-size cylinder, which provides about a 40-minute supply of oxygen.

A valve stem located on top of the cylinder is where the regulator is attached so that oxygen can safely flow out or where a filling device is attached to put oxygen back in. The valve stem has a special pin mount to prevent the cylinder from being filled with anything other than USP medical-grade oxygen. A washer is located at the connection point to help maintain a good seal; the washer is made of plastic, Teflon, nylon, or rubber with a metal ring.

The valve stem is used to turn the oxygen flow on and off. A handle may be built in, or a handle wrench may be needed. The handle wrench is supplied with the unit and should be securely attached with a chain.

When the oxygen supply runs out, most cylinders are refillable, although some are designed for one-time use and are disposable.

## Regulator

A regulator is a device that attaches to the valve stem and decreases the content pressure to a safe delivery rate. Delivery rate is expressed in liters per minute (LPM or L/M). The regulator is tightened against the valve stem by turning a T-handle at the side of the regulator, and the oxygen flows out of the regulator through a tapered hose barb. You should know about and recognize the various types of regulators available so you can select the one that is appropriate for your level of training. In the United States, emergency oxygen systems must use a fixed flow regulator.

Regulators come in three types:

■ *Fixed flow* is the required regulator for use with emergency oxygen. Depending on the setting (6 or 12 LPM), such a system delivers a fixed flow of oxygen at a precise rate that cannot be adjusted. The oxygen constantly flows out at the fixed rate until it is turned off.

■ *Variable flow* is the most common regulator used by medical professionals. It requires the user to set the amount of oxygen delivered from 0 to 25 LPM based on the patient's need, the delivery device used, and protocol. The oxygen flows out constantly at the adjusted rate until it is turned off.

■ *Demand regulators* deliver oxygen only when the person breathes in or, if fitted with a mechanical ventilator, when the provider pushes a button (similar to the function of a scuba regulator). This delivery system is highly efficient but requires specialized training and is for use by licensed medical professionals or specialized rescue personnel.

## Gauge

The gauge (see figure A.3) indicates how much oxygen is available, but all gauges don't measure the same way. Become familiar with how the gauge on your system indicates the content level. The most common indicators are an empty-to-full scale, the pressure level inside the cylinder, or the time remaining in minutes.

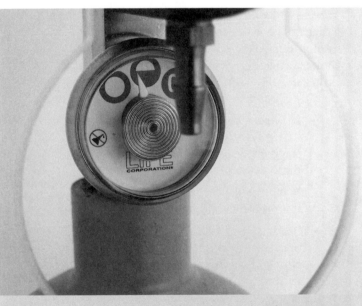

**FIGURE A.3** An example of one type of gauge found on an emergency oxygen system.

If the gauge is built into the valve stem, it will read even when the flow is turned off. If the gauge is located on the regulator, the oxygen system must be turned on before the gauge will activate.

## Tubing

The oxygen flows from the regulator to the delivery mask through crimp-proof plastic tubing. The tubing is attached to the regulator by slipping it over the hose barb, and it is attached to the delivery mask by slipping it over an oxygen inlet port.

## Delivery Mask

Several types of oxygen delivery masks are available. You must know about and recognize the various types so you can choose the delivery mask appropriate for your level of training and the condition of the victim.

- Barrier (CPR) mask. The device most commonly used with emergency oxygen systems is a *barrier mask* with an oxygen inlet and one-way valve. The barrier mask is the same one you use for CPR, but it is fitted with a port or inlet to which the oxygen tubing attaches. It is the ideal mask for delivering oxygen to either a breathing or nonbreathing victim. Sold under many brand names (Rescue Mask, Pocket Mask, SealEasy, to name a few), this mask is the one to consider for all emergency oxygen administration. Advantages of using a barrier mask with an oxygen inlet to deliver emergency oxygen include:
  - It is easy to teach and learn its use –simply attach the tube from the oxygen system to the port on the mask.
  - It eliminates direct contact with the nonbreathing victim's mouth or nose.
  - It is easy to seal and to deliver rescue breaths supplemented with emergency oxygen to the nonbreathing victim.
- Nasal cannula or simple face mask. A *nasal cannula* or *simple face mask* is included with some emergency oxygen systems and

is designed for use with victims who are breathing. A nasal cannula is a section of tubing that fits around the head and administers small quantities of oxygen directly into the nose. A simple face mask usually has an elastic strap that fits around the head and large ventilation holes in the mask that allow the oxygen flow to be diluted with air. Advantages of a nasal cannula or simple face mask to deliver emergency oxygen include:

- The device can be held in place without assistance.
- It doesn't cause claustrophobia by covering the mouth and nose.
- It is nonthreatening.
- It is used for victims who are breathing with mild to moderate respiratory distress.

- Bag-valve mask. A *bag-valve mask* requires specialized training that is included in CPR courses for health care providers and professional rescuers. It is used only with nonbreathing victims to administer artificial ventilations. When connected to a supplemental oxygen source capable of delivering high-flow oxygen, the device stores oxygen in a bag that is filled from an oxygen reservoir. One rescuer holds the mask in place, and another rescuer squeezes the bag to deliver the oxygen. Advantages of bag-valve-mask to deliver emergency oxygen include:
  - When connected to a high-flow (12 to 15 LPM) oxygen source, it delivers close to 100 percent oxygen.
  - It eliminates the need for any mouth-to-mask contact.
- Nonrebreather mask. A *nonrebreather mask* requires specialized training and is to be used in a clinical setting by a licensed medical professional. Lifeguards should not use a nonrebreather mask to deliver emergency oxygen.

## Case

Keep your emergency oxygen system in a case to protect the components from damage and to provide easy access during an emergency. The most common types of cases are a wall-mounted hard case, a portable hard case, and a fabric bag with a carrying strap.

# Assembly of Emergency Oxygen

Keep your oxygen system assembled and ready for immediate use. The only time you should take the system apart is for refilling, cleaning, or replacing parts. Follow these general steps when you want to remove the cylinder from an emergency oxygen system:

1. Turn the system off.
2. Loosen the regulator.
3. Lift the regulator off the valve stem.

Follow these steps when you assemble the components of an emergency oxygen system:

1. Remove the protective seal on the cylinder valve stem (if present).
2. Connect the handle wrench, if the handle is not built in.
3. Quickly open and close the valve to test the flow, and clean out any debris around the valve. Be sure the exit port (where the oxygen comes out) is directed away from you.
4. Check to make sure the sealing mechanism (gasket or washer) is in place on the regulator or at the connection to the tank stem.
5. Attach the regulator to the cylinder valve stem. Hand-tighten only.
6. Attach one end of the tubing to the hose nipple of the regulator.
7. Attach the other end of the tubing to the oxygen nipple or port of the mask.
8. Turn the system on and listen for oxygen flow.
9. Turn the system off and store for use.

# Oxygen Safety

Emergency oxygen systems have three main safety concerns:

1. Oxygen inside the cylinder is compressed and highly pressurized.
2. Oxygen is chemically reactive and can interact with other chemical substances.
3. Oxygen supports combustion when a source of flame or spark is present.

Although oxygen cylinders are durable and safe under normal use, they are susceptible to damage from unprotected falls or inadvertent strikes. For example, if an oxygen cylinder should fall from a height and strike a hard surface, the valve head might break, causing rapid release of the contents (2,000 pounds per square inch [psi] or greater). The cylinder could "rocket," causing significant damage and personal injury or death depending on the contents' pressure.

Although oxygen is not flammable, it can react with other chemicals and create enough heat to initiate combustion or, in some cases, explosions. Oxygen also feeds a fire, substantially increasing the rate at which flammable materials burn.

In the United States, the Occupational Safety and Health Administration (OSHA), Compressed Gas Association (CGA), and other regulatory agencies have the same specific regulations for safe handling, use, and disposal of **all** compressed gas cylinders. Carefully read the material safety data sheet (MSDS) that accompanies the product. For locations outside the U.S., follow the international regulations that apply to safe handling, use, and disposal.

Improper use of plastic gaskets or washers has been proven to be a major factor in cases where regulators used with oxygen cylinders have burned or exploded, in some cases injuring personnel. The plastic crush gaskets commonly used to create the seal at the cylinder valve or regulator interface should **never** be reused. Reuse can deform the plastic gasket, increasing the likelihood that oxygen will leak around the seal and ignite. Also take the following general safety precautions:

■ Always "crack" cylinder valves (open the valve just enough to allow gas to escape for a very short time) before attaching regulators in order to expel foreign matter from the outlet port of the valve.

■ Always follow the regulator manufacturer's instructions for attaching the regulator to an oxygen cylinder.

■ Always use the sealing gasket specified by the regulator manufacturer.

■ Always inspect the regulator and seal before attaching it to the valve to ensure that the regulator is equipped with only one clean sealing-type washer (reusable metal-bound rubber seal) or a **new** crush-type gasket (single use, not reusable, typically nylon) that is in good condition.

■ Always be certain the valve, regulator, and gasket are free from oil or grease. Oil or grease contamination can contribute to ignition in oxygen systems.

■ Tighten the T-handle firmly by hand; do not use wrenches or other hand tools that may overtorque the handle.

■ Open the post valve slowly. If gas escapes at the juncture of the regulator and the valve, quickly close the valve. Verify the regulator is properly attached and the gasket is properly placed and in good condition. If you have any questions or concerns, contact your supplier.

Reports have been made of patients and their bedding being set on fire during defibrillation when oxygen was in use. The oxygen concentration necessary to produce ignition will typically extend less than a foot (30 cm) in any direction from the oxygen source and will quickly disperse when removed. Therefore, you should remove the mask from the victim's face, place it several feet from the victim, and shut off the oxygen flow when delivering shocks. Leaving a device that continues to discharge oxygen near the victim's head before defibrillation is dangerous.

## Other Safety Guidelines

Read and follow the specific maintenance, safety, and operating instructions provided with your system. These warnings apply to all oxygen systems:

■ Never use oil, grease, adhesive tape, or other petroleum products on or near an oxygen cylinder or its components. A violent reaction can occur.

■ Never smoke or use a match or lighter near oxygen systems.

■ Turn off the oxygen flow and remove the oxygen system when delivering a shock with an AED.

■ Emergency oxygen systems are not designed to be used in rescue situations as an air supply to the rescuer.

■ Do not use emergency oxygen systems in oxygen-deficient atmospheres as a respirator or an air supply.

■ Do not use emergency oxygen systems in a fire situation. Remove the victim from such dangers before using oxygen.

■ Do not use emergency oxygen systems in hazardous or explosive environments. Remove the victim from such dangers before using oxygen.

## Safe Storage Requirements

Here are some guidelines for storage of emergency oxygen:

■ Do not place containers where they might become part of an electrical circuit or arc.

■ Do not expose compressed gas cylinders to extreme temperatures (more than 125 degrees Fahrenheit, or 51.6 degrees Celsius).

■ Keep valve protection caps on cylinders at all times except when cylinders are secured and connected to dispensing equipment.

■ Do not store containers near readily ignitable substances or expose them to corrosive chemicals or fumes.

■ Do not store containers near elevators, walkways, building entrances or exits, or unprotected platform edges or in locations where heavy moving objects may strike or fall on them.

■ Secure all compressed gas cylinders in service or in storage at user locations to prevent them from falling, tipping, or rolling. Store and use them valve end up.

■ Secure compressed gas cylinders with straps or chains connected to a wall bracket or other fixed surface or on a cylinder stand.

All compressed gases **must** be stored in areas away from heat, spark, flame sources, and explosive environments. If your facility maintains an extra supply of emergency oxygen cylinders, store them in a manner consistent with the guidelines described previously. Label the areas for **full** and **empty** cylinders.

# Maintenance of Emergency Oxygen

Emergency oxygen systems are relatively maintenance free, but they need to be inspected on a regular basis to ensure the systems are ready for emergencies. After use during an emergency, the cylinder will need to be refilled (unless it is a disposable cylinder), and the components will need to be properly cleaned.

## Inspections

Make inspection of your emergency oxygen system a regular part of your safety routine. Document your findings in a log. Conduct a visual inspection at least monthly that includes the following:

- See that no damage is visible to cylinders, regulators, or other components. Report damage to your safety or department manager immediately.
- Examine the content indicator gauge. Report cylinders that have not been used but that read "low" on the content indicator gauge as possibly having a leak. This helps ensure there is an adequate supply on hand when needed.
- Make sure the mask is present and that the one-way valve is attached and secure.
- Check that the tubing is not crimped and is securely attached to the hose barb on the regulator and the oxygen inlet on the mask.
- Ensure that any necessary handles or pins are present and attached to the device.
- Make sure the components are clean and dry.
- Check the stability of the unit mount, rack, or holders.

Conduct an operational inspection when you first obtain your emergency oxygen system and after reassembly, or at least every six months. Be sure to

- turn the system on,
- confirm oxygen flow, and
- turn the system off and store it for use.

## Refilling and Testing

When the gauge on your emergency oxygen system indicates less than half full, it's time to refill the cylinder. Any medical or industrial gas distributor that uses CGA's #870 pin-indexed universal coupling for oxygen can refill cylinders. Look for these distributors in your phone directory under *welding equipment* and *gases.* Another option for refilling is to contact your local fire department or hospital and ask if they offer refill service for emergency oxygen systems.

Federal regulations in the United States and most countries require that an oxygen cylinder be visually inspected (internally and externally) and pressure tested every five years or at any time the cylinder shows evidence of dents, corrosion, cracked or abraded areas, leakage, thermal damage, or any other condition that might render it unsafe for use. After a successful pressure test and inspection, a date is stamped into the cylinder. A cylinder is checked for a valid test date before it can be refilled. Federal regulations also require those who perform these cylinder tests to be currently approved to do so. Disposable cylinders do not have this requirement, but they **must not** be refilled under any circumstances.

## Cleaning

When an emergency oxygen system is used to provide care, the components are considered contaminated and must be replaced or cleaned. Cleaning procedures should follow bloodborne pathogen exposure and decontamination guidelines.

As with any item contaminated with blood or other potentially infectious material, a reusable oxygen cylinder or oxygen delivery device (mask, tubing, cannula) or other component that is visibly contaminated must be handled by a trained person who is wearing proper personal protective equipment. The cylinder or component can be initially surface-cleaned using warm, soapy water. It must be cleaned and disinfected with at least a 1:100 bleach-and-water solution or a commercial solution approved for use against biohazards.

Dispose of blood-soaked disposable components as biohazardous waste, or disinfect them as described previously in chapter 3 and dispose of them as regular waste. Consider asking EMS personnel if they will dispose of any contaminated materials for you. Have a policy in place for how you intend to dispose of these materials.

Now that you know how to operate an emergency oxygen system, let's explore how to integrate its use during an emergency.

## Considerations for Oxygen in an Emergency Action Plan

You must answer at least these questions in order to be prepared to administer emergency oxygen:

- How much oxygen should be kept on hand?
- Where should the emergency oxygen unit be mounted or stored?
- Who will bring emergency oxygen to the scene?
- When will emergency oxygen be used?

Answer these questions **before** an emergency occurs, then practice your emergency action plan regularly. You don't want an emergency situation to be the first time you've put your plan to the test.

When you are deciding how much oxygen to keep on hand, a good rule is to determine the average EMS response time to your facility and have enough to last twice as long as the response time. In most circumstances, 30 minutes' to 1 hour's supply is sufficient. Also have an extra full cylinder to replace any that are off site being refilled or tested.

When you are deciding where the emergency oxygen unit should be mounted or stored, start with the storage guidelines listed previously in this appendix. Then identify a location that meets these guidelines and is easily accessible at all times. Do not store your emergency oxygen system in a locked closet. If it is necessary to lock up the system overnight, be sure that part of your daily opening procedure is to bring the system to a predetermined accessible location.

When you are deciding who will bring the emergency oxygen to the scene, you must consider the number of people who will likely be present should an emergency occur. If you are the only trained person who will respond, you will either have to take the emergency oxygen with you when you first recognize an emergency or ask bystanders to bring the emergency oxygen to the scene. If another trained person will usually be on site to respond, you must consider how an emergency situation will be communicated so that person will bring the emergency oxygen.

When you are deciding your protocol for when to use emergency oxygen, here are two good general rules to follow:

1. Use emergency oxygen any time a person has been submerged and is experiencing signs of respiratory distress, and any time a person has been submerged and requires rescue breathing or CPR.

2. Use emergency oxygen as soon as reasonably possible under the circumstances.

Chapter 11 explains how to administer emergency oxygen to an unresponsive drowning victim.

## ⭐ Knowledge Into Practice

If your workplace has emergency oxygen equipment, you need to be prepared to provide care within the scope of responsibility.

## ✜ On the Job

These are the tasks related to delivering emergency oxygen that you will be expected to competently perform while working as a lifeguard:

- ▶ Recognize the situations in which it is appropriate to use emergency oxygen.
- ▶ Assemble an emergency oxygen system.
- ▶ Safely handle emergency oxygen.
- ▶ Provide routine maintenance and checks of emergency oxygen systems.
- ▶ Integrate emergency oxygen into the emergency action plan (EAP).

# BIBLIOGRAPHY AND RESOURCES

## Chapter 1

Van Beek EF, Branche CM, Szpilman D, Model JH, Bierens JJLM. November 2005. A new definition of drowning: Towards documentation and prevention of a global public health problem. *Bulletin of the World Health Organization* 83(11): 801-880.

Wendling R, Vogelsong H, Wuensch K, Ammirati A. November 2007. A pilot study of lifeguard perceptions. *International Journal of Aquatic Research and Education* 1(4): 322-328.

Witman D. November 2008. Invited review: U.S. adoption of the uniform definition of drowning. *International Journal of Aquatic Research and Education* 2(4).

## Chapter 2

Aquatic Safety Research Group. 2011. Note & float: Free lifesaving program for aquatic facilities. Available: http://www.aquaticsafetygroup.com/NoteAndFloat.html

Biswick C, Mattucci, M. 2011. Vested interest: One facility's experience with a life-jacket required policy shows why it's worth consideration–and the fringe benefits that can result. *Aquatics International*. Available: www.aquaticsintl.com/2011/may/1105_rm.html

Fielding F, Pia F, Wernicki P, Markenson D. November 2009. Scientific review: Avoiding hyperventilation. *International Journal of Aquatic Research and Education* 3(4).

Hsiao R. February 2009. An analysis of risk management implementation in aquatic centers in Taiwan and a review of selected law cases. *International Journal of Aquatic Research and Education* 3(1): 38-65.

Hsiao R, Kostelnik R. August 2009. Are university swimming pools safe? A model to predict the number of injuries in Pennsylvania university swimming pools. *International Journal of Aquatic Research and Education* 3(3): 284-301.

Langendorfer S. February 2010. Lightning risk and indoor pools. *International Journal of Aquatic Research and Education* 4(1).

## Chapter 3

American Safety and Health Institute with Human Kinetics. 2007. *Complete emergency care.* Champaign, IL: Human Kinetics.

Health and Safety Commission and Sport England. 2003. *Managing health and safety in swimming pools* (HSG 179). Sudbury, UK: HSE Books.

Hlavsa M. 2009. Three state programs that helped prevent outbreaks. 2009 World Aquatic Health Conference, Recreational Water Illness (RWI) Prevention Seminars.

International Life Saving Federation. 1999. Statement on communicable diseases. Available: http://www.ilsf.org/sites/ilsf.org/files/filefield/medicalpolicy02.pdf

Sackett D, Lachocki T. 2006. Preventing recreational water outbreaks. *Recreation Management.* Available: http://recmanagement.com/200607gc01.php

U.S. Department of Health and Human Services Centers for Disease Control and Prevention (CDC). June 1997. Preventing allergic reactions to natural rubber latex in the workplace. Available: http://www.cdc.gov/niosh/docs/97-135

U.S. Department of Health and Human Services Centers for Disease Control and Prevention (CDC). 2011. Recreational water illness. Available: www.cdc.gov/healthywater/swimming/rwi

## Chapter 4

Avramidis S. August 2007. The 4W model of drowning. *International Journal of Aquatic Research and Education* 3(1): 89-100.

Avramidis S, Butterly R, Llewellyn D. February 2009. Drowning incident rescuer characteristics: Encoding the first component of the 4W model. *International Journal of Aquatic Research and Education* 3(1): 66-82.

Avramidis S, Butterly R, Llewellyn D. August 2009. Where do people drown? Encoding the third component of the 4W model. *International Journal of Aquatic Research and Education* 3(3).

Avramidis S, Butterly R, Llewellyn D. August 2009. Who drowns? Encoding the second component of the 4W model. *International Journal of Aquatic Research and Education* 3(3): 224-235.

Griffiths T. 2007. Disappearing dummies and the 5-Minute Scanning Strategy. *Lifeguard vigilance training DVD*. Champaign, IL: Human Kinetics.

## Chapter 5

Brener J, Oostman M. May 2002. Lifeguards watch, but they don't always see. *World Waterpark Magazine*. Available: http://poseidon-tech.com/us/pressArticleWWA0205.pdf

Griffiths T. 2007. Disappearing dummies and the 5-Minute Scanning Strategy. *Lifeguard vigilance training DVD*. Champaign, IL: Human Kinetics.

Griffiths T. February 2008. Invited review: Reaction to Hunsucker and Davison's "Vision and signal detection." *International Journal of Aquatic Research and Education* 1(1).

Griffiths T. 2011. Oral presentation: The supervision myth. In *World conference on drowning prevention program and proceedings*, J. Scarr, editor. 127.

Griffiths T, Fenner P, Oostman M, Pia F. 2006. Lifesaver surveillance and scanning: Past, present and future. In *Handbook on drowning*, J Bierens, editor. Berlin Heidelberg, Germany: Springer-Verlag.

Hunsucker J, Davison S. February 2008. Invited review: How lifeguards overlook victims—vision and signal detection. *International Journal of Aquatic Research and Education* 1(1).

Mills P. Lifeguard vigilance and drowning detection systems. January/February 2005. *Recreation*. Available: www.imspa.co.uk/recreation/documents/REJan05pp36-39Lifeguard.pdf

Pia F. 1984. The RID factor as a cause of drowning. First published in *Parks & Recreation*, June: 52-67. Available: www.pia-enterprises.com/RID.pdf

Poseidon Technologies. September 2001. Executive summary: Bibliographic study on lifeguard vigilance. Available: http://poseidon-tech.com/us/vigilanceStudySummary.pdf

Poseidon Technologies. September 2001. Lifeguard vigilance bibliographic study. Available: http://poseidon-tech.com/us/vigilanceStudy.pdf

Smith T. November 2006. Seeing is believing; a technique called vigilance voice can help your lifeguards identify problems at your pool. BNet: The CBS Interactive Business Network. Available: http://findarticles.com/p/articles/mi_m1145/is_11_41/ai_n27079997

## Chapter 6

American Safety and Health Institute with Human Kinetics. 2007. *Complete emergency care*. Champaign, IL: Human Kinetics.

European Emergency Number Association. 2011. What is 112? Available: www.eena.org/view/en/About112/whatis112.html

National Emergency Number Association. 2011. 911 tips and guidelines. Available: www.nena.org/911-tips-guidelines

Spengler J, Anderson P, Donnaughton D, Baker T. 2009. *Introduction to sport law*. Champaign, IL: Human Kinetics.

## Chapter 7

International Life Saving Federation. 1999. Statement on who needs further medical help after rescue from the water. Available: www.ilsf.org/sites/ilsf.org/files/filefield/medicalpolicy05.pdf

Leclerc T. February 2007. A comparison of American Red Cross and YMCA preferred approach methods used to rescue near drowning victims. *International Journal of Aquatic Research and Education* 1(1): 34-42.

## Chapter 8

American Heart Association. 2010. 2010 American Heart Association and American Red Cross international consensus on first aid science with treatment recommendations. *Circulation* 122:S934-S946 (supplement 2). Available: http://circ.ahajournals.org/content/122/16_suppl_2/S582.extract

Clement A, Otto K. February 2007. Who is the head first plaintiff? Critical findings from court decisions for aquatic specialists. *International Journal of Aquatic Research and Education* 1(1): 6-17.

Dworkin G. 2001. The need for collaborative agreements between fire and rescue agencies and aquatic recreation and lifeguard agencies. Available: www.lifesaving.com/issues/need-collaborative-agreements-between-fire-and-rescue-agencies-and-aquatic-recreation-and-lif

## Chapter 9

American Heart Association. 2010. 2010 American Heart Association and American Red Cross international consensus on first aid science with treatment recommendations. *Circulation* 122:S934-S946 (supplement 2). Available: http://circ.ahajournals.org/content/122/16_suppl_2/S582.extract

American Safety and Health Institute. 2011. *Basic first aid*. Eugene, OR: Health and Safety Institute.

American Safety and Health Institute with Human Kinetics. 2007. *Complete emergency care*. Champaign, IL: Human Kinetics.

ASTM International. 2009. Standard guide for defining the performance of first aid providers in occupational settings. ASTM Standard F2171-02.

U.S. Department of Labor, Occupational Safety and Health Administration. 2006. Fundamentals of a workplace first-aid program. OSHA 3317-06N.

# Chapter 10

American National Standard. 2009. Criteria for accepted practices in safety, health, and environmental training. ANSI Standard Z490.1.

American Safety and Health Institute. 2011. *CPR pro for the professional rescuer*. Eugene, OR: Health and Safety Institute.

ASTM International. 2009. Standard guide for defining the performance of first aid providers in occupational settings. ASTM Standard F2171-02.

Australian Resuscitation Council. 2008. Guidelines of the Australian resuscitation council: Any attempt at resuscitation is better than no attempt. Available: http://www.resus.org.au/arc_compression_only_cpr_advisory_statement.pdf

International Liaison Committee on Resuscitation. 2010. 2010 international consensus on cardiopulmonary resuscitation and emergency cardiovascular care science with treatment recommendations. *Resuscitation* 81:E1-E330.

Nolan J, Nolana J, Soarb J, Zidemanc D, Biarentd D, Bossaerte L, Deakinf C, Kosterg R, Wyllieh J, Böttigeri B, on behalf of the ERC Guidelines Writing Group. 2010. European resuscitation council guidelines for resuscitation 2010. *Resuscitation* 81:1219-1276. Available: www.cprguidelines.eu/2010

U.S. Department of Labor, Occupational Safety and Health Administration. 2006. Fundamentals of a workplace first-aid program. OSHA 3317-06N.

Vanden Hoek TL, Morrison LJ, Shuster M, Donnino M, Sinz E, Lavonas EJ, Jeejeebhoy FM, Gabrielli A. Guidelines for cardiopulmonary resuscitation and emergency cardiovascular care. 2010 American Heart Association. *Circulation.* 122: S829-S861.

# Chapter 11

Advisory Council. February 2010. Scientific review: Subdiaphragmatic thrusts and drowned persons. *International Journal of Aquatic Research and Education* 4(1).

Australian Resuscitation Council. February 2005. Guideline 9.3.2 Resuscitation of the drowning victim. Available: http://www.resus.org.au/policy/guidelines/section_9/guideline-9-3-2feb05.pdf

Hunsucker J, Davison S. May 2010. Development of in-water intervention (IWI) in a lifeguard protocol with analysis of rescue history. *International Journal of Aquatic Research and Education* 4(2):186-198.

International Liaison Committee on Resuscitation. 2010. 2010 international consensus on cardiopulmonary resuscitation and emergency cardiovascular care science with treatment recommendations. *Resuscitation* 81: E1-E330.

International Life Saving Federation. 1999. Statement on automatic external defibrillation use by lifesavers and lifeguards. Available: www.ilsf.org/sites/ilsf.org/files/filefield/medicalpolicy03.pdf

International Life Saving Federation. 1999. Statement on who needs further medical help after rescue from the water. Available: www.ilsf.org/sites/ilsf.org/files/filefield/medicalpolicy05.pdf

International Life Saving Federation. 2001. Statements on in water resuscitation. Available: www.ilsf.org/sites/ilsf.org/files/filefield/medicalpolicy07in-waterresuscitation.pdf

International Life Saving Federation. 2003. Statement on critical CPR skills for lifesavers. Available: www.ilsf.org/sites/ilsf.org/files/filefield/medicalpolicy10.pdf

International Life Saving Federation. 2003. Statement on positioning a patient on a sloping beach. Available: www.ilsf.org/sites/ilsf.org/files/filefield/medicalpolicy09.pdf

International Life Saving Federation. 2003. Statements on the use of oxygen by lifesavers. Available: www.ilsf.org/sites/ilsf.org/files/filefield/medicalpolicy08.pdf

International Life Saving Federation. 2010. Statement on compression-only CPR and drowning. Available: http://www.ilsf.org/es/news/articles/new-medical-position-statement-compression-only-cpr-and-drowning

Krin C. April 2010. Surviving drowning: What EMS providers need to know about treatment of drowning and immersion injuries. *EMS World*. Available: http://www.emsworld.com/print/EMS-World/Surviving-Drowning/1$12665

Leclerc T, Canabal J, Leclerc H. February 2008. The issue of in-water rescue breathing: A review of the literature. *International Journal of Aquatic Research and Education* 2(1).

Vanden Hoek TL, Morrison LJ, Shuster M, Donnino M, Sinz E, Lavonas EJ, Jeejeebhoy FM, Gabrielli A. 2010. Guidelines for cardiopulmonary resuscitation and emergency cardiovascular care. Part 12: Cardiac arrest in special situations. 2010 American Heart Association. *Circulation.* 122: S829-S861.

Yarger L. May 2008. Emergency oxygen: Use in aquatic and recreation facilities is overdue. *International Journal of Aquatic Research and Education* 2(2).

## Chapter 12

Avramidis S. February 2009. Lifeguard leadership: A review. *International Journal of Aquatic Research and Education* 3(1): 89-100.

International Life Saving Federation. 1999. Statement on sun dangers for lifeguards. Available: www.ilsf.org/sites/ilsf.org/files/filefield/medicalpolicy04.pdf

Park District Risk Management Agency. 2011. Aquatics policy and training guide: 3 points of contact (pamphlet). Wheaton, IL: Park District Risk Management Agency.

Skin Cancer Foundation. 2011. The Skin Cancer Foundation's response to the release of the FDA's final regulations on sunscreens. Available: http://www.skincancer.org/the-skin-cancer-foundations-response-to-the-release-of-the-final-fda-monograph.html

Wendling R, Vogelsong H, Wuensch K, Ammirati A. November 2007. A pilot study of lifeguard perceptions. *International Journal of Aquatic Research and Education* 1(4): 322-328.

## Chapter 14

Bramblett D, White B, White J. 2007. *StarGuard triathlon and open water race manual*. Savannah, GA: Starfish Aquatics Institute.

Fawcett P. 2005. *Aquatic facility management*. Champaign, IL: Human Kinetics.

Griffiths T. 2012. *Safer beaches*. Champaign, IL: Human Kinetics.

Lepore M, Gayle W, Stevens S. 2007. *Adapted aquatics programming*. Champaign, IL: Human Kinetics.

Pound R, Cassidy S, Cliff H, Rodeo S, Rose E. April 12, 2011. Open Water Review Commission recommendations. Available: www.usaswimming.org/_Rainbow/Documents/7446603a-b37d-44eb-b8c2-18b5eece7ca3/Open%20Water%20Review%20Commission%20Recommendations.pdf

## Chapter 15

International Association of Amusement Parks and Attractions. 2011. Waterpark safety. Available: www.iaapa.org/safety/WaterParkSafety.asp

Saferparks. 2009. Injury trends for waterpark attractions. Available: www.saferparks.org/safety/injuries/byrt_waterpark_attractions.php

## Chapter 16

Griffiths T. 2012. *Safer beaches*. Champaign, IL: Human Kinetics.

Krin C. April 2010. Surviving drowning: What EMS providers need to know about treatment of drowning and immersion injuries. *EMS World*. Available: http://www.emsworld.com/print/EMS-World/Surviving-Drowning/1$12665

# ABOUT THE AUTHOR

**Jill E. White** founded the Starfish Aquatics Institute in 1999 with the mission to reduce drowning and save lives by providing reputable, responsive aquatic safety training programs to the public. She has consistently been named one of the Top 25 Most Influential People in Aquatics by *Aquatics International* magazine. In 2010 she received the prestigious Al Turner Memorial Commitment to Excellence Award from the World Waterpark Association.

White has authored textbooks on lifeguarding, lifeguarding instruction, and swim instruction for the National Safety Council, Jeff Ellis & Associates, and the American Safety & Health Institute and served as the aquatic education division director for Human Kinetics. She has firsthand experience in training, supervising, and managing lifeguards and has taught thousands of lifeguards and hundreds of lifeguarding instructors.

White has collaborated in drowning prevention and standards development initiatives and is a frequent speaker at national and international industry conferences.

White enjoys reading, hiking, and aquatic sports. She lives in Savannah, Georgia, with her husband, Robbin.